The Wedding Night

After enduring many hardships, Psyche accepts the embrace of the god of love and settles into a passionate, yet stable union. A 17th-century neoclassical sculpture by Antonio Canova. (Réunion des Musées Nationaux/Art Resource, New York.)

The Wedding Night

A Popular History

Jane Merrill and Chris Filstrup

 PRAEGER

AN IMPRINT OF ABC-CLIO, LLC
Santa Barbara, California • Denver, Colorado • Oxford, England

Library of Congress Cataloging-in-Publication Data

Merrill, Jane.
   The wedding night : a popular history / Jane Merrill and Chris Filstrup.
      p. cm.
   Includes bibliographical references and index.
   ISBN 978-0-313-39210-8 (hard copy : alk. paper) —
ISBN 978-0-313-39211-5 (ebook)   1. Marriage customs and rites.
I. Filstrup, Chris. II. Title.
  GT2665.M47   2011
  392.5—dc22   2011002672

ISBN: 978-0-313-39210-8
EISBN: 978-0-313-39211-5

15 14 13 12 11   1 2 3 4 5

This book is also available on the World Wide Web as an eBook.
Visit www.abc-clio.com for details.

Praeger
An Imprint of ABC-CLIO, LLC

ABC-CLIO, LLC
130 Cremona Drive, P.O. Box 1911
Santa Barbara, California 93116-1911

This book is printed on acid-free paper ∞

Manufactured in the United States of America

Contents

Acknowledgments

The debts owed for a book of this kind are far ranging and considerable, both because of the interdisciplinary nature of the subject and because ours is the first book to focus on it. Our abundant thanks are due to the many scholars, experts, librarians, and curators who helped us to swim rather than sink in the extensive material we encountered. We are especially grateful to our colleagues at the public library in Litchfield, Connecticut, and the university libraries at Stony Brook University. For reading over chapters and for his comments on chapter 6, we thank Rabbi Howard S. Hoffman. We thank Barbara Lencheck, a superlative copy editor, and Laurie Filstrup for formatting and proofreading the entire book.

We also toast as if with flutes of bubbly the following individuals and institutions, listed in alphabetical order: Franco Barbacci, a gentleman of many parts; Martha Tomhave Blauvelt, social historian; Lynn Brickley, a historian of New England; Janie Chang, for letting us quote from *When We Lived in Still Waters*, a sparkling trove of stories of her Chinese family; Helen Cooper, professor of Medieval and Renaissance English, University of Cambridge; Jean De Jean, professor of French, University of Pennsylvania; John Endicott for *le mot juste*; Joanne M. Ferraro, for the pleasure of reading her study *Marriage Wars in Late Renaissance Venice*; Henry F. Graff, scholar of presidents and biographer of Grover Cleveland; Trebbe Johnson, sui generis authority on the folklore and psychology of the feminine; Sherry Goodman Luttrell, Director of Education, Berkeley Art Museum; the Mashantucket Pequot Museum and its highly informed staff; David Lee Miller, Spenserian and professor of English and Comparative Literature at the University of South Carolina; Carolyn Niethammer, esteemed interpreter and scholar of Native American societies; Barbara Penner, cultural history nonpareil and lecturer in architectural history at the University College, London.

The finest pieces of virtual wedding cake are also due to the outstanding reference team of the Westport Public Library in Westport, Connecticut.

Finally, several rosettes to our very special publisher, and especially to our very cool editor, Michael Wilt, for entrusting us with this unusual subject.

Introduction

Le sort d'un mariage dépend de la première nuit.
(The fate of a marriage depends on the first night.)

—Honoré de Balzac

A kaleidoscopic array of cultural expressions constitutes the history of intimacy. In this book we summarize a large literature in order to bring attention to an elusive yet identifiable moment—the couple's traditional first night. What follows the ritual party? What leads to the honeymoon? The wedding night is not the icing on the cake but the jam that holds together the layers of the wedding experience.

Each thing that the bride or groom is told or thinks of doing or that wedding guests or members of the community think of doing with regard to the wedding night has more tradition than anyone may imagine at first blink. For instance, men have been carrying their brides over the threshold at least since ancient Greece. Finnish philosopher and sociologist Edward Westermarck's massive study of marriage customs, *The History of Human Marriage*,[1] finds the practice all over the world. The sill on the ground, which separates the outside from the inside of a house and over which people pass daily without a thought, on the wedding night takes on a magical quality. One of Westermarck's examples comes from Wales, where "it was very unlucky for a bride to place her feet on or near the threshold," and "trouble was in store for the maiden who preferred walking into the house."[2] From this example, we sense evil spirits lurking at the bride's feet. However, as we see in chapter 2, the larger explanation is that in the classical world the threshold defined the space that the household gods and goddesses protected; in the Western world, the wedding night life unconsciously reenacts this ancient belief in household deities.

Wedding customs come and go, but the practice of carrying the bride over the threshold is among those that endure. That may be because the more flexible the custom, the more it "customizes" for the individual couple. The threshold custom can hold a variety of meanings for newlyweds. Most men still lift the bride over the threshold, but they may do it with a flourish, romantically or ironically as a shared nod to tradition. The "how" also has variants. Does the groom use the "underhand carry" or the "fireman's carry"? The underhand carry is instinctive and the one most men execute unless they know the other method from lifesaving classes or summer camp. The fireman's carry is a more dramatic way to get the bride across the threshold. Either way, the bride may utter an "Oooo!" Traditions are like that: although the bride knows generally it's coming, she's emotionally as well as literally swept off her feet.

Just as carrying the bride over the threshold holds multiple shades of meaning, so does the entire wedding night—this is what makes it fascinating, yet elusive. In the past, it was often the most terrifying night of a young woman's life, shrouded in ignorance, frequently anticipated as pain rather than pleasure, and darkened by the fear of dying during childbirth. For the young man, the prospect was often arid, a test of male prowess without an expectation of an emotional union or an equal life partner.

The imprint of the past gives today's wedding night an importance but does not define it. Today the night extends the festive behavior of the day or evening; because unseen and largely unplanned, it stands in counterpoint to the wedding itself. Whereas the wedding culminates a great deal of preparation and, above all, means to the couple having people important to them gather in one room, the wedding night signifies to the newlyweds sheer privacy. And they want everything about their wedding, including the first night (even if "it's no big deal"), to have a special weight that will carry their marriage to a successful future. The bride wears something old and something blue, the groom has a best man present the wedding band to him because tradition matters to each of them. She wants to know what other couples are doing and have done in past to confirm their bond. Most young people long to commit to each other for a lifetime marriage. Most couples vow to keep faith through thick and thin with the wedding partner, and one way to do this is to make the rituals count.

Our weddings are often elaborate affairs, after which the bride and groom are as likely to fall asleep as to fall into each other's passionate embrace. Instead of a sprint, the average wedding is a marathon that starts on the day of the engagement and continues until the couple or their parents have spent to the limit, dozens or hundreds of wedding guests have departed the ballroom, and the couple is alone and wed at last. But one thing has not changed: the wedding night has a mystique, sometimes sacred, sometimes cultural, sometimes familial, as the moment at which the intimate part of matrimony starts.

This book fills a surprising gap in wedding literature. There are articles and books on the traditions of the day—but what of the night, the unorchestrated but much anticipated segue to married life? The wedding nights of other people, whether in the historical past, in other cultures, or in our own, lie off the standard wedding map. The chapters that follow answer questions such as: what is the origin of giving away the bride? Why did Renaissance English kings give away their beds the day after the wedding? What were 18th-century courtiers doing in the royal bedroom after the wedding? What's an epithalamium? Did Queen Victoria approach her wedding night as a "Victorian"? Where have the newlyweds eaten a mixture of chocolate and champagne? What happened on your grandmother's wedding night? Why did Uncle Luther short-sheet the bridal bed? What did Milton Berle have to say about wedding nights?

What this book does not do is tell the bride and groom how to have sex. The odds are excellent that they've already learned about lovemaking with each other. Instead, we have taken a look at the history of marriage manuals to show how the social norms set expectations (e.g., the advent of the birth control pill made staying a virgin less consequential). *The Wedding Night* concentrates on the Western world, starting with the Greeks, using the available facts as a foundation from which to explore the universal human drive to find a partner and secure an intimate relationship.

Viewing the chapters across an intellectual spectrum, at the academic end the book deals with the first night as a guarantee of paternity in the event the wife becomes pregnant. The wedding night looms large in the evolutionary development of the two-parent family unit. As a marker event, it predates the wedding rite of passage. Until birth control was widely practiced, sex was fraught with the possibility of conception and the responsibilities of rearing children. It is no exaggeration to say that the first marital sexual intercourse brings into play the entirety of humanity's struggle for survival and eventual dominance.

Related to paternity and also at the serious end of the spectrum, we bring to the bedside table descriptions of royal wedding nights in which dynasties vested their survival and, by contrast, the practical perspectives of early American settlers and Native Americans. We also draw back the curtains to show how different classes and communities verified the bride's virginity and promoted conception and how the public dimensions of the wedding spilled into the bedroom. Also at this end of the spectrum is the story of Tobias, a diaspora Jew whom the angel Raphael aids in his quest for a bride and in his conquest of a demon who has killed her previous husbands on their wedding nights.

In the middle of the intellectual spectrum, we describe and reflect on wedding-night advice proffered to women by a wide variety of marriage manuals. The sexiest chapter of the book, this is not a how-to but a what-did-they-expect.

On the lighter end of the spectrum, you will find descriptions of clothing, both for the bed and for the bride, the intimate meal and special foods, pranks played on the newlyweds, and imaginary wedding nights. In *The Thousand and One Nights*, each night Scheherazade ends a story just short of a climax so that the Persian king will spare her until the next night. She keeps him in a state of unresolved desire. The place of literature, including *The Arabian Nights*, poetry, novels, and cinema, primes our excitement by drawing us into imaginary worlds.

Our final chapter, "Do Not Disturb," records contemporary as-told-to accounts of unusual and ordinary, ludicrous and disappointing, and truly romantic wedding nights. Today, only a fraction of men and women are virgins at their weddings, but the wedding night is no less vibrant with expectations and possibility.

The wedding night is about commitment and exclusivity over the long run. In traditional Freudian terms, on the wedding night, the bride and groom bring to bed their parents. That is, they bring to the union a rich, unruly subconscious where their deepest values jockey for dominance. Within the act of sexual consummation lie humans' most rooted drives, and around the act hover social standards that sustain or inhibit these drives. In recognition of the wedding night as a rite of passage, we close the book with our back-to-the-present chapter, which looks at the subjective dimension, where personal experience mirrors a larger pattern or archetype and where couples recall what was special about their own wedding nights.

NOTES

1.   Edward Westermarck, *The History of Human Marriage*, 3 vols. (1891; New York: Allerton, 1922).

2.   Ibid., vol. 2, 536–37.

CHAPTER 1

It Takes Two to . . .

Clearly, the naked ape is the sexiest primate alive.
—Desmond Morris, *The Naked Ape*[1]

Humans are the naked apes of Morris's book. We have less hair, and our sex lives differ radically from those of most other animals, even our closest evolutionary ancestors. Chimps have sex more often, in fact many times a day, but chimp copulation lasts only a few seconds and appears to stimulate little pleasure in the female.[2] It is purely reproductive. Gorillas may go without sex for several years, and, even though the males come in at 300 to 400 pounds, their sex organs are smaller than humans'.[3] Bonobos and gibbons have sex face to face, but humans are the only primates to transform a reproductive act into a highly pleasurable staple of adult life. Though chimpanzees and humans have in common 96 percent of their DNA, the sex lives of the two species are very different. How did this happen?

For some, the answer comes from the Bible: this is how God made humans, different from chimps and gorillas. Until Charles Darwin published *The Origin of the Species*, in 1859, this was the standard answer. Rooted in many centuries of reading the first chapter of Genesis and in Christian theology, which posited an all-knowing, all-powerful Creator, most people held that God made each species with its own, immutable behaviors. Humans and chimps differed in the past, differ in the present, and will differ in the future. In this view, accepted by some of today's creationists, the multitude of the world's species have been here from the beginning, and differences among species are hardwired and permanent. In addition to a long tradition, belief in the God-given differences among species has an appealing simplicity. The natural world is the way it is because God makes it so. While this belief is comfortable, it is hard to square with science. Since this belief system describes the world, it is legitimate to test it against scientific observation: what evidence does science bring to bear on the origins of the human species?

On his famous voyage, Darwin found continuity among species of finches. In the Galapagos Islands, looking at the various kinds of finches, he observed and deduced that one species had evolved from another, that a change in location or climate can change members of one species into something qualitatively different. When seen in this light, the fossil record available to Darwin indicated that species came and went. Dinosaurs, which had roamed the world millions of years ago, disappeared millions of years ago. The fossil record showed that many species were extinct and could be dated to particular geologic periods. If Darwin and his successors had left the matter of species change to nonhuman animals, it would have stirred little controversy. Traditionalists could have argued that animals are one realm and humans another. But Darwin and the large majority of scientists who study human origins include humans in the large process of evolution, of species emerging from other species over long periods of time. In this perspective, it is useful and interesting to compare specific features of various species.

According to this view, humans have a long prehuman history. We are a recent species of hominids that split off from a common ancestor of chimpanzees about 7 million years ago.[4] About 3.5 million years ago, even while hominid brains were small, about the size of a chimp's, hominids learned to walk and run on two legs. This upright position afforded our prehistoric African ancestors the ability to work with their hands. They began to make tools out of materials such as stone to remove flesh from animal bones and to crush the bones to extract marrow.[5] Our ancestors also learned to hunt in groups in order to survive in an environment that included both large cats, with claws and teeth for killing and eating meat, and large grass- and leaf-eating animals, such as elephants and buffalo, which dominated the plains and forests.[6] Until very recently, about 10,000 years ago, when humans began to domesticate crops such as wheat and animals such as goats, our ancestors were hunter-gatherers in direct competition with other animal species. Along the way, hominid brains grew and grew.

What does this have to do with wedding nights? As human brains grew larger and larger, plenty. Let's look at two famous women named Lucy.

The discovery, in 1974, in northern Ethiopia, of the hominid Lucy opened modern eyes to an amazingly long history of human evolution.[7] Lucy—let's call her Lucy A after her species, *Australopithecus afarensis*, meaning "southern ape of Afar" (Afar being the region in Ethiopia where she was discovered)—lived 3.2 million years ago. That's about 100,000 generations. Like us, Lucy A had a pelvis and knees that allowed her to walk on two feet. This is what made her famous, because paleoanthropologists—khakied men and women who dig up the remains of early humans and their smaller-brained ancestors—at the time surmised that the earliest bipedals (animals that walk on two feet) had lived only 2.5 million years ago. Lucy was a million years older, and we moderns have an insatiable interest in our ancestors—the older, the better. It helped Lucy's fame that the paleoanthropologists named her after the Beatles' song *Lucy in the Sky with Diamonds*.[8]

Unlike us, Lucy A had the torso and brain of a chimpanzee. She stood only three and a half feet tall, and she had long, curved fingers that enabled her to swing through the trees. She was both a tree-swinger and a ground-walker. But she probably lacked a grasping big toe, meaning not only that she moved through the trees with just her arms but also, and more important, that her babies could hang on with only their arms. This probably indicates that she carried her young while standing upright. She was a walking, not a swinging, mom. She was transiting from trees to ground, arms to legs, and ape to human.

Lucille Ball—let's call her Lucy B—was a star comedienne of the 1950s. Desi Arnaz was a star band leader. Their courtship, in the late 1930s, was tumultuous, with each accusing the other of pursuing other love interests. But Desi, age 23, was determined, and, in November 1940, while his band was performing at the Roxy in New York City, the dashing Latino whisked Lucy B, age 29, off to Connecticut to be married by a justice of the peace. On their wedding night, the younger but macho Desi woke up Lucy B to ask her for a glass of water. Lucy later recalled wondering, "Why the hell he didn't get it himself."[9] Desi and Lucy's program *I Love Lucy* ran from 1951 to 1957 and brought into American living rooms their domestic squabbles and Desi's coping with Lucy's zany ways.

In their hit 1953 movie, *The Long, Long Trailer*, the famous couple spend a wedding night in a 40-foot trailer. The movie begins with Tacy (Lucy) persuading her fiancé Nicky (Desi), a traveling engineer, that they can live more economically in a trailer than in a series of hotels. They go shopping at a big house-trailer show, where they find that the economical trailer that figured in Tacy's money-saving budget is too cramped. Tacy persuades Nicky that they should make a down payment on a 40-footer. After the wedding, the pair jump into their convertible and fitfully pull the trailer toward their honeymoon destination, a trailer park. Nicky attempts to carry Tacy over the trailer door threshold when close-by neighbors—that is, almost everyone in the trailer park—ask why he is doing this. She turned her ankle, Nicky fibs, so a crowd of helpers "bob up," and, before Nicky can say "Let's snuggle," the "trailerites" transform the wedding-night trailer into a party. The camaraderie is overwhelming. One guest remarks that he lived in a house for 15 years without knowing his neighbors, but in the trailer park "you get to know everyone right off." As the guests depart, a woman informs Nicky that she gave the bride a sleeping pill. The wedding night is undone!

The next morning, Nicky surprises Tacy with breakfast in bed, and they agree that in the trailer park they lack the privacy appropriate to a honeymoon. So they take to the open road and head for the woods, ideal for a romantic night alone. But it rains, and the trailer becomes mired in the mud, at a tilt. Tacy cannot cook a meal on a slanted stove, so they settle on a meal of wine and cheese. In this romantic moment, Tacy tells Nicky that she fell in love with him when she saw him at a freeway entrance with a button missing from his shirt and decided she would take care of him for the rest of his life.

Nicky, exhausted from trying to right the leaning trailer, falls asleep before he can hear Tacy tell him how romantic she finds the rain on the roof. Since the Code was still operative, Tacy completes the movie's wedding night trying to sleep on a tilted twin bed.

Between the two Lucys lies the extraordinary evolutionary history of the human species. Lucy A certainly had a mate, but not a husband or lover. Lucy B not only had a husband; she brought him into millions of other people's homes. I Love Lucy rode a wave of broadcast technology and a long tradition of popular drama. Lucy B had tools and culture utterly unavailable to and unachievable by Lucy A. This rest of this chapter takes a look at five big changes that separate the two Lucys across the 100,000 generations that divide them: stay-at-home fatherhood, social cooperation, female ovulation, private sex, and the missionary position.[10]

DOMESTICATED FATHERS

In *Male and Female,* the pioneering feminist anthropologist Margaret Mead argues that a key characteristic that distinguishes humans from our chimpanzee ancestors is the role of the male in caring for females and children.[11] The female chimp bears the male's young but has little value to him beyond her sexual role. Like all species, humans must reproduce. Like most males, human males are blessed with a strong sex drive. In most animal species, males tend to conceive as many offspring as possible. We see this in fish, birds, and mammals. But conception and survival of the young are different matters. Females who bear the offspring are less interested in numbers and more interested in making sure each offspring survives. It takes little time or effort for a male to impregnate a female, but, in animals that conceive internally, the female makes a heavy investment in gestation and in the subsequent rearing of the offspring.

Among most primates (monkeys, apes, lemurs), the male copulates and goes his way. He has little or nothing to do with raising the young beyond providing protection. But human males and females learned that for their offspring to survive, they needed two parents to gather food, build and maintain shelter, and protect them. Of course, males have a stronger tendency to stray than females, but the norm of one sexual partner was very strong and generally practiced. Human reproduction is not a series of one-night stands.

As humans developed large brains, children required a long period of training. Unlike chimps, which start gathering food as soon as they are weaned, young humans endure years of dependency before they can fare for themselves. This meant that, millions of years ago, raising the young became a two-person job, a job for daddies as well as mommies. Anthropologists theorize that a basic division of labor between hunting and caring for the hearth developed so that the father and mother could contribute different skills to the survival of their young. Females, who carried the fetus and nursed the baby, could not hunt as effectively as the males. They could mash nuts and cook meats while tending to the child, but on the range they were decidedly inferior hunters. They were also somewhat smaller than their male partners. Until the postindustrial age, this division of labor was almost universal, and it still is very common.

SOCIAL COOPERATION

As humans developed the intelligence and tools to hunt animals as well as gather plants, they gathered together to live in groups. But, unlike chimps and most apes (and lions), they sustained two-parent units within the group. Among chimps, paternity is unknown because the female copulates with many males. This is her strategy for protecting her offspring: the males cannot be certain that the babies are not carrying his genes. The combination of two-parent caregiving and communal living required strict rules about paternity. Rather than expending their energies fighting over access to the females, humans figured out rules to minimize this kind of conflict—imperfectly, of course, but sufficiently to set the ground work for sexual loyalty as a norm. From the cradle of paired male and female adults in a society of other adult males and females came the institution of marriage, of a primary bond that excluded sex with other adults. Again, cheating was and is common, but the genesis of marriage reaches way back to the unusual combination of pairing and communal living (we say "unusual" because some shore birds stay paired while living in large colonies).[12]

OVULATION

Unlike other primates, human females do not restrict sexual intercourse to their periods of ovulation. Many female monkeys and apes advertise their fertility. The female baboon's genitals turn bright red. When ovulating, female chimps present themselves to many males. But human females do not restrict their sexual availability to a few days a month. Their ovulation is hidden to males and, to a considerable degree, to themselves. Of course, a modern woman can count backward from her menstruation to more or less pinpoint her ovulation, but, through the long history of humans, sex and ovulation were unlinked. Even newlyweds who have a vigorous sex life without contraceptives have only a 28 percent chance of conception in each menstrual cycle. This means that humans developed sex as a regular activity, a form of affection, and a bond that separated each couple from other couples.

PRIVATE SEX

Humans normally do not copulate in public. It is offensive to our moral code and deserves the retort that the copulating couple are behaving like "animals." Actually, "chimps" would be more germane, for they are close evolutionary cousins who engage in quickies wherever. Orgies notwithstanding, humans have a strong proclivity for engaging in sexual intercourse out of the view of others. Doing it so that others can see or watching others in sexual embrace is prurient. Although humans can copulate at any time of the day, pair bonding moved the activity to night, to the straw or the bed. Sexual intercourse became a private act, acknowledged by the larger community but occurring in the dark, in private space. Of course, male and female responses to copulation differ, but the fullness of daily tasks and the steady responsibility of raising children, the extended nature of sexual arousal, and postcoital release all combined to move sex into the night and into the relative privacy of where the couple slept. In terms of social dynamics, moving sex out of the public view reduced male aggression against other males. By limiting sexual intercourse to one or a few known women, males could channel their natural sexual aggression into hunting with the guys and feeding the group.

MISSIONARY POSITION

Yes, it's old fashioned, but, yes, it's efficacious. As Lucy A and her descendants found their two feet and left the trees forever, sexual intercourse repositioned to the front. With a few exceptions, monkeys and apes do it "doggy style." Face to face, chest to chest, and pelvis to pelvis—that's how we humans usually like it. Moreover, humans usually embrace (from the French "to hold with both arms") when they copulate. Among chimps, the act is quick, and the female chimp experiences nothing like the human female orgasm. After intercourse, she matter-of-factly moves on to other business. No romantic glow.

In the long evolution of hominids, erogenous zones moved front and center. Females developed hypersensitive clitorises, and the male took longer to ejaculate so that the female associated copulation with intense pleasure. In simian sex, the heads are far apart and facing away from each other. Hence, kissing is unimportant. Chimps kiss, but the most sensitive area of their lips is inside the mouth—good for tasting food, but not related to sexual sensation. Human lips have the vermillion, which is loaded with nerves. A kiss on someone else's lips can have all the zing of sexual intercourse.

Once the female hominid was walking upright, her vagina shifted to the front to accommodate frontal intercourse. To increase the chances of conception, the female lay on her back, giving the sperm a horizontal swim to the uterus. The female orgasm leaves the female at rest on her back, so sexual intercourse has a postcoital as well as a precoital phase. The embrace continues after climax.

Returning to the naked ape, as our ancestors evolved, they lost most of their body hair. Anthropologists surmise that hominids lost their hirsute covering as they developed into hunters on the savannah. What remains is pubic hair, full of pheromones, in the crotch and armpits. As hominids lost their hair, they developed sweat glands as a cooling system. These glands are also full of sexually powerful scents.

THE PREHISTORY SETTING

We are now closing in on the wedding night. By the time homo sapiens, our species of hominid, emerged in Africa about 150,000 years ago, we had grown large brains. Making tools and hunting in groups seem to be the main factors in making human brains much larger than the brains of apes. The combination of large-brained offspring who required many years of care before they could survive on their own and the increasingly complex organization required to hunt animals pushed humans into a sexual behavior radically different from that of most animals and especially from that of other primates, such as apes. Human females formed mostly exclusive bonds with one member of the opposite sex to produce and rear offspring. Part of the bond was regular sexual intercourse unrelated to pro-creation. Face-to-face intercourse provided intense pleasure to the female, as well as to the male. The exclusivity of the bond—the male wanting to be sure the offspring carried his genes, the female wanting to ensure that the male was not only the father but also a caregiver—pulled copulation into private space. This reduced interest in other males in the bonded fe-male. And, because of the rigors of daily life, the private sexual act moved to nighttime and the bed and often occurred before sleep.

The stage is almost set for weddings and wedding nights. First, humans needed to take two more big steps. The first was to shift from practices based on sheer survival to practices that combined survival and culture, involving ritual and public expressions of deep feelings of awe and fear, of wonder and curiosity.[13] After a long hominid evolution of something like 5 million years and a stable period of human existence of more than 100,000 years, about 40,000 years ago, homo sapiens suddenly developed sophisticated tools like needles and awls; they greatly improved their hunting abilities by making barbed harpoons and spear throwers; and they expressed themselves artistically in cave paintings, designs on pot-tery, and figurines of fertility. With a firm command of fire, humans were able to live in larger groups. Survival rates increased. Humans drove their rivals, the Neanderthals, into extinction. And these humans migrated to every part of the world except Antarctica. They traded goods. Dia-mond's "trinity" of distinctive human characteristics were in place: pos-ture, large brains, and sexual behavior.[14] Humans were ready to create recorded history.

NOTES

1.   Desmond Morris, *The Naked Ape* (New York: McGraw Hill, 1967), 63.

2.   Jared Diamond, *Why Is Sex Fun? The Evolution of Human Sexuality* (New York: Basic Books, 1997), 78–79.

3.   Jared Diamond, *The Third Chimpanzee: The Evolution and Future of the Human Animal* (New York: Harper Perennial, 2006), 73.

4.   Diamond, *The Third Chimpanzee*, 21.

5.   Ker Than, "Lucy the Butcher? Tool Use Pushed Back 800,000 Years," *National Geographic News*, August 11, 2010, http://news.nationalgeographic.com/news/2010/08/100811-lucy-human-tools-meat-eating-nature-science/.

6.   Diamond, *The Third Chimpanzee*, 68.

7.   Donald Johanson, *Lucy: The Beginnings of Humankind* (New York: Simon and Schuster, 1990), 16–18.

8.   Ibid., 18.

9.   Stefan Kamfer, *Ball of Fire: The Tumultuous Life and Comic Act of Lucille Ball* (New York: Knopf, 2003), 79.

10.   Diamond, *The Third Chimpanzee*, chapter 3; Diamond, *Why Is Sex Fun?*, chs. 1, 4, 5; Morris, *The Naked Ape*, ch. 2.

11.   Margaret Mead, *Male and Female* (New York: New American Library, 1955), ch. 9.

12.   Diamond, *Why Is Sex Fun?*, 7–8.

13.   Diamond, *The Third Chimpanzee*, 47–57.

14.   Diamond, *Why Is Sex Fun?*, 9.

CHAPTER 2

The Classical Three-Step: Establishing the Wedding Pattern

. . . Is it true
that new brides hate Venus? Or are the tears pretended
with which they frustrate a hopeful husband's joys,
those copious sobs inside the bridal chamber?
So help me the gods, their grief is feigned, not real.[1]

—Catullus (first century B.C.E.)

Desire conquers, bright, from the eyes of a happily wed bride, sharing in
the reign of all great powers, for the goddess Aphrodite is invincible in her
play.

—Sophocles, *Antigone*[2]

MESOPOTAMIANS

The last big step in human development takes us to the threshold of recorded history. About 10,000 years ago, humans who had moved out of Africa into the Fertile Crescent domesticated plants such as wheat and barley and animals such as goats and sheep. They moved from hunting and gathering to growing crops and raising animals. They enjoyed some respite from fighting daily for their survival. Over the next millennia, they had the leisure to invent writing. They recorded deeds and laws and songs on clay tablets. They created rituals. They carved cuneiform and images into hard cylinders of lapis lazuli and obsidian to make impressions

Romans held hands to symbolize the bride's new familial loyalty. Second-century C.E. marble relief. (© The Trustees of the British Museum/Art Resource, New York.)

on clay. They created governments and specialized bureaucracies. They built cities and monuments. With wheeled vehicles, they created powerful armies. Against the long prehistory of humans, some 6,000 generations, these settled people were the first moderns.

The very first record of a wedding night comes in the form of songs and hymns from the fourth millennium (3000–2000 B.C.E.).[3] They are written in Akkadian, a Semitic language that resembles Hebrew and Arabic. The wedding is between two gods—Inanna, the goddess of the storehouse, and Dumuzi, the god of agriculture. In one of the songs, Dumuzi wants to take a tumble with Inanna, but the lady wants marriage. The battle of the sexes goes back a long way! In another song, probably sung by women as they did their work, Inanna's brother brings to her a proposal for marriage from an unknown suitor. The proposal comes in the form of "Let me bring you flax." But Inanna is a lady of leisure, unskilled in weaving. She counters her brother by asking who will spin the flax. The brother answers that he will bring spun flax. This back-and-forth continues until the brother agrees to bring to his sister the final product, a bleached sheet. It is only then that Inanna asks the identity of the suitor, and her brother tells her that it's Dumuzi. Inanna rejoices: "He is the man

of my heart." That is, she accepts the fullness of the harvest into the fullness of her storehouse bed. In another song, Inanna welcomes Dumuzi to
her home, the storehouse, with this:

> Not only is it sweet to sleep hand in hand with him
> sweetest of sweet is too the loveliness of joining heart to heart.

In other hymns, Inanna sweetens her loins by taking a bath and making the bridal bed comfortable before she invites the groom in. Or, in a
hymn which portrays the gods as rulers, she compares her pubic delta to
a watered field ready for the god to plow. "My parts piled with levees well
watered / I, being but a maiden, who will be their ploughman? . . . You
lady, may the king plow them for you!"

These hymns were sung in city-state temples throughout the Fertile Crescent. There is no wedding prior to or separate from the wedding night. The hymns center on the bridal bed. Given the evolutionary
background to the first human settlements, this is no surprise. These early
hymns recognize the centrality of the sexual bond, which at the heavenly
level ensures good crops and at the worldly level guarantees the well-
being of the city-state and its citizens. At one level, the bridal bed is
where the crops come into the storehouse. This is the level of myth and
ritual. Unlike their hunter-gatherer ancestors, the settled people of the
Fertile Crescent articulated their awareness of larger realities in terms of
gods and goddesses, of heavenly personalities worthy of worship and celebration. These people developed elaborate religious rituals celebrating the
arrival of spring and the fall harvest. In the city-states of Mesopotamia,
professional clergy performed rituals and wrote texts to guide all levels of
society in their relations with heavenly forces.

At another level, the hymns reflect a social reality of well-established
wedding practice. The man proposes; the woman has conditions; the man
accepts; the woman welcomes him to her bed. In another hymn, a bridal
party of four men (farmer, shepherd, fowler, and fisherman) accompa-
nies the groom. Except for the formal representation of specific working-
men, the bridal group is familiar to us 4,000 years later. The myth imitates
worldly practice. Finally, these songs and hymns are a wonderful mix of
desires for security and for pleasure. The wedding night is both a contract
for sharing wealth and children and a celebration of erotic pleasure. For
kings, the wedding night secured their lineage. For farmers and shepherds
and women weavers, the wedding night brought social status and a dura-
ble partnership through which to survive the hard as well as to enjoy the
easy times and to raise a family. As noted earlier, the inhabitants of the
Fertile Crescent were the first people to write and create important docu-

ments such as laws and contracts. By 1800 B.C.E., marriage contracts on clay tablets were common.

GREEKS

Just as the wedding night goes back to the beginnings of recorded history, so the basic structure of the wedding harks back to early Greek civilization. Although we mostly know the Greeks through the wild stories about their gods, what the early Christians labeled "myths," the Greek weddings and wedding nights were founded in largely private family religious practices. According to Numa Denis Fustel de Coulanges,[4] the ancient Greeks believed that each person had a soul that stayed alive after death. If the deceased had a proper burial and resting place, the soul would remain in the vicinity, not wander, and "live" happily ever after. If the person did not have a proper grave, the soul would wander in misery, bereft of family ties. The souls of the deceased also required regular sacrifices at the family altar. In short, the family bore daily responsibility for the well-being of its deceased.

Although the Greek city-states had official religious events, each family's collection of gods and goddesses and each family's practices were particular to that family. The Greeks, and later the Romans, and, later still, most Europeans married outside their immediate family. This meant that the woman left her childhood home and moved to the home of the husband. This move from one family to another was a rite of passage, a set of formalities that led the woman from one status to another.

This marriage rite of passage had four parts. Anthropologists describe three of these as separation, transition, and incorporation.[5] The fourth, consummation, though not part of the rite proper, gave the marriage its legal and communal grounding. In the first part, the father gave the daughter to the husband. This ritual occurred before the altar of the husband's home. The giving-away ritual formally cut off the daughter from the protection of the family gods and absolved her of responsibility for the deceased members of her family. The second part of the ritual was a procession to the husband's home. This community event featured family and friends, led by the city-state herald, who held a torch lit at the family hearth and who escorted the daughter from one home to another. Members of the procession played drums and flutes and sang songs. The *Iliad* gives us a glimpse of an ancient wedding procession when it describes the depiction on Achilles' shield: "and they were leading brides from their bridal chambers under / shining torches throughout the city, and the loud wedding song."[6] Along the way, spectators threw fruits and sweetmeats at the bride. Usually the bride wore a white dress and a veil. The music and

singing marked both the community's blessings and joy and their excitement in the couple's new sexual life, as the songs were often ribald and
the jokes pointed.

The third part of the marriage ritual began at the doorstep of the bridegroom's home. Here a ritualized struggle often took place. The groom
physically seized the bride, and the bride's family resisted, protecting the
bride from the unknown world she was about to enter. This ritual struggle reflected the bride's anxiety over leaving a known home and entering
a new one. The anxiety is beautifully captured in a fragment of one of
Sophocles' lost plays. The wife, Procne, laments:

> But when we reach puberty and can understand, we are thrust out
> and sold away from our ancestral gods and from our parents. Some go
> to strange men's homes, others to foreigners, some to joyless homes,
> some to hostile. And all this once the first night has yoked us to our
> husband, we are forced to praise and say all is well.[7]

In most quarters, this struggle was a faint remembrance of bride-
capture. Memories of bride-stealing appear throughout the classical world
and, later, in Europe. According to Plutarch, in ancient Sparta, the ritual
carried darker tones of ritualized rape. The abducted girl was consigned
to a woman, called a *nympheutria*, who had expertise in marriage ceremonies. She shaved the girl's head, dressed her in a man's cloak and sandals,
and laid her down on a straw mattress in a dark room. The man who was
to be her husband dined with his comrades in the mess room as usual and
then came into the room, undid her belt, and took her. After this brief
consummation, he returned to sleep with his comrades. Plutarch disap-
provingly describes this wedding night against the widespread Spartan
practice of homoerotic sex in which the basic division is not between
male and female but between active and passive. The *nympheutria* prepared the bride to outwardly resemble a young male, a common premarital
sexual partner for young men.[8]

Back in Athens, at the end of the ritual struggle in front of the husband's
home, the groom picked up the woman and carried her through the door,
careful that she not touch the sill or threshold that separated his home from
the outside world. In the Greek family religion, the threshold separated the
sacred from the profane. Crossing this boundary required a ritual heft of the
bride into a world of new responsibilities, obligations not just to a husband
but to his ancestors and his gods. To mark her new duties, the groom sprinkled the bride with water and the bride touched the sacred altar fire. The
water and the fire marked the end of the bride's former existence and her
entrance into a new home, a new religious practice, and a new life. Some-

times a basket of nuts, dates, figs, and dried fruit was upended, signifying the contribution the bride would make to her new household.[9]

The fourth part of the rite of passage occurred at night. Greek marriages typically took place in early evening, so the couple consummated their union at night in the nuptial bed. Before turning in, the husband and wife shared a loaf or cake of grain, a sacred food. The bride carried a piece of fruit into the bedchamber, a ritual remembrance of the pomegranate that Persephone ate in Hades, thereby separating her from her earthly mother. Often, a *nympheutria,* a woman with expertise in marriage ceremonies, led the bride to the bedchamber and ritually prepared the bed for the bride's first night. The bed in the *thalamos* or bedchamber often was curtained. Once the newlyweds were alone in the bedchamber, one of the bridegroom's friends stood guard, symbolically preventing the bride's rescue. Also standing outside the door were the bride's closest unmarried friends, singing *ephithalamia,* or wedding songs, through the night to comfort the bride as she embraced her husband and a new life.[10] On a darker note, the Greek poet Theocritus noted that the singing drowned out the bride's cries during her first intercourse.[11] One of Sappho's songs has the bride saying goodbye to her virginity:

> Bride: Maidenhood, maidenhood, where did you go and leave me?
> Maidenhood: I will never come back to you, never come back.[12]

Decorations on some classical vases show a baby in the bride's bed, suggesting that the baby was placed as a fillip to a fertile sexual life or even that the bride slept with a baby the first night. The Greek historian Pollux describes the custom of both the bride and the groom sleeping one night with a child of the opposite sex.[13]

Procreation was so important that the Greeks and, later, the Romans passed laws discouraging celibacy. In Sparta, during the rule of Lycurgus, who brought the military-oriented reformation to Sparta in the seventh century B.C.E., unmarried men were denied the rights and protections of citizenship. Another Spartan practice was to delay consummation for one night. In Sparta, where the entire population served the state and its military readiness, men were encouraged to spend the first night apart from the bride. This delay was said to increase the potency of the husband and to improve the chances of conception, especially conception of a son. In Athens, women sometimes underwent a similar preparation. Before consummating the marriage, the bride slept in a dormitory devoted to the worship of Artemis.[14]

The morning after the wedding featured the *epaulia,* the presentation of gifts by family and friends. Pausanias, a second-century lexicographer, describes the gifts such as a "basket . . . unguents, clothing, combs, chests, bottles . . . sandals, boxes, myrrh, soap."[15] In this description, the basket indicated the bride's contributions to the household, and the other gifts were intended to help her sustain her attractiveness to her new husband.

ROMANS

The Romans recognized as binding several types of marriages.[16] An official clergyman married the most important citizens. This ceremony, *conferratio*, took its name from the central ritual in which the bride and groom shared a cake made of grain (*ferr*).[17] In a more common ceremony, the father of the bride passed her from his hand (*manus*) to the hand of the groom. This ceremony emphasized the bride as an asset passed from one family to another. A third and popular form of marriage gave legal status to the couple after one year of cohabitation in which the bride was not absent for more than three nights at a time. If the couple lived together for less than a year or if the bride was absent for more than three consecutive days, the marriage could dissolve without legal action; if the couple was together for more than a year and there were no absences of more than three consecutive nights, dissolution required a divorce.

Unlike the Greeks, the Romans placed great stock in auguries, in signs that allowed them to forecast the future by inspecting the clouds or, more famously, the entrails of birds. The *auspex* (the root of our word "auspicious") looked for signs that the marriage met the favor of the gods and would succeed.

Roman weddings followed the Greek script, but with variations. As in Greek weddings, relatives and friends accompanied the bride as she proceeded from her childhood home to the husband's. Before departing, she probably dedicated her childhood dolls and toys to her household god.[18] She dressed in a white robe, bound by a woolen girdle fastened by a thick "Hercules" knot just below the breasts. The Roman bride wore a veil and coiffed her hair either in braids tight on her head or, like the Vestal Virgins, with curls hanging down the side of her face. On her head she wore a wreath of herbs such as verbena, marjoram, and myrtle. Whereas the Greek bride passively enjoyed fruits and sweetmeats thrown by well-wishers, in Rome the groom responded by casting walnuts at the boys in the street, and the bride carried three coins—one for her husband, one for the *penates*, the household gods she was about to embrace, and one for the *lares*, gods at the crossroads. The songs sung along the procession were called hymenals. They entreated the god of marriage, Hymen, to favor the union. Hymenals were popular songs, not hymns. A more formal poem, inherited from the Greeks, was the *epithalamium*, or wedding poem.

When the bride arrived at the groom's home, she rubbed the doorpost with animal fat and tied a ribbon to it. As in Greek weddings, the groom lifted the bride over the threshold, but the Romans kept the legend of Sabines in mind. In this famous legend, often depicted in paintings, the Romans, newly arrived in Italy and in need of wives, invited the neighboring Sabines to a feast and, in the midst of revels, abducted their guests' women. As the story goes, the Sabine men debated among themselves so long that the Roman youths escaped without consequence. The Romans later offered the Sabine women their freedom to return, but most chose to stay, preferring their new virile husbands to their passive former spouses. Clearly a Roman story! And a strong memory of bride-capture as a founding event.

In the Roman groom's house, the groom sprinkled the bride with sacred water, and she ran her fingers through the sacred flame. Then followed a feast accompanied by bawdy as well as romantic songs. The most honored bridesmaid escorted the bride to the nuptial couch, which was decorated with garlands of flowers. When the bridesmaid departed, the groom entered.

Whereas modern Europeans and Americans tie the knot, the husband in the classical Roman world began consummation by untying the Hercules knot that bound the bride's garment. The groom also removed her veil. The next morning, it was possible that the bride would be "angry with her husband," meaning that he, like the Spartans, postponed sexual intercourse in order to avoid the evil eye. And, like the Spartans, the male might prefer anal or oral sex. Romans considered these variations legitimate forms of intimacy, and guests gathered for a morning feast would joke about the bride's unhappiness, which could end in procreative intercourse as early as that afternoon, a daytime and libertine exception to the usual nighttime activity.[19]

NOTES

1. Catullus, *The Poems of Catullus; a Bilingual Edition*, trans. Peter Green (Berkeley: University of California Press, 2005), 161.

2. Quoted in John Oakley and Rebecca Sinos, *The Wedding in Ancient Athens* (Madison: University of Wisconsin Press, 1993), 47.

3. Thorkild Jacobsen, *Treasures of Darkness* (New Haven: Yale University Press, 1976), ch. 2.

4. Numa Denis Fustel de Coulanges, *The Ancient City: A Study in the Religion, Laws and Institutions of Greece and Rome* (Baltimore: Johns Hopkins University Press, 1960), parts 3–4.

5. Martti Nissinen and Risto Uro, eds., *Sacred Marriages: The Divine-Human Sexual Metaphor from Sumer to Early Christianity* (Winona Lake, IN: Eisenbrauns, 2008), 150.

6.   *The Iliad of Homer,* trans. Richard Lattimore (Chicago: University of Chicago Press, 1961), 18:490–96.

7.   Mary R. Lefkowitz, *Women's Life in Greece and Rome: A Source Book in Translation* (Baltimore: Johns Hopkins University Press, 1992), 12–13. This is from a fragment of a lost play.

8.   Joseph Braddock, *The Bridal Bed* (New York: John Day, 1961), 134.

9.   Ellen Reeder, *Pandora: Women in Classical Greece* (Baltimore: Walters Art Gallery, 1995), 127.

10.   Ibid., 128.

11.   Oakley and Sinos, *The Wedding in Ancient Athens,* 37.

12.   Ibid., 37.

13.   Ibid., 20, 37.

14.   Lefkowitz, *Women's Life in Greece and Rome,* 284.

15.   Oakley and Sinos, *The Wedding in Ancient Athens,* 38.

16.   E. Roylston Pike, *Love in Ancient Rome* (London: Frederick Muller, 1961), 11ff.

17.   For a contemporary enactment, see http://portadigiano.net/forumnovum/viewtopic.php?f=14&p=9455.

18.   Pike, *Love in Ancient Rome,* 41ff.

19.   Pascal Dibie, *Ethnologie de la Chambre à Coucher* (Paris: Grasset, 1987), 50.

CHAPTER 3

Virginity to Consummation: The Rite of Passage

I like my body when it is with your
body. It is quite so new a thing.

—e. e. cummings (1894–1962)

RELIGIOUS BELIEFS AND PRACTICES

The metaphor of a marriage to Christ originated in Paul's second letter to the Corinthians (11:2): "I betrothed you to Christ to present you as a pure bride to her one husband." Paul, who never married, is proposing that, just as a bride comes to her husband intact, so does the Christian remain virginal in order to enter the kingdom of God. For mystics, Christ was the desired bridegroom. Unity with him was personal and expressed sensually, and virginity was a lofty abstraction.

In monastic practice, a nun could aspire to be a bride of Christ through pure living and devotion. The union became passionate and emotionalized for women mystics, notably in Germany. The term *Brautmystik*, or "mystic bride," refers to erotic and bridal imagery describing the soul that cleaves to God.[1]

Religious traditions regarding consummation were also prevalent, and some are still followed today. Jewish law and tradition (as observed among Orthodox and Conservative Jews) require that, before the wedding, the bride immerse herself in a *mikveh*, or ritual bath. She and the groom do not see each other on the wedding day until they meet under the *chuppah*,

The curtain is drawn back on this medieval couple in the act of consummation. From a 15th-century manuscript. (Bildarchiv Preussischer Kulturbesitz/Art Resource, New York.)

or marriage canopy. Both fast on the wedding day. Immediately after the ceremony, they observe *yichud*, or complete isolation from others, in a room in the wedding hall, where they break the fast together. Following the wedding, the bride and groom go to their new home, where they are expected to perform intercourse for the first time. There are no rules about the form of the intercourse, and the couple may do whatever satisfies their desire. But a religious injunction comes into play right after the coupling, when the bride immediately enters a state of *niddah* ("menstruant," literary, "one set aside"), and she and her new husband discontinue marital relations for seven days.

Before the Church deemed marriage a sacrament that had to be presided over by a priest, in many places the betrothal was the couple's free pass to have sex. Low material stakes made of the contract itself much ado about nothing. A mid-19th-century history of the French family describes the attitude among the French peasants:

When a couple became engaged, the priest blessed them and this blessing gave them the right . . . to sleep together as man and wife. The child that was eventually born and proudly carried to the baptismal font was never considered to be a bastard, even if the wedding ceremony had not yet taken place. If the couple had been lax enough to forget about the service until they had had several children—as sometimes happened—their progeny were made to attend the belated ceremony hidden under a cloak near the baptismal font.

VIRGINITY: THE MEDIEVAL TESTS

Tests for virginity usually required that the woman's body be inspected for signs of sexual activity. Midwives checked the size and shape of vagina or cervix, looking for the intact hymen but also for signs of a widened passageway or of conception. Easier than checking the woman's genitalia was an examination and "reading" of her urine. Those who were virgins were expected to have clear (and sparkling) urine; when virgins urinated, a delay and then a hissing sound might reveal their uncorrupted state.

Other tests, recorded in religious and secular literature, were more farfetched. During sleep, if certain names were placed between her breasts, a false virgin would tell the truth about adultery. Likewise, if a virgin drank an infusion of jet stone in water, she urinated it at once. Or an astrologer might read the evidence of a woman's concourse with a man in the conjunction of the stars.

The standard test was postcoital bleeding. This was common enough that medieval literature describes how to cheat. Leeches could do the trick; so could a bird's intestine positioned to break at an optimal moment. An 11th-century medical text gave instructions:

> This remedy will be needed by any girl who has been induced to open her legs and lose her virginity by the follies of passion, secret love, and promises. . . . The day before her marriage, let her put a leech very cautiously on the labia, taking care lest it slip in by mistake; then blood will flow out here, and a little crust will form in that place. Because of the flux of blood and the constricted channel of the vagina, thus in having intercourse the false virgin will deceive the man.[2]

THE VIRGINAL PRIZE

When the birth control pill was new, it suddenly became a badge of honor at my women's college not to be a virgin. A friend offered me a month's supply of pills, which I kept, viewable, in my top bureau drawer—as if I had attained the status of an experienced woman. Along the same lines, in some societies, the woman or girl has traditionally been deflowered by somebody other than her mate.

Sometimes a feudal lord had the right to sleep with the bride on her first night as a married woman. In his history (1527), Hector Boece recorded the *jus primae noctis* (Latin: "law of the first night") as the custom in ancient Scotland. The law permitted King Evenus to sleep with any bride in the land on her wedding night, and all his lords were permitted to do the same with their vassals. In the 11th century, Malcolm III was persuaded by his wife, Margaret, to abolish this custom. Thenceforth, the price of redemption of the bride's chastity at her marriage was a gold or silver coin.[3]

THE RISKS OF DEFLOWERING

In Italy, young people have tended to live at home with their parents until they marry. This leads to a lot of secretive sex among the unmarried. The novel *The Monster of Florence* describes sex in parked cars as an Italian "national pastime . . . one out of every three Florentines alive today was conceived in a car. On any given weekend night the hills surrounding Florence were filled with young couples parked in shadowy lanes and dirt turnouts, in olive groves and farmers' fields."[4]

A recent deflowering was often seen as having drawing power for supernatural sprites. But a couple bonded by consummation could ward off the spirits by sleeping with clasped hands or by exchanging love bites or a magical token of hair. They were demonstrating their physical union and telling the goblins, "Too late, you can't have us." English gypsies warded off evil spirits by scattering bread on the bride and groom or by having the couple carry grains of wheat.[5] A final moment of the wedding ceremony sometimes involved mixing the urine of bride and groom with brandy and a pinch of dirt in a wooden wedding cup. The young couple would drink from the cup, and the minister would ask if either the bride or the groom could separate the mixture. As neither could, the marriage was declared also not to be dissolved. We surmise that customs involving the magic use of urine came from northern India, where, for example, some men drank urine daily for good health.

FAILURE TO CONSUMMATE

Sigmund Freud had a patient, a middle-class lady of 30 years, divorced for 10 years, who came to him with an obsession—not the kind of obsession we have with high heels, chocolate, or white-water rafting but a medically disabling neurosis. Numerous times a day, the lady ran from her bedroom to the living room, took a stand by a table in the middle of the room, rang for her housemaid, and then sent the maid out on a pretext or dismissed her. Playing the mind detective, Freud talked out the crazy behavior with the woman until, in one session, she suddenly came up with the explanation.

On her wedding night, her husband had run into her room again and again to try to consummate their marriage, without success. In the morning, he said angrily that he'd be embarrassed in front of the help, so he poured red ink from a bottle that happened to lie on a table onto the bed sheet.

Freud concluded that the woman identified with or felt compassion for the man who had been her husband. She was taking his role when she "showed" the maid a big stain on the doily on the living room table. Freud comments on the symbolism: "Table and bed together stand for marriage, so that the one can easily take the place of the other." The poor woman was trapped in her action, by which she was subconsciously "making her husband superior to his past mishap." What, asks Freud, could have more of an imprint on a young lady than what occurs on her first night with her new husband?[6]

TEENAGE READING IN BED

When I was a teenager, being a virgin felt like being on the shore looking out at another continent. It was not sheer ignorance or lack of experience of one physical function, as one might be ignorant of how to whistle a tune. While fantasizing about the transition from virginity to womanhood, I came across a strange French novel, *Les Chants de Maldoror*, by Isidore Ducasse (whose pen name was the Comte de Lautréamont).

The voice is a young man's, but it is not callow; he has passed puberty and abounds in sexual energy and sensitive feelings. But the narrator has not yet had sex with a woman, and this preoccupies him: "Whenever he sees a man and woman strolling down some grove of plane-trees he feels his body split in twain from head to foot and each new part yearns to embrace one or another of the strangers. But this is only an hallucination and reason is not slow in repossessing her empire. For this reason he mingles neither with men nor with women, for his excessive modesty, which has derived from his feeling that he is nothing but a monster, prevents him from bestowing his warm sympathy upon anyone."[7] He broods about his state and has an inkling of changing it: "I sought a soul that might resemble mine and I could not find it. I rummaged in all the corners of the earth: my perseverance was useless. Yet I could not remain alone. There must be someone who approved of my character; there must be someone who had the same ideas as myself."[8]

The youth continues his wanderings on the earth and in his dreaming. He sits on a rock during a hurricane and sees from the shore the water swirl around a ship that founders and sinks. He feels very sad, but the wild awareness of life and death stirs him. As he watches the ship sink, sharks enter the scene and start to make a meal of the human detritus. Suddenly the youth sees "on the surface of that crimson cream" a pretty lady shark surrounded by three sharks that are in fierce combat with her. His will rises up with courage, and he takes a gun and shoots first one, then the other monster sharks, freeing his brave "maiden" from their jaws.

Being a shark, she has deadly teeth, but he swims out, and they come together in harmonious coupling—a pubertal dream of the unknown. Here is what happens between the human and shark that conjugate after the hurricane.

The swimmer and the female shark rescued by him find themselves together. For a while they look at each other eye to eye; each is astonished to find so much ferocity in the aspect of the other. They swim around in circles, neither losing sight of the other, and each murmurs: "Hitherto I have been mistaken: here is someone more evil than I." Then, by mutual consent, they glide toward each other, with mutual admiration, the female shark parting the waters with her fins, Maldoror beating the waves with his arms; they hold their breath, each desirous of contemplating for the first time a living portrait of the self. Arriving within three yards of each other, effortlessly, suddenly they come together like two magnets and kiss with dignity and gratitude in an embrace as tender as that of a brother and sister.

Carnal desire follows this demonstration of friendship. In Maldoror's dream, two sinewy thighs clasp tightly about the viscous skin of the monster; arms and fins interlacing, they cleave with love, with the human throat and chest quickly fusing into one fishy mass smelling of seaweed: "In the midst of the tempest that continues to rage, illuminated by its lightning's and having for a nuptial couch the foamy waves, borne upon an undertow as in a cradle, and rolling upon one another towards the depths of the ocean's abyss, they join together in a long, chaste and hideous coupling!

"At last I had found someone who resembled me! Henceforth I should not be alone in life! She had the same ideas as I! I was face to face with my first love!"[9]

The young boy can only imagine sex, so the author casts his sexual initiation in extravagant and outlandish imagistic terms.

As a teenager, I didn't just read exotic French novels. I also loved the English tradition and took to bed John Cleland's novel *Fanny Hill,* the picaresque story of the most famous trollop in English literature. Identifying with Fanny gives us insight into why finding a special person to mate with feels brand-new.

Fanny is by turns brazen, plucky, crafty, decadent, purely sensual/materialistic, and completely in control of the erotic episodes of her story. Just as when we read *The Odyssey* it seems that Odysseus delays his return to Penelope but we feel all is well when he is back at his palace in Ithaca at the end, so, too, when Fanny reunites with her first lover, Charles, she asks us to discount or forget the barrage of erotic episodes that has gone before in the crescendoing passion of the present.

Charles, at the story's end, is reduced to his essential self, with no financial assets to show for his years in India. Charles and Fanny meet by accident at an inn, and, after they eat and catch up, the innkeeper shows them to the room with the best bed he has. It is then that Fanny shows, for the first time, shyness about sex: "And here, decency forgive me! if, once more I violate the laws and, keeping the curtains undrawn, sacrifice thee for the last time to that confidence without reserve, with which I engaged to recount to you the most striking circumstances of my youthful disorders."[10]

The very modern Fanny observes that being with Charles, the combination of feeling lovesick and yearning for him, tempered by sudden diffidence and modesty, "all held me in a subjection of soul incomparably dearer to me than the liberty of heart which I had been long, too long! the mistress of, in the course of those grosser gallantries." Only Charles has the "secret to excite" the emotions that "constitute the very life the essence of pleasure." Moreover, it is not merely Charles's prepossessing manliness and lovemaking but her "distinction of the person" that affects her "infinitely more . . . than of the sex." She goes on to detail the ecstasy her lover's "scepter-member" brings her through her "sentiment of consciousness of its belonging to my supremely beloved youth." Love and sensation are streams that mingle and "poured such an ocean of intoxicating bliss on a weak vessel, all too narrow to contain it, that I lay overwhelmed, absorbed, lost in an abyss of joy, and dying of nothing but immoderate delight."[11]

Invariably, Fanny brings the reader down to earth—here with the image of the narrow passage containing Charles's "organ of bliss"—but the feeling that soul and sensation coming together, the in-body and out-of-body experience, reconsecrates her as a virgin being deflowered of cynicism is true to female psychology. A woman who recalls a certain night as being like a wedding night is saying that it's the love inside oneself that counts and that a sexual experience can be transformative without regard to the presence or absence of marriage vows.

After Fanny confesses her vices, Charles forgives her and asks her to marry him. Their night in the inn is, therefore, their real wedding night. This was not, however, enough to redeem the story in the eyes of the law, and, for more than two centuries after John Cleland wrote the novel in 1748 while in debtors' prison, it was banned for obscenity.

A person experiences the "wedding night" as it relates to the spiritual or transformative side of sex once or several times in his or her life, not necessarily the one that follows a wedding ceremony. The case of Fanny's reunion with Charles is current and important because she views this special night with a man as unique, unforgettable, transformative, sacred, and colored by regret but not diminished by guilty feelings about her past.

AMOR AND PSYCHE

In many myths, when gods consort with humans, it's a rapid fling, like the mating of two dragonflies in the sky or a mad chase ending with the god's angry wife or some other deity objecting to the match and changing the innocent one to a tree or water lily or both the human and the transgressive god into heavenly bodies. The love story of Amor (Cupid) and Psyche is a world apart from this pattern of predator and prey. In it, the human girl and the male god Amor make love, have a blow-up, and suffer estrangement. When they get together again, they lovingly accommodate each other's nature. In the version by the second-century Roman author Apuleius in *The Golden Ass*, their conjugal love is celebrated by a host of gods at the end.

But the night precedes the wedding, and that is the most indelible and famous part of the story. It has inspired artists and sculptors for more than 2,000 years, and I [Jane] carried the edition with Erich Neumann's commentary with me for years. A psychologist friend once told me that all of us have one fairy tale or myth that seems our own, and for me that has been the story of Psyche ever since a friend gave me a book with the story of Amor and Psyche in college. I identify with Psyche's life and always have.

Bound to a cliff by order of the jealous goddess Venus, beautiful Psyche is resigned to her fate when she is seen by Venus's son Amor, the god of love, who instantly falls in love with her. As Psyche faints into his arms, Amor flies away with her to his fantastical palace, where they are the perfect lovers. Only one thing does he ask of her—that she not look upon him. He comes to her in the night and leaves before dawn.

She is utterly happy for a time, but then she invites her sisters, who prove cruel and jealous and tell her that her husband is a monstrous serpent. They counsel her to shine a light on the mystery man at night to see how dreadful he really is. And Psyche does this one night and sees that Amor is in fact of ineffable beauty. As she holds the lamp, a drop of oil falls on Amor, who awakens and berates her. Abandoned, she throws herself off a cliff, but the shepherd god Pan saves her, and advises her not to give up and to win back the heart of Amor.

This is when Psyche has life struggles of an order that would likely destroy anyone. She passes all the tests—the sorting of the seeds does seem very feminine compared with, say, the tasks of heroes like Hercules. Her travails, the last of which her beloved helps her to complete, are hair-raisingly onerous. Psyche begins as not a very conscious or developed person, but, in the course of the story, she dares to stretch herself spiritually and becomes worthy of the sublime connection that was too much for her when she was a passive little thing. Interestingly, when you read the story or see the iconography, you think that she had her wedding night as soon as Amor spirited her to his castle, but in fact she was still passive and mute. It is only after her physically and emotionally terrible trials that she and Amor have their real wedding night, with the blessings of the same gods who made a fuss and put her through her paces, including Venus.

Analytic psychologist Trebbe Johnson explains:

> Jung called the psychological equivalent of the culmination of Psyche's difficult journal the "coniunctio." This is the inner marriage, in which all the diffuse, fragmented parts of the self (or psyche) are united and one discovers a new sense of passion, wholeness, and joy. . . . With the god, it is eternally the wedding night and rarely a domestic partnership. . . . If it were possible to remain in the embrace of the god, we would simply curl there, as Psyche did at first, in an undifferentiated tangle of bedding and empyreal demands and we would never strike out into the world on a sacred path of our own creation. We have to be separate from the god in order to keep striving, time and again with a heart full of joy, into our holy longing. When we do we walk into the world as into the arms of a waiting lover.[12]

DOUBLE WEDDING NIGHTS

Sometimes a folk variation of a myth gives only the bare bones that have come down through the ages, so one or another point especially stands out. Such is the case with the "double wedding night" of Amor and Psyche, of which a delightful retelling is "The Man Who Came Out Only at Night," by Italo Calvino. In the Italian story, the groom tells the bride that very night that he is under an evil spell and is doomed to be a tortoise. The only way to break the spell is for him to leave right away, without carrying through with making her his wife, and to travel around the world as a man by night and a tortoise by day. The bride is willing to stay the course, so he gives her a magical diamond ring that has secret powers. The rest of the tale is about the Psyche character, who uses the ring in wily ways to fend off advances by several men. She even defeats the police when the men denounce her to the authorities—the female police officers box one another's ears, and the male police who then pursue her are made to play leapfrog "by the power of the diamond"—that is, by the strength of her love for her husband. While the game of leapfrog is in force, the tortoise comes crawling back. "He saw his wife, and behold! He was again a handsome young man, and a handsome young man he remained, by his wife's side, up to a ripe old age." She has used her wits to survive; he has evolved in a parallel fashion.[13]

The true wedding night in a spiritual sense is the "double one" in the template of all the Amor and Psyche myths. People used to say that a woman who bore with a difficult marriage was a "patient Griselda." By this they meant that she epitomized the uncomplaining wife. Indeed, on the surface, the ineffably long-suffering wife of the lord who doesn't trust women is a passive victim. However, she evolves from stupid to smart, from a will o' the wisp to a proud woman. In mastering the art of showing nothing, she also learns to keep her own counsel. After years of being on probation and enslaved to another's will, she emerges from her shell and shows great strength and an integrated self. In the story, the lord (her husband) who has banished her children as infants brings them back and pretends that the daughter will be his new wife. Griselda for the first time stands up to him and says, "Okay, but only if the treatment she receives is better than what I received"—and that confrontation breaks the spell. Now Griselda and the lord are equals and can, in a metaphysical sense, truly marry. In case we didn't get that this story was about female individuation, the lord states that he wasn't humiliating Griselda all those years, only testing her.

EARLY TO SEX, LATE TO COMMIT

Today, most people lose their virginity before the wedding night. The sexual picture has changed enormously in the past 40 or 50 years. Once upon a time, couples waited until the nuptials to live together. The couple came to each other barely touched, and, given the secularization of our diversions and even our schools, often a newlywed didn't really know his or her new spouse well; they hadn't lived together or had sex. Actress Lynn Redgrave

(1943–2010) heard from her mother that her maternal grandmother, Beatrice Kempson, had told her that the honeymoon night was awful: "She knew nothing! Zero! Zip! And my poor virgin grandfather Eric whispered to her, 'I've got something really awful that I have to ask you to do!'"[14]

Sigmund Freud went with the idea that, after a first sexual experience with a man, a woman was emotionally in a state of "bondage" to him. "Some such measure of sexual bondage is, indeed, indispensable to the maintenance of civilized marriage and to holding at bay the polygamous tendencies which threaten it, and in our social communities this factor is regularly reckoned upon."[15] Nowadays couples may have lived together or had a long relationship and a sexual relationship, and the significance of the wedding night is about making a commitment.

According to adolescent and adult psychiatrist Dr. Martha McFadden, because the two can have all these things before marriage, people are much more commitment-averse than they were decades ago. "It's a matter of taking the next step to adulthood, and moving from adolescence to adulthood is about closing down options. A lot of moving out of adolescence has to do with the acknowledgment of the ability to close down options. People who don't get on with it are perpetual adolescents who never settle down. They think if they keep their options open they'll never get old."

The wedding night is then the first true commitment, the one the man and woman do not expect to reverse. As a major rite of passage of being grown up, marriage has shifted the options. The pair make a commitment for life. Divorce is a back door; nevertheless, when they conjugate now they do something very different from what they did before the wedding.

According to Dr. McFadden, in the past the wedding night carried effectively less weight, not more. Now the issue of permanence looms large:

> One or the other may be ambivalent, they have discussions, they may even go to couples therapy. So the wedding night is exciting and scary, depending on how much you've come to terms. If you are more ready to take the step, it's exciting. When you're ready and come to terms you welcome this step—"I'm leaving the adolescent stage. I've made a choice of one man or woman, and can go ahead and have a family, and buy a house or decide where we'll live, and this is the permanent person I'm going to spend the rest of my life with.". . . If they are scared they're not ready.
>
> The excitement is not sex that night, but that sex can become different than previous encounters because it's for keeps. The sex represents more intimacy . . . 'till death do us part.' Also there can be much more real planning. I see young people who, instead of going

on the honeymoon that is the most conventional, will decide they want to hike in the Rockies, or spend three weeks helping the poor. It's exciting to do this collectively, acting as a team. They also plan for their future—the two become one. A lot of that goes into today's wedding night.

The wedding used to be momentous, an incredible party that ushered in a feeling that "I can do what I want," making a person *feel* grown up. Now people are making the decision to be grownups, and the celebration is not just a party with all the friends out for them but an affirmation that "we are a magical team."

Some will put this off for a long time but once they do they have made a true decision to move on in their development (and not just have the next stage of liberty, i.e., having sex with my boyfriend). Again it's that rite of passage—"I'm really grown up"—almost like a school graduation. And on the wedding night both of them are going to be aware that "I can't do whatever I want to do now.". . . The momentous part is the self-awareness of being a team. This is what young people deliberate about today, about making the connection, not about the sex as an amazing experience . . . . It's like "We've been doing this for a long time."[16]

A woman in her 30s, married and the mother of three, described to me, from the vantage of more than a decade having passed, how sweet and romantic her wedding night was. Neither she nor her sweetheart, both 18, expected the summer romance to last through college. She said it was as if this trusted male friend "led me out on a dance and I'm still dancing."

Perhaps the only trend about virginity is that a young person raised secure in the love of family and honoring his or her body is going to be, as it is said in French, "bien dans sa peau" (comfortable in his or her skin) when it comes to the first intercourse. I think the major aspect of being on the brink of initiation is the yearning to overcome all past disjunction between two persons and to achieve a perfect connection with another self. The act of losing one's virginity is, naturally, awkward, because it is unpracticed. I remember planning with my boyfriend to "do it" in a borrowed apartment in the only graduate student high-rise at Harvard. I realized that the couple who lent us the apartment for the night knew what we were about and looked on it benignly, being much advanced and already married. The awkwardness that came into play was that, being so happy to be in an apartment with a nice kitchen to eat in and a lovely sofa to lie on, we waited for the sex part until about midnight. I had to keep rallying to awakeness as we proceeded. I became acutely conscious we were in a borrowed bed when we positioned a towel underneath me. I thanked Venus when it was over and we could sleep.

The next morning I felt jubilant, because we went down the elevator and out into the Cambridge street and bought coffee, donuts, and the *New York Times*. This was the life! Reading the newspaper together! Being quiet with a person who, unlike a mere date, was there, companionably, in the morning. No longer tired, I rejoiced in walking, as I imagined, like a peasant woman, hip-heavy and more womanly than before, when I was back on my campus. For sure, sharing the Sunday paper made me feel more grown up and no longer a virgin. I think each of my daughters feels "bien dans sa peau" as well, and, like mothers and daughters since time immemorial, we do not diminish the mystery about being a virgin and then being a virgin no longer by discussion of it.

NOTES

1. Katharina M. Wilson, *Women in the Middle Ages: An Encyclopedia* (Westport, CT: Greenwood, 2004), 1:122–24.

2. Kathleen Coyne Kelly, *Performing Virginity and Testing Chastity in the Middle Ages* (New York: Routledge, 2000), 32.

3. James George Frazer, *Folklore in the Old Testament* (London: Macmillan 1919), 489.

4. Douglas Preston with Mario Spez, *The Monster of Florence* (New York: Grand Central Publishing, 2008), 19.

5. Edward Westermarck, *The History of Human Marriage*, 3 vols. (1891; New York: Allerton, 1922), 2:482–83.

6. Sigmund Freud, *Introductory Lectures on Psychoanalysis* (New York: W.W. Norton, 1977), 325.

7. Maldoror Lautréamont, *Les Chants de Maldoror* (New York: New Directions, 1943), 71.

8. Ibid., 103.

9. Ibid., 113.

10. John Cleland, *Memoirs of a Woman of Pleasure* (New York: G.P. Putnam's Sons, 1963), 288.

11. Ibid., 291.

12. Interview with Trebbe Johnson, April 2010. Also see her "Wedding Night with the God," *Parabola* (Spring 2004): 83–88.

13. Italo Calvino, *Italian Folktales* (New York: Harcourt Brace Jovanovich, 1980), 12–14.

14. http://www.oprah.com/relationships/Lynn-Redgrave-on-Her-Latest-Play-Nightingale.

15. Sigmund Freud, "The Taboo of Virginity," in *The Standard Edition of the Complete Psychological Works of Sigmund Freud*, ed. James Strachey (London: Hogarth Press, 1957), 11:193–94.

16. Interview with Dr. Martha F. McFadden, March 2, 2010.

CHAPTER 4

Proceeding to the Royal Bedroom

I see them leaning in and moving me around the board.
—Victoria to Albert, in the film *Young Victoria*

CHESS AND PORTRAITS

Like many princesses' marriages before her, Victoria's depended on the affairs of state, which she compares to a chessboard in the epigraph. Leopold was the king of Belgium, and Albert, Victoria's husband, was his nephew. Leopold was determined to keep England in the anti-German camp. In this lovely movie, Victoria cannot step outside the interests of politically powerful people in England or Belgium, but she does have a say in her marital future and asserts herself sufficiently to choose a man in whom she has a romantic interest. At first, the young queen is dependent on the doubtful advice of Lord Melbourne, but, as she matures, Victoria learns her role in the British political system. In this process, she comes to rely on Albert for his more neutral good sense and for his total devotion to his wife.

In the chess scene, Albert and Victoria continue a long European theme comparing romance to chess. Originating in India and traveling across the Middle East to Europe, chess was popular among royals and aristocrats from the 11th century. During the highly circumspect Middle Ages, chess represented the equally serious game of romance. The queen could move forward, sideways, and diagonally, so the game bespeaks Victoria's maneuvers to establish her independence in court.

In the movie, Albert teaches Victoria how to use a bow and arrow. This is another medieval representation of romance. Medieval art and literature feature many hearts pierced by the lover's arrow. And, in a wonderful reversal, while Albert courts the princess, she draws his portrait. As we will see in this chapter, the portrait of a prospective queen plays a major role in English history.

FAMILIES THAT MARRY EACH OTHER

In the first chapter, we considered some theories about the emergence in prehistory of the two-parent family and its responsibility for raising children. That chapter included current anthropological research on both patrilineal and matrilineal families. In the second chapter, we saw how various kinds of governments and religious bodies in the classical world took an interest in marriages as an essential institution of settled communities, especially in ensuring that property passed to the father's children.

The wedding of Marie de Medici to Henry IV, the king of France, celebrated by Pope Clement VIII, was one of the grandest events of the 16th century. Painting by Jacopo da Empoli. (Scala/Art Resource, New York.)

In this chapter, we take a look at royal weddings where the stakes were large and the drama high. Throughout history, powerful families have married each other. This was especially true of royal families. There are modern exceptions, such as Edward VIII's abdication, in 1937, to marry Wallis Simpson, but, as long as monarchs have wielded power, members of one royal family have usually married members of another royal family. Royal weddings were about the survival of ruling families—the production of an heir—and their ability to dominate or at least survive the constantly shifting international balance of power. What happened or did not happen on royal wedding nights directly affected the well-being of entire nations. A lot was at stake.

THE EDUCATION OF A PRINCESS

First, let's look at the royal culture that bred and educated princesses. The brides were young, usually in their mid- to late teens. They were sent abroad to marry men they had not met. These women were pious, sexually inexperienced, and, by our standards, appallingly ignorant of sexual behavior. To a large degree, their mates were equally ill prepared to begin the intimate side of married life. They knew their realms, their uniforms, the rules of court, but the bedroom was terra incognita. The youth and the strangeness of the newlyweds to each other led to wedding nights notable for their raw unpredictability.

Although royal children were often destined to serve the purposes of the monarch or ruling class, their education sometimes included the literature of courtship and passionate love. All royalty believed that pious living ensured the blessings of God on conception. No matter how involuntary or pragmatic the politics of marriage among royal families, the woman's dependence on the grace of God for a successful match was unquestioned.

And, finally, the medieval notion that sex was inherently sinful hovered over every marriage. Nuptial sex was better than sex out of wedlock, but the surest way to salvation could be found in the lives of the clergy, celibate and devoted to prayer and good works. In short, a boggling mix of youth, international power politics, ideals of passionate love, and ecclesiastical and popular discomfort played havoc with the pleasures of sex.

DANCING GIRL TO EMPRESS

The earliest record of a royal wedding night harks back to Byzantium and the Empress Theodora (500–548). Theodora is one of history's extraordinary Cinderellas. The daughter of a royal bear-keeper who left the family penniless when he died, Theodora became a dancing girl. The nature of the stage performances at the time was bawdy, and she became famous for her X-rated acts. Theodora caught the attention of a Byzantine high official, became his mistress, and followed him to North Africa. When the relationship foundered, she made her way back home to Constantinople on her own, a journey of more than 1,000 miles.

When Theodora resumed her dancing career in Constantinople, Justinian, the crown prince, fell for her, and, when he became emperor, to the shock of the imperial circle, he proposed. In fact, not only did he seek out and wed the dancing girl; he made her an equal partner in his long rule.

On their wedding night (in 525), after Justinian showered his bride with gems and jewelry, including a precious belt of gold coins, and a great number of major property deeds, Theodora wrapped around him and asked for one more thing. The next morning, a decree went out that all of Theodora's counterparts in all the brothels and all the prostitutes who were in business for themselves in Constantinople be married within a year or give up their property and rights. The former actresses could convert to Christianity, find husbands, and have all their former blemishes wiped out. Nobody was to remind Theodora or the citizens of her embarrassing, although colorful, past. The whole marriage was understated and discreet so as not to irritate Justinian's father, but the couple's feelings were "lofty" and would affect the population of the vast area of the empire.[1]

In the Middle Ages, royals usually married other royals or powerful regional rulers. Although St. Paul and the early Church fathers preferred celibacy to marriage, by the 9th century the Church had included marriage as a sacrament, and by the 12th century it had included rules of marriage in canon law and then firmly established its authority to give legitimacy to these unions, which were monogamous and in theory dissolved only upon the death of the husband or wife. In the late Middle Ages, nation-states such as England and France emerged as centralized governments, and marriages played an important role in international politics

INGEBORG TAKES A STAND

The French king Philip II (ruled 1180–1223) was a contemporary of England's Richard the Lion-hearted and the Holy Roman Emperor Frederick I Barbarossa. The three of them led the Third Crusade, which featured the famous battles between Richard and the Muslim ruler, Saladin. Back in Europe, however, France and England were rivals. To strengthen his alliance against England, Philip, widowed, proposed marriage to the

Danish king's daughter, Ingeborg (1175–1236). King Valdemar agreed and sent Ingeborg to France with a large retinue of attendants and dowry gifts. Philip met her in Arras, and they proceeded to Amiens, where they were married in August 1193. However, Philip had second thoughts—evidently the result of a combination of sexual attraction to another woman and political ambition—and, within days of their wedding night, he announced that the marriage was invalid and offered to return Ingeborg and her retinue and gifts to Denmark. He requested that Pope Celestine III annul the marriage on the grounds of nonconsummation *per maleficium*, the result of sorcery.[2] While waiting for the pope's approval, Philip married a German princess, Agnes of Merania, in 1196. However, Ingeborg did not return to Denmark but took shelter in a French nunnery. From the historical sources, it is not clear whether this was completely voluntary or was coerced by Philip. Whether or not she was there by her own free will, Ingeborg did not take her dismissal casually. She began a long campaign to restore herself to the French throne by writing a series of petitions to the pope asking that he recognize her marriage to Philip and annul his marriage to Agnes. In her letters to Celestine, Ingeborg argued that Philip's decision to send her back to Denmark was the work of the devil and evil princes.[3] Although Celestine did not act on her behalf, in 1198 a new and vigorous pope, Innocent III, sided with Ingeborg. In 1199, he declared Philip's marriage to Agnes null and void. Philip argued that the marriage with Ingeborg had not been consummated and refused to reinstate her as queen. The pope excommunicated Philip and placed France under interdiction, meaning that the king's countrymen and -women, as well as the king himself, could not take the sacraments. Wherever Philip traveled, the clergy, loyal to the pope, darkened their churches. The excommunication was authoritative enough that the king could not attend his own son's wedding, which had to be celebrated outside his royal domain.

Eventually, the pope and his allies wore Philip down, and in 1200 the king of France recognized Ingeborg as queen and separated from Agnes. The pope lifted the interdiction, but Philip did not invite Ingeborg to Paris. Instead, he locked her up in the castle of Estampes and continued bedding Agnes, who bore him several children. The pope called a council, which promised Philip that it would render a just decision on the legitimacy of his children by Agnes if he would reinstate Ingeborg. Philip acquiesced, and this time, the king and the restored queen rode pillion (two asaddle) to court in a public display of her royal status. Ingeborg won the crown but likely never shared Philip's bed again. She was an active queen, supporting churches and hospitals, and commissioned an illustrated Psalter that survives. After Philip's death, in 1223, her stepson, Louis VIII, and her step-grandson, Louis IX, supported her until her death, in 1237.

FERDINAND AND ISABELLA:
ROYAL MATCHMAKERS

In the 15th and early 16th centuries, three of the monarchs most active in marrying their children to other royal families were Ferdinand of Aragon and Isabella of Castile, in Spain, and Henry VII, in England. Ferdinand and Isabella ruled from 1469 to1516 and Henry from 1485 to 1509. Ferdinand and Isabella were wed in 1469, when they were 17 and 14 years old. Teen marriages were common when the average life span was but 40 or so years. The marriage of Ferdinand and Isabella consolidated the northern half of Spain, and their combined Catholic forces eventually defeated the Muslim kingdom in the southern half. Contemporary chronicles report that, on their wedding night, officials from both Castile and Aragon huddled below the young couple's bedroom to hear the sounds of sexual intercourse.[4] These were the sounds of teenagers who had first met a few days earlier and who had no sexual experience and, because their parents were devout Catholics, little knowledge.

When the consummation was complete, these officials swept into the bedroom, pulled the spotted sheet from the bed, and, to fanfare, displayed it to the court.[5] Such was the Spanish custom of checking the bride's virginity and of celebrating the sexual intimacy necessary for the endurance of the new regime. The property holders in these strongly paternalistic societies in Europe and the Middle East routinely examined the bridal bedclothes for evidence that the woman was a virgin on her wedding night.

Isabella bore a son and three daughters who survived into maturity. All four children were chess pieces to be moved in the earnest game of international diplomacy. In 1490, they sent their oldest child, Isabella, age 20, to Portugal to marry Prince Alfonso. Alas, he died soon after the wedding and before Isabella conceived. Isabella was later sent to marry Alfonso's brother, King Manuel. With the king, Isabella conceived, but both baby and mother died during the baby's birth. Queen Isabella and King Ferdinand then sent their youngest daughter, Maria, to wed the same King Manuel. The royal couple sent another daughter, Juana, to the Netherlands to marry the Archduke Philip, son of the Holy Roman emperor, Maximilian. Philip in turn sent his sister, Margaret, to Spain to marry Ferdinand and Isabella's son, Prince Juan. Before being dispatched to Spain, Margaret had already been dealt to Francis, the king of France. But Francis was not satisfied and returned Margaret to her parents. En route to

Spain, the Dutch fleet hit stormy weather, and Margaret limned a wry epitaph:

> Here lies Margaret, the willing bride
>   Twice married—but a virgin when she died

Happily, Margaret's fleet found a safe harbor, and Margaret enjoyed her wedding night and soon produced an heir.

A GRAND WEDDING AND A CONTROVERSIAL WEDDING NIGHT

Ferdinand and Isabella's youngest daughter, Catherine, gives us our first look at a grand wedding and a controversial wedding night. In 1499, seven years after Columbus discovered the new world, the Spanish king and queen contracted with England's Henry VII to marry Catherine to Prince Arthur, the English heir apparent. The prospective bride was 14 and the groom, 13. Catherine remained in Spain with her parents until 1501, when she sailed to England for the wedding. It was a grand affair celebrating the alliance of two great nations. London bedecked itself in lights and banners. Guilds performed skits. Church bells rang. At the wedding, the bride's vow included "to be bonny and buxom in bed and at board." At the wedding celebration, Arthur's brother, Henry, age 10, stole the show. He cast off his princely coat and in his jacket danced, much to the court's delight and, in retrospect, in contrast to the less vigorous groom.[6]

English court tradition involved an extensive preparation of the bedchamber. The Yeoman of the Guard had the honor of "rolling up and down" the straw litter. At the summons of the Lord Great Chamberlain, court ladies left the wedding feast to supervise the preparation of the bed. The ladies covered the straw with a protective canvas, followed by a featherbed, a fustian or blanket, a lower and upper sheet, another blanket, and, finally, several rugs, one of ermine. In royal marriages, the court is never far away, and the elaborate preparation of the bed showed the strong interest of the court in the success of the newlyweds' first night.[7]

Once the bedroom was ready, Catherine's ladies-in-waiting brought her to the bedchamber, changed her into her nightgown, and put her to bed. She waited while Arthur and his companions drank and sang lusty songs. Finally, the groomsmen arrived with Arthur and dressed him for bed. With about a dozen people in the room—Henry VII and his queen and various officials from both courts—Arthur sat beside Catherine. Then the officiating bishop, following the protocol established in Salisbury during the Middle Ages, entered the bed chamber and blessed the bed. He intoned: "Bless, O Lord, this marriage bed and those in it . . . that they live in your love and multiply and grow old together in length of days." The blessings dispelled any curse that might injure the couple's fertility. Specific to the ensuing night, the priest invoked God "to watch over your servants as they sleep in this bed, protecting them from all demonic dreams." Demonic forces were never far away. Since conception was the work of God, its absence was the work of the devil. The priest then sprinkled the bride and groom with holy water.

After the blessing, the married pair shared a cup of posset, a wedding-night beverage described along with other drinks and foods in chapter 15.

The entourage of well-wishers departed, save two maids and two groomsmen who remained to play a traditional sport with the royal couple. This was the Tudor version of today's garter fling. The two maids gathered up Arthur's stockings, and the two grooms did the same with Catherine's. The two maids and the two groomsmen then sat on opposite sides of the bed facing away from the newlyweds. Over their shoulders,

The Bishop blesses the Marriage Bed

A 15th-century woodcut showing a bishop blessing the nuptial bed of a high-born couple. (From *Warm and Snug: The History of the Bed*, by Lawrence Wright. © Routledge and Kegan Paul, 1962. Reproduced by permission of Taylor and Francis Books UK.)

the maids threw Catherine's stockings at Arthur, and the grooms threw their stockings over their shoulders at Catherine. Whoever hit the bride or groom was sure to marry in the near future.[8]

MUCH ADO

A century later, Charles I (1600–1649) rebelled against the stocking throw and locked the doors before the maids and groomsmen could enter so that the king and his bride, Henrietta Maria, could embrace without further ado. But his son James II (1633–1701) personally escorted his daughter, Mary, to the nuptial bed to be shared with her new husband, William, Prince of Orange. Mary's tutor, Dr. Edward Lake, recorded her wedding night as follows: "At nine o'clock at night the marriage was solemnized in her highness's bed-chamber. The King, who gave her away, was very pleasant all the while. . . . At eleven o'clock they went to bed, and his majesty came and drew the curtains, and said to the prince, 'Now, nephew, to your worke! Hey! St. George for England!'"[9] A wedding poem celebrating the marriage of Charles Leigh, in 1719, begins:

Draw, draw the Curtain, fie, make haste,
    The panting Lovers long to be alone,
    The precious Time no more in talking waste,
    There's better business going on[10]

The royal stocking custom stopped altogether when George III married Charlotte in 1761, the same day the two met for the first time. The lack of stockings in the air did not diminish this marriage, which was a happy one and produced 13 surviving children.

Returning to Arthur and Catherine, after the maids and groomsmen left, the royal couple had some, but probably not total, privacy. For, as in Spain during the wedding night of Catherine's parents, Ferdinand and Isabella, it was also the custom in England for officials from both sides of a royal marriage to gather at the door or under the bedroom to listen for the sounds of sexual intercourse and the promise of an heir. There is no record that the English examined the bed sheet, which is just as well because Catherine was an avid horseback rider who had accompanied her mother on Isabella's active schedule of inspecting estates and even riding with the army, and it is possible that Catherine's hymen was no longer intact.

What occurred on Arthur and Catherine's wedding night became a matter of grand dispute. The first mention was a servant who recalled that the next morning, Arthur had requested "a cup of ale, for I have been this night deep in Spain."[11] As we shall see, Catherine disputed this penetration many years later. Unfortunately, Arthur died seven months after wedding Catherine, and she had not become pregnant.

HENRY'S WIVES

Arthur's brother, Henry, was now heir apparent. With his father's blessing, he asked for Catherine's hand. Since she was Henry's former sister-in-law, he needed the pope's dispensation, which was granted. Unlike Catherine's first wedding, this one took place in a "closet," that is, a private chamber, followed by a private wedding night. In contrast to Arthur's wedding, at this one, his own, Henry did not dance. But, if the wedding ceremony was modest, the marriage was a great Renaissance match. Both had education; both knew their Church doctrine; both loved to ride and hunt; both were close to their mothers. And Catherine secured from her father, Ferdinand, an enormous dowry. In the first nine years of their marriage, Catherine was pregnant six times. (Two of the births were stillborn, and a son and a daughter died in childhood.) Only a daughter, Mary, lived to maturity. By her late 30s, Catherine was beyond childbearing and showing her age. Henry began to look for another queen.

Henry, a pious Christian, considered the marriage a failure because of Catherine's inability to deliver and raise a son to maturity. To give him that son, Henry fixed on one of Catherine's ladies-in-waiting, Anne Boleyn. He asked the pope to annul his marriage to Catherine. (This was the same pope who had given him dispensation to marry Catherine in the first place.) This was a common royal request, but the pope refused. Why? Simply put, the pope wanted Spain to be "deep" in Henry's court. In a long negotiation with the pope, Henry's churchmen justified Henry's desire for a divorce by citing Leviticus 20:21: "If a man shall take his brother's wife, it is an unclean thing . . . they shall be childless." By this argument, Henry's marriage to Catherine was flawed from the start and lacked God's favor, a favor that would have produced a son. It is easy to see this as empty rationalization for Henry's desire for a new and young wife, but we need to keep in mind that, although arrogant and headstrong, Henry was pious.

In response, Catherine claimed that her marriage with Arthur had not been consummated, either on the wedding night or afterwards. Therefore, the biblical injunction did not apply. Catherine claimed that she had shared Arthur's bed only seven times in their five-month marriage and had not known him carnally. She was still a virgin, as "intact and uncorrupted by hie, as she from her mother's womb."[12] However, at the divorce hearings, several courtiers testified that, the morning after the wedding night, Arthur had boasted that he had been "deep in Spain." Most historians side with Arthur. Even though the marriage was short—only seven months—it seems likely that Arthur penetrated the Spanish princess.

Whatever the state of Catherine's maidenhead, Henry decided to divorce his wife of 24 years. This led to the split of the Church of England from Rome, and thus began the famous sequence of "divorced; beheaded; died; divorced; beheaded; survived." Before turning to this sequence of wives—Catherine of Aragon/Anne Boleyn/Jane Seymour/Anne of Cleves/Catherine Howard/Catherine Parr—let's take a peek at the wedding nights of Henry's sister, Mary Rose Tudor.

When Mary was 19, her brother, Henry VIII, married her to the aged (for those times; he was 52) Louis XII, king of France. In fact, Mary married Louis twice. The first was a proxy wedding that took place in England in 1514, where Louis was represented by the Duc de Longville. At the wedding ceremony, the duke stood in for Louis and Mary represented herself. After the ceremony came a proxy consummation. Mary dressed in a nightgown and sat in the bed, legs exposed. The duke removed his red hose and with his leg touched Mary's leg: a flesh-to-flesh proxy consummation. Then Mary traveled to France to wed the gouty Louis in person. Louis was delighted and hoped that Mary would bear him a son, for his second wife, Anne of Brittany, had borne him only daughters, and, by the terms of the Salic law current in France and other nations on the continent, only males could wear the crown. After the wedding, Louis's daughter, Claude, four years younger than Mary, led her to the bedchamber, already blessed by a priest, and there Louis consummated the union. The next morning, Louis declared that he had "performed miracles." An Italian official spelled this out in more detail: Louis "thrice did cross the river."[13] Three months later, Louis died, and Mary was not pregnant. Rather than face the same fate as the Dutch Margaret, Mary subverted her brother's diplomatic wishes and, while still in France, eloped with the Duke of Suffolk, solemnizing the match in a small church in Cluny. Henry VIII was irate, but the duke was wealthy and through a large cash gift regained Henry's favor and permission to return to England with his new bride.

While married to Catherine, Henry courted Anne Boleyn, but Anne was not an easy catch. She played hard to bed—so that when Anne retreated from the court to her family home, Henry sent her a dead buck with a note reminding her that he was a hunter! Anne refused his bed for seven years, but, once she was confident that Henry would carry out his divorce of Catherine, she allowed him between the sheets. Given the controversy over Henry's divorce of Catherine, Henry wed Anne in a secret ceremony in January 1533, and, again, there was no dancing. When she ascended to the throne five months later, Anne was six months pregnant. In Henry's royal sensibility, she was pregnant with a son. Henry was so confident that the baby would be a son that he arranged a great celebration. Instead of a son, the babe was a girl, Elizabeth. The marriage never recovered, and, because she came from a powerful family, Anne had powerful enemies, who persuaded Henry that she was unfaithful and therefore a traitor. After a trial, she was beheaded.

Henry's marriage to Jane Seymour, also from a powerful family, was an equally quiet affair. Jane bore Henry a son, Edward, but she died from the aftereffects of childbirth less than two years after marrying Henry. Henry now had three heirs—in order of succession, Edward, Mary, and Elizabeth. But Edward was a sickly child, and Henry wanted another son. Rather than find another lady-in-waiting in his court, Henry sent his courtiers to the continent in search of a woman who would both bear him a son and strengthen his position as a Protestant king facing the Catholic powerhouses of France, the Holy Roman Empire, and Spain.

Whereas Anne Boleyn had caught the king's eye as a lady-in-waiting, the other Anne, raised in the German duchy of Cleves-Juliers to marry into the aristocracy, was presented to Henry through an oil portrait by the hand of Hans Holbein the Younger.[14] Anne of Cleves was the daughter of John III, who ruled Cleves and Maria, heiress to Juliers. Both were Protestants and allies against the Catholic French and Spanish, whom Henry feared would unite and invade England. This suited Henry, who had broken with the Catholic Church but viewed the Lutherans as a threat to his Church of England, which retained many of the Catholic sacraments. In the 16th century, there were three ways to gain information about a prospective foreign bride. One consisted of reports from officials who visited the intended in her home. Another, more romantic alternative was for the prospective groom to visit the court of the prospective bride in disguise. And the third was to commission a portrait. A face-to-face interview was diplomatically fraught. Henry's emissaries brought back favorable reports about Anne, and Henry commissioned Holbein to paint a portrait. Henry was pleased with the Holbein rendering, and his representatives negotiated the marriage. Part of the negotiation was the assertion of Anne's brother, William, that Anne's previous engagement to Francis of Lorraine had been formally annulled. In the diplomatic game, such engagements were commonly made and abandoned as international alignments shifted. Like the claims and counterclaims over the maidenhead of Catherine, whether or not the previous engagement of Anne of Cleves was legally intact became the ostensible if dubious argument when Henry later sought to divorce her.

After a stately procession through northern Europe to Calais, Anne sailed to England and proceeded to the castle of Rochester, newly refurbished for her arrival. Henry showed up somewhat disguised in a hooded, mottled cloak to see Anne in the flesh. Anne was caught off guard and ignored the stranger's flirtations. She did not recognize her betrothed beneath the civvies. Henry was schooled in the rituals of courtly love, which delighted in such games. According to medieval romance literature familiar to Henry, lovers could recognize the beloved at a glance whatever the obstacles. For example, a lady might catch the eye of a knight though he was covered in armor. In Henry's mind, this pure love disguised as profane flirtation distinguished the nobility from the rest of humanity. But Anne was unschooled in these matters and appropriately retreated to the proper etiquette of ignoring an uninvited advance.

Henry was displeased. He also found Anne less attractive than her portrait. He complained to his officials and asked for a way out of the marriage. But Henry, fearing that France and Spain were about to join forces to invade England, lacked resolve. He could not endanger his alliance with Cleves and other Protestant powers in Europe. So, though unhappy at the prospect, Henry decided to go ahead with the wedding.

Henry and Anne married on Epiphany, January 6, 1540, a little more than two years after the death of Jane Seymour. Henry was 49, and Anne was 25. The wedding date was inauspicious because the church forbade marriages between Advent in November and Epiphany. Like all of Henry's weddings, this one was modest by royal standards. It took place at Greenwich, rather than in London, again in a "closet." For the bride, Henry had ordered his workshop to make a new bedhead. In full relief were central carvings of the letters "H" and "A" and to the side of the initials stood a priapic cherub and a pregnant cherub.[15] In chapter 13, we will pat the panes of some other wedding beds. The facts of their wedding night are well known because of what did not happen: Henry was unaroused and did not go deep into Cleves.

There were three reasons for this. One was that Henry abstained in order to follow the letter of the law—it was Epiphany—and thereby increase his chances of a male heir. Though capricious, Henry was God-fearing. The second was related to the first. Henry claimed he was rendered temporarily impotent by doubts over whether the officials in Cleves had actually repudiated Anne's contract to marry Francis of Lorraine. Though it was requested several times, Cleves never delivered the relevant documents. In Henry's mind, if Anne was not clearly available to marry in the eyes of the law, her ability to conceive a son would be in doubt. The third reason was that the royal eye that admired the portrait of Anne was disappointed by Anne in person and in bed. After a couple of nights in her bed, Henry complained to his advisers, "Surely I liked her before not well, but now like her much worse. For I have felt her belly and her breasts and thereby I can judge, she should be no maid. When I felt them, I had neither will nor courage to proceed any further in other matters."[16] At the time, "belly" could refer to the vagina as well as the stomach, but it seems unlikely that Henry searched for the intact hymen. Anne's surface was sufficient evidence that the marriage lacked God's favor and she failed to arouse Henry's sexual interest.

As in the case with Catherine of Aragon, we have to resist the temptation to see the link between Anne's belly and breasts and her legitimacy as Henry's queen as pure rationalization on Henry's part. Henry shared the common belief that the outward world directly reflected the divine. Empirical science was still in its infancy. Physicians had only the scantest knowledge of human physiology. It would be 100 years before William Harvey figured out that the heart was a pump and 400 years before physicians could treat problems in human reproductive systems scientifically. On subsequent nights, Henry continued to find himself unaroused and blamed Anne. As the weeks passed, Henry confessed to Thomas Cromwell, his principal secretary, that an "obstacle" prevented consummation. To ward off suspicion of impotence, Henry claimed he had nocturnal emissions. Outwardly, the couple regularly retired to the bedchamber together, but, below the grand bedhead of "H & A," Henry did not go "deep in Germany."

Anne confided to her ladies-in-waiting that Henry was affectionate in bed, giving her kisses, and seemed to think that such expressions of affection could eventually result in an heir. After one of these conversations, one lady lectured Anne that "there must be more than this, or it will be long ere we have a Duke of York."[17] Once Henry was sure that Cleves would not abandon its support against the French and Spanish enemies, Henry proceeded to divorce Anne on the basis that her previous engagement to Francis of Lorraine was still technically valid. Anne was crushed to hear of Henry's decision, responding that Henry was her "true lord and husband." A convocation of parliament declared the divorce in July 1540, ending a marriage of only half a year.

In return for a generous settlement, Anne agreed to the divorce and to remain in England. She retired to a country castle and lived another 17 years. Though Henry quickly married Catherine Howard and returned to an active life, the king declared Anne his "servant and sister." Anne joined Henry and Catherine at the wedding dinner, and, after Henry retired early, the two ladies danced with each other. For as long as he lived, Henry saw to Anne's financial well-being. After Henry had Catherine Howard beheaded for infidelity, Anne expressed her desire to return to Henry's marital bed. But Henry was no longer looking for an heir and married Catherine Parr, who was beyond her childbearing years. Anne considered this an insult. She lived long enough to survive Henry. She died at the age of 42, during the reign of the Catholic Queen Mary, and received a Catholic funeral in Westminster Abbey, where she is buried; there you can visit her grave. Anne was raised to marry a prince. Instead, she married a king. But her wedding night betrayed her as his wife, and instead she became his sister.

DRESS REHEARSAL

One way to work out all the political kinks of an important political union is to hold a proxy marriage before the actual one—a sort of dress rehearsal. The families commit in principle and agree to work out the details before the official event.

Thus, in 1660, the young dauphin of France, soon to be Louis XIV, journeyed with his mother, Anne of Austria, to Spain. His bride-to-be, Maria Theresa, came up from Madrid with her father, Philip, who was Anne's brother and Louis's uncle. Louis and Maria Theresa both lodged with their retinues on their respective sides of the border. At the proxy ceremony, in Fuenterrabia, Spain, Anne and Philip met for the first time in 44 years. The young Louis was keenly interested in catching a glimpse of the little blond foreign princess and so took it upon himself to ride by the windows of the grand chamber where the proxy ceremony was taking place.

As the story goes, he asked that the door be opened. He was let in, and his mother asked Maria Theresa how she liked the stranger. Her father, Philip, replied this was not the time to say. "And when can she say?" asked Anne in Spanish. "When she has walked through that door," said Philip, meaning the border. Louis's mischievous younger brother, known as Monsieur, then asked how the princess liked the door, to which she replied, "Muy linda, muy buena me parece la puerta" (the door looks very handsome and good to me).[18]

The widowed Anne had her wishes for an alliance between France and her own country fulfilled. She had been at loggerheads with her husband, Louis XIII, and obligated to endure his wars, much as the French wife of her brother Philip had had to endure wars between Spain and France from her side. The birth of Louis XIV (1638–1715) was a near miracle. Queen Anne had suffered a number of miscarriages and her husband, Louis XIII, usually slept with a mistress. However, a storm interfered with the king's travel itinerary and billeted him with his wife, instead of a mistress. With her the future Sun King was conceived.

When it was time for the dauphin Louis to marry, Anne arranged a proxy wedding. This was a way to commit in principle to a marital and political union and work out the details later—a sort of dress rehearsal. In fact, Anne had been married to Louis by proxy when she was only 11 years old. Anne, now Regent of France after the death of Louis, took her son to the border of Spain. The dauphin's bride-to-be, Maria Theresa, came up from Madrid with her father Philip, who was Anne's brother. Louis and Maria Theresa both lodged with their retinues on their respective sides of the border. At the proxy ceremony, in Fuenterrabia, Spain, sister and brother Anne and Philip met for the first time in 44 years, for France and Spain had been at war. The young Louis was keenly interested in gaining a sighting of the little blonde foreign princess and so took it upon himself to ride by the windows of the grand chamber where the proxy ceremony was taking place.

As the story goes, he asked that the door be opened. He was let in and his mother asked Maria Theresa how she liked the stranger. Her father, Philip, replied that this was not the time to say. "And when can she say?" asked Anne in Spanish. "When she has walked through that door," said Philip, meaning the border. Louis's mischievous younger brother, known as Monsieur, then asked how the princess liked the door, to which she replied, "Muy linda, muy buena me parece la puerta" (the door looks very handsome and good to me).

Several days later, Louis and Maria Theresa officially wedded at St. Jean-de-Lus, near Bordeaux. After dinner, Louis retired and requested his bride to join him in the bedchamber. To hasten their union, Anne dismissed the bride's retinue from the bedchamber and personally drew shut the curtains of the bridal bed.

To have all the top courtiers watching "the first time" was not something that Anne wanted for her son. The next morning, they were discovered cooing. Louis announced that the new queen would share his room as they traveled to Paris. He spoke little Spanish and she spoke little French, but they were compatible on the sexual plane. The king continued to sleep with Maria Theresa throughout the marriage; she tolerated his mistresses, and it is recounted that the queen had a habit of clapping her hands at her "lever" (morning wake-up ceremony) whenever she had spent a night with the king.

Ironically, after the royal folderol of the wedding night of Maria Theresa and Louis, and within a year after the queen's death, in 1683, Louis secretly married his pious mistress, Madame de Maintenon, a wedding that was so secret that no one knew exactly when it occurred or where. When they saw Madame de Maintenon attending mass sitting in the queen's box and when she remained seated when a member of the royal family entered the room, however, it was clear to everyone that it had occurred.

As for Louis's brother, Monsieur, it is recounted by biographer Antonia Fraser, relying on the confidences of his second wife, Liselotte, that he required the inspiration of rosaries and holy medals draped in strategic places to perform the act.

NIGHTS OF NOTHING

Henry VIII was not the only royal who could not perform on his wedding night. Two hundred years later, the dauphin of France, the future Louis XVI (1754–1792), failed on his wedding night to enter his young Austrian bride, Marie Antoinette. What ensued was one of the longest wedding nights on record and a testimony to bridal perseverance.

Marie Antoinette and Louis were married by proxy in a palace outside Vienna on April 19, 1770. She was 14 and her husband 15. Since this was a proxy marriage, rather than retire to a wedding chamber, the dauphin and the dauphine traveled to Paris for the official ceremony. Two large wagons went ahead of the procession in relays so that wherever the dauphine stopped, she would have one of two bedrooms, with armchairs, screens, folding stools and a twin bed covered with a white satin coverlet.

The wedding was held on May 16 under a silver brocade canopy in the Royal Chapel at Versailles. The wedding night commenced in the Hall of Mirrors, where the newlyweds played a long game of *cavagnole*, a board game like bingo in spades. A late banquet followed in the opera house; only a handful of courtiers supped, while the others watched politely. After the banquet, at which the groom ate heartily and the bride scarcely anything, royal fireworks lit up the sky, and then the bridal pair were led to the bedchamber. There the archbishop blessed the nuptial bed, Louis XV handed his grandson his nightshirt, and the Duchess of Chartres assisted Marie Antoinette as she put on her nightgown. The bride and groom reclined behind the bed hangings, and then the curtains were drawn aside for public viewing. The courtiers bowed and followed out the king out, leaving the sleepy dauphin to fall into a noisy sleep.

Prince Louis wrote a famous one-word entry in his diary the following day—"Rien" (nothing). Courtiers blamed this lack of activity on overeating at the wedding feast. However, Louis's diary recorded "Nothing" night after night. Marie Antoinette's mother preached patience, but when the month of festivities was well past and Louis was still inattentive, Marie Antoinette confronted him. Undaunted, Louis promised to fulfill his marital duty when they went to Compiegne in August; at that point, he would have turned 16. He assured her that "the time limit I set myself has been reached. You will find that at Compiegne I shall live with you in the fullest intimacy that you could wish."[19] Perhaps he imagined that all the exercise at his hunting lodge, away from the formality of Versailles, would give him fortitude. But he didn't carry through and spent his time at Compiegne hunting and enjoying banquets as usual.

The king intervened and asked his grandson about his "frigid condition." The dauphin answered that he found his wife charming and loved her but still needed time to overcome his timidity. Conjecturing that he had a sluggish body and poorly functioning endocrine system, doctors at court advised him to exercise more and to eat heartily, which only made him plumper. Marie Antoinette's mother continued to fret: "If a girl as pretty as the Dauphine cannot stir the Dauphin, every remedy will be useless."[20] The years passed with no pregnancy. Marie Antoinette poured her energies into a court life lavish with clothes, parties, and intrigues. Marie's brother, the Holy Roman emperor Joseph, investigated and reported:

> In his conjugal bed he has normal erections; he introduces his member, stays there without moving for about two minutes, then withdraws without ejaculating, and still erect, bids goodnight. This is incomprehensible because he sometimes has nocturnal emissions, but while inside and in the process, never; and he is content.[21]

Whatever the cause of Louis's nonperformance, Joseph beseeched Marie to remain affectionate and available, and, in August 1777 the queen wrote her mother that Louis had consummated the union. The long wait had fed rumors in court and ribald broadsides in public suggesting that the king was unable to control his consort and that Marie Antoinette was cuckolding him. Historians find no evidence of this and instead speculate that Louis had a physical impediment to erection. Whatever the reason for the long delay, Marie Antoinette bore him a daughter and two sons. Louis ascended to the throne in 1775 as Louis XVI and was the first king of France in 200 years not to have a royal mistress. And, no, Marie Antoinette did not say, "Let them eat cake."

WAITING FOR THE GROOM

The dauphin was not the only prince who did not perform on his wedding night. In 1744, the German Sophie Fredericke Auguste, 15 years of age, traveled to Russian and married Karl Peter, the Grand Duke and heir apparent to the Russian throne. Sophie converted to the Russian faith and changed her name to Catherine. Under the keen eye of Peter's aunt and of a daughter of Peter the Great, Empress Elizabeth, the court staged a grand wedding. Celebrations lasted 10 days before the ceremony. The Russian Orthodox service was grand, and the evening meal and ball extended beyond midnight. Finally, Catherine retired to the nuptial bedroom and slipped out of her massive wedding clothes and heavy crown and jewels and slipped into her nightgown. The empress now delivered Peter, embraced the young couple, and departed. Alas, Peter also departed, probably to play with his toy soldiers. In her memoirs, Catherine, by then Catherine the Great, described her wedding night as follows:

> Everybody left me and I remained alone for more than two hours, not knowing what to expect of me. Should I get up? Should I remain in bed? I truly did not know. At last Mme Krause, my new maid, came in and told me very cheerfully that the Grand Duke was waiting for his supper which would be served shortly. His Imperial Highness came to bed after supper and began to say how amused the servant would be to find us in bed together.[22]

Schooled by her mother on what to expect on her wedding night, Catherine soon realized that Peter was not up to the task and turned over and went to sleep. The marriage remained chaste for a number of years, but Catherine, with the empress's approval and so that she would produce an heir, took lovers. Of her married life with Peter, Catherine recorded in her memoirs: "my beloved spouse did not trouble himself in the slightest degree about me, but was constantly with his valet, playing at soldiers, exercising them in his room, or changing his uniform twenty times a day."[23]

After several miscarriages of questionable paternity, in 1754, she delivered a son, who resembled the Grand Duke. In the first year of his rule as emperor, Catherine staged a coup, sent Peter into exile and to an unnatural death, and ruled her adopted country with vigor. And, no, she never slept with a horse.

LOVE ME, LOVE MY DOG

Malmaison, the home of Napoleon and Josephine during their 13-year marriage (1796–1810), is a time capsule of the Empire style, an interior style befitting a great, if ruthless, conqueror. However, when Josephine and Napoleon met, in 1795, the sleek ornamental Empire style was yet to come. Josephine was a widow with two children. Napoleon was a major general on the rise. It was passion from the start, but neither was inclined to faithful monogamy. Napoleon wrote her steamy love letters about how her kisses set him on fire and how he wished he could assist at her undressing. "To live within Josephine is to live in the Elysian fields."[24] The wedding took place on March 9, 1796, and Josephine dressed in contemporary style, in a white muslin dress and a tricolor sash, "the picture of republicanism."[25] In her hair was her only wedding present from Napoleon—a gold enameled medallion engraved with the words "To Destiny." The ceremony was set for seven, and Napoleon arrived at the mayor's office three hours late. One of the witnesses on the bride's side was her former patron and lover, Paul Barras. The mayor had fallen asleep, and Napoleon had to shake him by his shoulders to waken him.

When the brief ceremony was done, the newlyweds rode in her carriage, led by the two black Hungarian horses that Barras had given her from the royal stables, to her pretty little house with a garden. The servants lit the way with lanterns as the newlyweds went up the three steps to the porch with stone lions on either side. They continued up a spiral staircase into her room, and there, on the nuptial couch, slept the poodle Fortune. The poodle bit Napoleon on the leg, yet Josephine's pet spent the night with them all the same. Thirty-six hours later, Napoleon left Josephine and rode off to his command, the army of Italy, and then to his invasion of Egypt. In European painting, dogs usually connote fidelity. The poodle in bed notwithstanding, Napoleon and Josephine were famously unfaithful to each other. Still, Napoleon divorced Josephine only when it was evident that she would not bear him a child.

A canine played a part in Napoleon's next wedding night, as well. Bent on correcting his tactical error of marrying for love, Napoleon fixed on a buxom girl with a long royal lineage as his next bride. Weirdly, by his alliance with Marie Louise, daughter of the Austrian emperor, Louis XVI and Marie Antoinette became his great-uncle and great-aunt.

Again the impatient bridegroom, when the never-seen bride arrived at the palace at Compiegne, Napoleon raced them through the ceremonies, which were held on April 2, 1810. Then Marie Louise went to her apartments in the palace, where she found her little pet dog and canary, which she had left behind in Vienna but which were brought by the emperor, along with her unfinished needlework. Napoleon, supposedly drunk with excitement, wished to put her at ease on the big night. The table was set for three—Napoleon, Marie Louise, and a younger sister of Napoleon, Caroline Murat. After they supped, Caroline had the customary role of adviser on the facts of life but reported that the bride had already been "told everything at Vienna." Then Napoleon, "soaked" in eau de cologne, came back to join Marie Louise. The fragrance was lavender, rosemary, bergamot, and neroli, in grape spirits. He used several bottles a day. Perfume water was invented in the 18th century by an Italian barber in Germany and named by the French.[26] He told one of his favorite young generals, Gaspard, Baron of Gourgaud, who wrote important memoirs when they were on Saint Helena, "I came to her and she did the whole thing with a laugh."[27]

THE UNVICTORIAN VICTORIA

Although the Victoria of "Victorian" comes to us dressed in black and morally pinched, the young queen was vivacious and deeply in love with her consort, Albert.

One of the Victorian habits of the Queen was keeping a journal. In it she described her wedding night: "Albert took me on his knee and kissed me. We had dinner in our sitting room; but I had such a sick headache that I could eat nothing and was obliged to lie down in the middle blue room for the remainder of the evening, on the sofa, but, ill or not, I never, never spent such an evening. He called me names of tenderness, I have never yet heard used to me before—was bliss beyond belief! Oh! This was the happiest day of my life!—May God help me to do my duty as I ought and be worthy of such blessings." The next morning: "When day dawned (for we did not sleep much) and I beheld that beautiful angelic face by my side, it was more than I can express! He does look so beautiful in his shirt only, with his beautiful throat seen."[28]

Equally giddy on her wedding night was Alexandra, Victoria's granddaughter. She married Nicholas, soon to become czar of Russia, in 1894. Like the union of Victoria and Albert, Alexandra's marriage was outwardly placid and privately passionate. On the day after their wedding night, she wrote in Nicholas's diary: "Never did I believe there could be such utter happiness in this world, such a feeling of unity between two moral beings. I love you, those three words have my life in them."[29]

NOTES

1.   Paolo Cesaretti, *Theodora: Empress of Byzantium* (New York: Vendome Press, 2001), 158–59.

2.   George Conklin, "Ingeborg of Denmark, Queen of France, 1193–1223," in *Queens and Queenship in Medieval Europe*, ed. Anne Duggan (Woodbridge, Suffolk, England: Boydell Press, 1997), 45.

3.   Katharina Wilson and Nadia Margolis, eds., *Women of the Middle Ages* (Westport, CT: Greenwood Press, 2004), 1:454–55.

4.   Leslie Carroll, *Notorious Royal Marriages* (New York: New American Libraries, 2010), 40.

5.   Retha Warnicke, *The Marrying of Anne of Cleves: Royal Protocols in Early Modern Europe* (Cambridge: Cambridge University Press, 2000), 161.

6.   Karen Lindsey, *Divorced, Beheaded, Survived: A Feminist Reinterpretation of the Wives of Henry VIII* (Reading, MA: Addison-Wesley, 1995), 17.

7.   David Starkey, *Six Wives: The Queens of Henry VIII* (New York: HarperCollins, 2003), 61.

8.   John Cordy Jeaffresson, *Brides and Bridals* (London: Hurst and Blackett, 1872), 1:248ff.

9. Mary Eden and Richard Carrington, *The Philosophy of the Bed* (London: Spring Books, 1961), 93.

10. "An Epithalamium on the Marriage of the Honourable Charles Leigh," in *Poetica Erotica: A Collection of Rare and Curious Amatory Verse*, ed. T. R. Smith (New York: Crown, 1949), 442–43.

11. Starkey, *Six Wives*, 63.

12. Ibid., 224.

13. Carroll, *Notorious Royal Marriages*, 96.

14. Warnicke, *The Marrying of Anne of Cleves*, ch. 7.

15. Starkey, *Six Wives*, 631–32.

16. Carroll, *Notorious Royal Marriages*, 166.

17. Ibid., 167.

18. Antonia Fraser, *Love and Louis XIV: The Women in the Life of the Sun King* (New York: Doubleday, 2006), 59.

19. Andre Castelot, *A Biography of Marie Antoinette*, trans. Denise Folliot (New York: Harper and Brothers, 1957), 45.

20. Ibid., 274.

21. Carroll, *Notorious Royal Marriages*, 276.

22. Virginia Rounding, *Catherine the Great: Love, Sex, and Power* (New York: St. Martin's Press, 2006), ch. 2.

23. Catherine II, *Memoirs of the Empress Catherine II* (New York: Appleton, 1859), 54.

24. Quoted in Christopher Hibbert, *Napoleon: His Wives and Women* (London: HarperCollins, 2002), 56.

25. Evangeline Bruce, *Napoleon and Josephine* (New York: Scribner, 1995), 162.

26. See http://www.jolique.com/perfume/origin_eau_cologne.htm.

27. Andre Castelot, *Napoleon*, trans. Guy Daniels (New York: Harper and Row, 1971), 391–92.

28. Carroll, *Notorious Royal Marriages*, 372.

29. Ibid., 411.

CHAPTER 5

Merriment and Pranks

Show us a glimpse of the House of Bliss!
—Arthur Upfield, *The Sands of Windee*[1]

Not only do we not tease those of higher social and economic status to their faces, but their power and money insulate them from ribs and jabs. In an office around the corner from mine [Jane], in a publishing company, was a reporter who dressed in dark suit and tie, more formal than the rest of us. He directed the annual roast for the top brass at IBM, and he would talk about what an exceedingly tricky job of diplomacy and politics it was. I also attest, as a former member of the Harvard Club of New York, that poking fun at anybody among that privileged crowd in any way requires as much care as one would take at a lunch with law partners. For this reason, this chapter turns to the common people as we take a look at pranks. When we enter their derring-do and teasing, we go to the heart of what has distinguished the wedding nights of ordinary people in Europe and America, especially country people, from those of the upper crust.

Arthur Upfield, a soldier in the British army, failed his surveyor's exam and disappointed his father. He decided to emigrate to Australia, where he became one of the best writers of detective fiction who ever lived. Upfield's chief detective, Napoleon Bonaparte, or "Bony," son of an aboriginal mother and a white father, was as interested in the land and the ways of all the people who made up Australia early in the 20th century as in solving crimes. In *The Sands of Windee* (1931), Bony celebrates a wedding

French youths carry a cauldron to rouse newlyweds for a wedding-night drink. (Reproduced with permission of the Bibliothèque Nationale de France.)

with ranchers in New South Wales and plays a green box-leaf at the "tin-kettling."

According to Upfield, that women and weddings were in short supply in Central Australia made nuptials all the more a red-letter day. The ceremony was modest and quiet, but then came the focal event, tin-kettling, which was actually "an adjunct to a housewarming party." Tin-kettling had the gaiety of a happy clown beating on a kettledrum: loud sounds and boisterous exchanges announcing the late-night guests to the bridal pair. Upfield commented that, rather than a casual, impromptu revelry, tin-kettling was very ritualized, down to what the person said who opened the door and how the bride and groom greeted their guests: "Tin-kettling a newly-wed pair is an event accompanied by a ceremonial of almost religious inflexibility, whilst with our modern motor transport a distance of eighty miles is but an evening's jaunt."

A portion of the scripted (unvarying) dialogue, according to Upfield's narrative, went as follows:

"Awake, ye sleepers in the House of Bliss! We are an-hungered and athirst. . . . Show us a glimpse of the House of Bliss!" . . . For the third time they came to the veranda steps and for the third time Stanton called: "Open ye dwellers in the House of Bliss!" And then a light sprang up in one of the rooms. A window was thrown open, and a voice raised in pretended anger came to them: "Enough! Who are you who should disturb the slumbers of those within the House of Bliss?" . . . "We are friends of the bride and friends of the groom. We are in need of refreshment and desire to rest," was Stanton's reply. "Gladly then will you all be admitted."

An oil lamp was suspended from the roof of the veranda, the door was thrown open, and the newlyweds, both dressed in white, invited the people in for a night of eating and drinking, music, and good company. The food was already on the table—stacks of sandwiches, buttered scones, cakes, and drinks. Yet, as if to emphasize the ritual nature of the custom, there was one more formal moment when the priest Father Ryan linked arms with the bride and then the groom and blessed the couple before the whole party: "Behold love which is God!"[2]

Pulling a prank is a tradition always waiting to be revived. Examples are the vaudeville turning in of a false fire alarm and giving the newlyweds' address so the fire brigade will shoot cold water through their window or attaching a telephone to the nuptial bed so that the bride and groom's sweet talk is broadcast to others. Playing pranks on a couple on the wedding night is a diversion for people, usually young men at loose ends, who have to create their own fun.

THE PRELUDE

The bachelor party or stag night foreshadows the wedding night. The archetype is of a surprise party given by the best man, with activities like watching a porn movie or hiring a stripper, and male bonding that includes heavy drinking. Not to be outdone, the bachelorette party is a version that bridesmaids give for the bride-to-be. The sexual content is essential to make the affair a stag party—and, with it, some element of humiliation for the soon-to-be-wed bachelor, who presumably needs a rite of passage from his exciting single life to a life of being "tied" to one female.

Interestingly, the fact that the party is a surprise and the tricks that will be played on the groom, the type of entertainment, and place a secret define it as a spoof of the wedding night.

In real life, the groom may be forcibly stripped himself or given a public lap dance by the stripper; in feature films that use stag parties in the plot, things usually go from playfulness to downright debauchery. For instance, in *The Hangover* (2009), the guys who attend the party wake up the next morning without memory of what happened and without the groom. At the end of the movie, they find out that the whole crazy night was captured in photos and agree to look through them once, then delete them.

PRANKS AT THE CEREMONY
AND PARTY

At many weddings, you have to hold your breath while somebody offers an outrageous toast that silences every partygoer. In the film *Four Weddings and a Funeral* (1984), Hugh Grant is hilarious as a best man whose toast calls to mind his last appearance as best man for a "nightmare of recrimination and violence that became their two-day marriage. . . . Anyway, enough of that. My job today is to talk about Angus. There are no skeletons in his cupboard. Or so I thought. I'll come on to that in a minute."

In the countryside, often pranks start right outside the church door—where an interruption is spectacular! Since most American wedding customs can be traced to the British Isles, we cite an example in Ireland—the arrival of the straw-boys, a spooky band that was part of goings-on as late as the 1960s. In certain Irish counties, at the close of the church ceremony, young men arrived, wearing costumes of straw, and swarmed around the wedding party. Although not invited guests, they expected to join in the celebration and to dance with the bride. If they felt they were well treated, they took off their masks and made a bonfire of their costumes in the yard. If the dancing and drink failed to amuse them, they threw their costumes into the highest trees around the place where the party was held. Snagged on branches, the costumes disintegrated as a negative commentary, or omen.[3]

Snatching the Bride or Groom

Stealing the bride is a most colorful caper when performed on horseback. In modern times, this cluster of customs that distinctly splinters the ceremony from the wedding night by removing one or the other of the newlyweds has ceased. In rural areas, however, such customs seem to have lasted.

Although stealing the bride or groom was a threat rarely fully carried out, it was often sport for a couple of hours. Most of the pranksters, however, were not known rascals but friends of the groom, who did their pranks with good humor—half the fun being to tell the story later.

Perhaps the custom is not as remote as we might assume. A Mrs. Job Marsh, a new bride in 1783 in Hadley, Massachusetts, was the last recorded bride in the United States to have been stolen. The perpetrators were a band of young friends of the groom. They carted her off to a nearby tavern, and there is no indication of an ensuing scandal or legal action.[4]

Replacing the Bride

An early episode of replacing the bride occurs in the Bible in Genesis 29:25. When it is time to marry, Jacob travels to the home of Laban, his uncle, where he falls in love with Rachel. Jacob lacks the sheep or gold needed to pay the bride price. Instead, he labors for seven years to earn the right of marriage. On the wedding night, Laban substitutes Rachel's older sister, Leah, for the bride in the nuptial tent. When Jacob realizes that he has consummated the wedding with the wrong woman, he complains: "What is this you have done to me? Did I not serve with you for Rachel? Why then have you deceived me?" But Laban defends the switch by stating that, among his people, the oldest daughter always marries first. Jacob still wants to marry Rachel and works another seven years in order to return home to his father, Isaac, with both women. Though more serious than a prank, this biblical nighttime swap disconnects the wedding from the wedding night in a fundamental way and represents the granddad of comedic nuptial trickery.

In Greek mythology, Mars, the god of war, confesses to a seemingly sympathetic goddess Venus that he is desperately in love with the goddess of wisdom and battle, Minerva, who has previously spurned him. Venus pretends that Minerva is ready to extend her favors. Mars prepares a bridal chamber, to which Venus, wearing a bridal veil over her face, is escorted. When Mars lifts the veil and sees the face beneath, he is outraged and ashamed, while Venus howls with laughter at his humiliation. Here the prankster is the woman who offers herself as a substitute, a fake lover. Unlike in the biblical story of Jacob, this switch of women does not entail consummation, only surprise. The woman, a goddess, has a voice, and, of course, Mars has not labored for this night and is not the marrying type.

Shakespeare's comedy *Measure for Measure* turns on a bed trick. Angelo, a judge who rules in the absence of the Duke, rejects Mariana, his betrothed, when her dowry is lost at sea. Angelo lusts after a novice nun, Isabella, who tells him she is willing to submit to him—if he will free her brother from prison in exchange—but in fact it is Mariana, his betrothed, whom Angelo caresses under the sheets. Mariana and Angelo have sex, a consummation of their betrothal, ensuring that they will marry.[5]

In many traditions, practical jokes where the bride is replaced with a proxy are means to delude the evil eye. In folklore, the replacement of a beautiful bride with an old hag occurs so frequently that it has a name: the false bride. In *And the Bride Wore . . .*, Ann Monsarrat reports on the different versions of this tale that are found across Europe. In Bavaria, a bearded man concealed in woman's clothes slips into bed; in Estonia, the bride's brother is the joking surprise left to lie in wait for the groom.[6]

Interrupting the Bridal Procession

Playing pranks on a couple on their wedding night has an undeniable edge. Sometimes the tomfoolery is a covert criticism of the marriage, and, like most teasing and trickery, it can contain a shade of envy. In effect, the mischief is a hot fudge sundae that the couple may experience as both hot and cold.

As we saw in chapter 2, on wedding nights in Greece and Rome, the bride processed from her household to the groom's. There the groom carried her over the threshold as a symbolic representation of her entrance into a new set of responsibilities, both social and religious. One explanation for the bride's being lifted over the doorstep or carried over the threshold is that it harks back to bride capture. But this pleasing custom took a diametrically opposite form among the Greeks of Macedonia. After a week of celebrating, the bride tried to lift the groom off the ground and carry him away, while he resisted. First, he had to be sure she wasn't a witch and that she truly wanted him.

The ancient Greek and Roman procession often included a mock battle between the bride's and the groom's families, invoking a ritual memory of bride capture. This ancient custom was the basis for pranks that interrupted the communal transfer of the woman.

In Eastern and Western Europe, it was a common custom to interfere with or to stop the bridal procession by throwing logs on the road or setting up barriers. For example, young scamps threw darts at the procession (from a safe distance and aiming to miss).[7] In the gentler version found today, friends stretch a rope or garland across the road and ask the bridegroom to pay the friends a token toll.

A Harvard professor and anthropologist, Laurence Wylie, did innovative research in the 1950s, in the Vaucluse, now chic but then a poor and remote southeastern mountain region of France. Wylie studied the ways of people by living alongside them instead of observing them from a sort of pinnacle. By Wylie's account, in the context of the goings-on connected with weddings, the customs that followed the ceremony splashed a bright douse of paint on the gray village life. Moreover, these customs were not staged like a play at a community theater but were traditional pranks inherited from previous generations. They were woven into the wedding fabric.

From the church, the procession started down the narrow village streets, but a crowd formed and barred the newlyweds' way with a long pole festooned with flowers and ribbons. The groom sprinkled coins onto a tray, located in the middle of the street, to "pay for their passage." Then children in the crowd would trail after, shouting "Vivent les novi!," and the couple would throw them candy. The wedding banquet took place at the house of the bride's parents or at a hotel. Toward the end of the meal, one of the men dived under the table. Everyone giggled, and the bride would squeal. The man would reach up and remove from her leg the wedding garter that she had put on for the occasion. What Wylie says about this custom holds true for so many wedding night customs: that this "had no special symbolic significance to the people of Peyrane who think of it only as a trick to be played on the bride to embarrass her." Old boyfriends and rejected suitors were "publicly reminded of their failure" when friends of the couple would go around tying bouquets of sage to the doors of their houses.[8]

What are we to make of these customs? Are they just good fun? Or do they express, in light fashion, deep competition for the woman? From a modern anthropological point of view, the ritual interruption of the procession reflects deep antagonism between the family losing the woman and the family gaining her and among the men who competed for her as a sexual partner and mother of their children. In Freudian terms, the custom works as a sublimation of illicit sexual desire—in the case of pulling off the bride's garter, the desire of the men of the village to sleep with the young woman. Being suggestive but not disruptive, the prank is an allowable form of sexual expression.

Sometimes an aspect of the prank is clearly intended to wish the bride and groom well. In Ireland in the days when Anthony Trollope was a horseback postal inspector there, some of the wedding guests used to race on horseback from the church to the home of the bride, where the couple would be spending the night, for a party. The winner of the race received a prize of whiskey or a garter belonging to the bride. If the prize was whiskey, the bride smashed the bottle before it was emptied; the scattered drops meant that the couple would have children. Again, the ritual race was a fun substitute for more earnest competition for a woman, while the whiskey routine illustrates that men other than the groom may enjoy a portion of the joy but not intimacy with the bride. The whiskey that falls to the ground undrunk ensures that the bride will reserve sex and procreation to the groom.

Throwing objects at the bride was customary in ancient Greece, with grains and fruit most clearly associated with fertility. In Rome, the bridegroom threw nuts at the well-wishers. Our association of nuts with male sexuality has ancient roots. In Israel, people throw cake at the bridal pair. Since the late Renaissance, in Europe, people also have thrown shoes at the newly married couple and their carriage, which they have to dodge. The Italian word "confetti" is related to "confectionery" and refers to the grain or nuts, covered in sugar, that were tossed at the bride and groom.

FOOLISH FOOD

Returning to the Vaucluse, after the procession and its ritual interruption came a banquet and then a dance, during which the bride and groom slipped away to the house of one or the other set of parents. In the wee hours, they heard a loud knock on the door. The noise increased until the groom went to the door to receive a boisterous group of his friends. The couple, thought to be in need of nourishment, was then presented with two bowls of onion soup.[9]

A NOBLEMAN'S HEADACHE

An old custom that is the opposite of the wedding guests blessing the newlyweds is in France called a *charivari* and in the rural American South "shivaree." The origin of the word is the Latin *caribaria*, or headache, for obvious reasons. The following account shows how wild it could get.

Talleyrand (1754–1838) was the supreme aristo-cat with nine lives, for he danced out of the shadow of the guillotine to hold high posts in government under Napoleon and after the restoration of the monarchy. But some members of the haute bourgeoisie had several lives, too. For example, Antoine-Vincent Arnault (1766–1834) had a father who was a functionary who worked for Louis XIV's brother, and his family lived at Versailles from the time he was five. The father died after short service to the king, but Antoine-Vincent's mother served as "femme de chambre" for Louis XVI's mother, so the family stayed at Versailles. As a young man, Antoine-Vincent was secretary (an honorific that allowed him to stick around at court) to the wife of the future Louis XVIII. Still later, he was on very good terms with Napoleon and his family, and he wrote it all up in his memoirs.

In 1792, France was in the aftershocks of the terrible bloodshed of the Revolution. Arnault took a trip of several days, going north from Paris to Amiens. He arrived at a village and asked directions. The grocer gave them but advised him to spend the night before continuing to Amiens. Arnault thus spent the night in an alcove type of bed in the grocer's store. Before he closed his eyes, he thought about the contrast between the bloodshed and tumult in the capital and the tranquility of the countryside he had traveled through and the hamlet where he was spending the night. When awakened by a terrible racket, he imagined the worst—violent revolutionaries:

> I'd been asleep a few hours when a terrifying racket, produced by a cacophony of instruments and singing, was audible around the house and woke me with a start. Had I been wrong I asked my-

self as I rubbed my eyes. Did this village too have its radicals, its Jacobin cannibals? For certain those were their death songs, their barbaric music. Who was their target? Was it myself? Nothing was more likely. They waited until I was in bed, in order to seize me more easily. There they were, they were coming to get me.

Then my door opened. "Get up, Sir, get up quickly," my host said. "'Why? What's the matter?" "A charivari, Sir, a charivari."

The marriage of a young man and an old woman had indeed stirred up this population of villagers. Armed with pots, pails, pans, and kettles, which the women were pounding with their tongs, and animal horns, in which the cowherds were blowing with all their might, the townspeople were celebrating in the noisiest possible manner the most ridiculous sort of wedding. These good people were laughing while, 10 miles away, thousands of families were in tears; these good people were having fun, while Paris was plunged into mourning and horror!

Arnault reported that, after a half-hour, the revelers tired of their sport; they wanted to sleep, so they let others sleep, and he slept soundly until the grocer came in to open his shop.[10]

A CONTEMPORARY CHARIVARI

Practical jokes and pranks on wedding nights have changed in the modern period, as customs will. Interviews done in the early 1970s with people between the ages of 17 and 80 living in the inland farming areas of New Brunswick and Maine reveal both the continuity and the change. In this area, newlyweds either set up housekeeping immediately after the wedding or stayed with the bride's parents the first night. Either way there would be a shivaree for them.

The afternoon before the wedding, the new husband bought treats—hard candy, peanuts in the shell, and a few boxes of cigars. In the early evening, people started coming from all directions, bringing noisemaking equipment such as pots and pans, horse bells, horns, and "almost always the blade of a circular saw with a piece of steel pipe for hitting it." When it was dark, the well-wishers gathered in the front yard of the bride's parents' house and started to make a racket. This went on for as long as the couple could stand it, with the couple probably retiring to a back room. Finally, the newlyweds came to the front door dressed in their wedding clothes. If they did not invite the merrymakers into the house, the company would burst through the front door and go right up the stairs with their "instruments" to the bedroom door. There the couple received the visitors, sometimes at the end of a receiving line that included close family members. Either the treats were handed out straightway or the bride and groom set them outdoors in washtubs for their visitors.

Other pranks involved the couple's car as they prepared to leave on their honeymoon. Fooling with the car might involve putting shaving cream on the seats or actually cutting the ignition wire or letting air out of the tires. If the couple was to remain at the bride's home, pranksters might rig the bed so that it would fall apart when slept on. Or someone might tie a bell to the ropes under the mattress or put squeaky toys under the mattress. Someone might cut holes in strategic places in the bride's nightgown or sew up the groom's pajamas or sew bells to them. Although stealing the bride or groom was very rarely fully carried out, it was often threatened.[11]

Shoes have had the potential to be sexy. In America, they are tied to the back of the honeymoon car. In *It's a Wonderful Life*, though the newlyweds, George and Mary, are spending their first night in a leaky house, a shot of the bedroom shows the couple's shoes sitting side by side on the floor beneath the nuptial bed—this sentimental movie's suggestion of the happy sex awaiting the pair. Sometimes the envy of the couple's neighbors can become distinctly weird. In rural France, a jealous suitor might tie the groom's laces in order to prevent the consummation of a marriage. A case is quoted in *Love and the French* of a man in 1591 who was fined 20 crowns and banished for having "tied laces not only to prevent young men, but even cats, dogs and other domestic animals from procreating."[12]

TESTING BRIDE AND GROOM

Near the Arctic Circle, Laplanders had a custom that was a game and also a test. To be a successful couple often takes more grit than flowery words, and Laplanders put that quality to a serious test. After a wedding, the guests would bury the bride and groom. This might be in a cave-like fold in a hill, enhanced by the snow that the guests piled up around them. Here the bride and groom stayed for upwards of a day and a night. Then together they tunneled out of the snow.[13]

In weddings in Europe and America that did not involve royalty and that preceded the Victorian era, the parties were very much simpler than anything touted in bridal magazines today. The community, by means of pranks, found a way to mark and celebrate the couple's change of status that didn't involve fancy gifts or clothes, an impressive ceremony, or an elaborate meal. In such unpretentious weddings, it was often the case that the bride and groom simply went home to the home of one of their families and started to work again the next morning. We think of the pranks as the rags tied on the tail of old-fashioned kites—building up the personal and communal story of the newlyweds, letting off youthful steam, possibly expressing old rivalries, and adumbrating the sexual union with a rip-roaring time. Moreover, the men who interrupted the progress to the nuptial chamber showed off their cleverness and reaffirmed their manliness, not unlike cats spraying a territory—and masculine prowess is a matter of great moment for a wedding night, even if the question of virginity has received much more commentary over the ages.

AN INTERLOPER IN THE NUPTIAL BED

It was terrible for the French to learn, from the second decade of the 19th century, that Napoleon was a ruthless general and ruler who was responsible for the deaths of 100,000 French soldiers and who created many enemies for France by invading their territory. The prior shock came to those dazzled by Empire style and Empire paintings and concerned Napoleon's consort Josephine herself—who was divorced, with two children, and on the move. She was apparently an unmitigated tart who had switched her favors for the money from Paul Barras, without any intention of being faithful to the Napoleon, not even after they were wed—and the same was true for him.

They had slept together, and he was captivated with her. He wrote steamy love letters about how her kisses set him on fire and how he wished he could assist at her undressing. The wedding took place March 9, 1796, six years after the storming of the Bastille and three years after Marie Antoinette went to the guillotine. To have aristocratic tastes was not in vogue, and Josephine was married in a white muslin dress and a tricolor sash, "the picture of republicanism," said one biographer.[14] In her hair was her only wedding present from Napoleon, a gold enameled medallion engraved with the words "To Destiny." The ceremony was set for seven, and Napoleon arrived at the mayor's office three hours late. One of the witnesses of the bride was her former patron and lover, Barras. The mayor had fallen asleep, and Napoleon had to shake him by his shoulders to waken him.

When the brief ceremony was done, Josephine and Napoleon drove in her carriage, the one led by the two black Hungarian horses that Barras had given her from the royal stables, to her pretty little Parisian house with a garden at 18, Rue Chantereine (no longer there). The servants lit the way with lanterns as the newlyweds went up the three steps to the porch with stone lions couched on either side. They went up a spiral staircase into her room, and there on the nuptial couch slept the poodle Fortune.

They began to get amorous, but the dog parked right in the middle of the bed. Napoleon, who didn't want to be in the doghouse himself, was the model of forbearance, according to his confidence to A. V. Arnault, a playwright and functionary of Napoleon:

> I wanted to boot him off it: a hopeless wish. I was told I must resolve to sleep somewhere else or agree to share. That annoyed me quite a bit, but it was "take it or leave it." So I resigned myself. The favorite, however, was less accommodating than I.[15]

Other sources say that the poodle bit the general on the leg. It is said he spent the night with them all the same. Thirty-six hours later, Napoleon left Josephine and drove off to his command, the army of Italy.

NOTES

1.   Arthur Upfield, *The Sands of Windee* (New York: Charles Scribner's Sons, 1931), 50–51.

2.   Ibid.

3.   Linda May Ballard, *Forgetting Frolic: Marriage Traditions in Ireland* (Belfast: Institute of Irish Studies, 1976), 123ff.

4.   Sylvester Judd, *The History of Hadley, Massachusetts* (Somersworth, NH: New Hampshire, 1976), 237–38.

5.   Act V, scene 1. Mariana says, "I have known my husband; yet my husband knows not that ever he knew me."

6.   Ann Monsarrat, *And the Bride Wore . . . : The Story of the White Wedding* (New York: Dodd, Mead, 1974), 109.

7.   Ibid., 111.

8.   Laurence Wylie, *Village in the Vaucluse* (Cambridge, MA: Harvard University Press, 1957), 132.

9.   Ibid., 133.

10.   Antoine-Vincent Arnault, *Souvenirs d'un Sexagenaire* (Paris: Honore Campion, 2003), 214–15.

11.   Monica Morrison, "Wedding Night Pranks in Western New Brunswick," *Southern Folklore Quarterly* 38 (1974): 285–97.

12.   Nina Epton, *Love and the French* (London: Cassell, 1959), 111.

13.   Documentary described to Jane Merrill by Franco Barbacci, an Italian automobile executive, which he saw on Swedish television in the mid-1980s.

14.   Evangeline Bruce, *Napoleon and Josephine: The Impossible Marriage* (New York: Scribner, 1995), 162.

15.   Quoted in Richard Zacks, *History Laid Bare* (New York: HarperCollins, 1994), 283–84.

CHAPTER 6

Tobias Nights

Oh, those naked nights at Chelsea! When will they come again?
I kiss both locks of hair every time I open my desk—
but the little curly one seems to bring me nearer to you.
—Charles Kingsley to his wife, Fanny[1]

MARRIAGE IN THE JEWISH BIBLE

In previous chapters, we have seen a number of unconsummated nights, unconsummated because something went awry. There is also a tradition of delaying consummation intentionally. This delay usually has strong religious overtones. It marks a night of sacrificing immediate pleasure in order to acknowledge a sacred obligation that lies outside the marriage. At the same time, the delay honors a deep anxiety over the big move to sexual union. This anxiety often takes the form of evil spirits that the couple is told to avoid by putting off sexual intercourse. In chapter 2, we saw that Athenian brides might spend a night in the temple of Artemis, asking the goddess's permission to leave behind the bride's virginal state— Artemis was a virgin deity and patron of all women—and accept a male sexual partner. In Sparta, some men delayed sexual intercourse for a night on the assumption that their pent-up energy would enhance their chances of impregnating the bride on the first night of sex.

From a traditional Judeo-Christian-Islamic perspective, Adam and Eve are the original couple. The first chapter of Genesis focuses on their fertility and biological dominance: "So God created man in his own image, in the image of God he created him; male and female he created them. And God blessed them, and God said to them, 'Be fruitful and multiply, and fill the earth and subdue it'" (Genesis 1:27).[2] The creation story of the first chapter of Genesis fills the Earth with, in order, day and night; sky; plants; sun and moon; creatures in the air, sea, and land; and, finally, man and woman. Following God's suit, the man and woman will multiply and establish human dominion over the animal and plant kingdoms.

The second chapter of Genesis focuses on the relatedness of Adam and Eve. Having created Adam—in this chapter, out of Earth—God reflects: "It is not good that the man should be alone; I will make him a helper fit for him" (Genesis 2:18). In this version of creation, God extracts a rib from Adam's side and fashions a woman to support the solitary male. The Jewish Bible has many affirmations of married life and looks askance upon celibacy, which men and women rarely voluntarily embrace. This second chapter of Genesis refers to Adam and Eve as man and wife, but there is mention of neither a wedding nor a wedding night. As long as Adam and Eve dwell in the Garden of Eden, they are a self-sufficient couple with, patently, no need to distinguish themselves from other couples. There is no need to publicly or legally lay claim to each other and no need to formally proceed from one household to another. They cleave to one another "as one flesh" (Genesis 2.18), and in their innocence, "the man and his wife were both naked, and were not ashamed" (Genesis 2.25).

Much changes in the third chapter when Eve eats the fruit of the tree of knowledge. This act of disobedience ends the couple's innocence; self-conscious, they cover their genitals. God evicts the primal couple from the Garden of Eden, and it is only now that they begin begetting. With the birth of Cain and his brother, Abel, biblical history begins with a sibling rivalry.

The family structure in the Jewish Bible is generally patriarchal—the "begats" list only men—and the patriarchs often travel to find an appropriate woman. Jacob journeys to Laban and lives with his future father-in-law while earning the right to marry Rachel (Genesis 29). Before leading the Hebrews out of Egypt, Moses remains with his wife's family in Midian (Exodus 2:15–22). The Jewish Bible presents us with many dramas between man and wife. Prominent examples include Sarah's gift to Abraham of her slave, Hagar, who will bear him a child on Sarah's behalf, and Sarah's subsequent eviction of Hagar (Genesis 16–21); Jacob's courtship of and marriage to Rachel (Genesis 24); David's lust for Bathsheba and his consequent strategy to eliminate her husband, Uriah (2 Samuel 11–12); and Solomon's marriages to foreign wives (1 Kings 11). The latter is especially problematic in the Jewish Bible because the Israelites were trying to survive as a community living among Moabites, Canaanites, Samaritans, and other foreign peoples. There are notable instances of men with multiple wives—Abraham, David, Solomon—but scholars agree that over the long course of composing the Jewish Bible, some 800 to 900 years, monogamy was common and increasingly standard. By the third century B.C.E. and into Christian times, monogamy was assumed.

Marriage was central enough to the lives of the Israelites that the prophets often compared the relationship of the Israelites to God to a marriage. In positive terms, in Isaiah 62:4–5, God affirms the vindication of His people in marital terms: "you shall be called My delight is in her, and your land Married; for the Lord delights in you, and your land shall be married. For . . . as the bridegroom rejoices over the bride, so shall your God rejoice over you." In negative terms, other prophets often compare the people to wives who are unfaithful to their spouses. Through Ezekiel, God recounts how he found Jerusalem as an abandoned baby girl, rescued her and helped her to grow to maidenhood, again found her naked and again rescued her, this time by marrying her, and in her married state provided as follows: "Thus you were decked with gold and silver; and your raiment was of fine linen and silk, and embroidered cloth; you ate fine flour and honey and oil" (Ezekiel 16:13). Yet, the bride turned harlot, associating with the Egyptians, Assyrians, and Chaldeans, provoking God's wrath and leading him to abandon his bride to foreign conquerors. Hosea, to dramatize God's forgiveness of a wayward people, takes as his wife the prostitute Gomer, who bears three children by other men and then abandons the prophet. Hosea takes her back, just as God renews his protection of Israelites who have turned to other gods: "I will heal their faithlessness; I will love them freely, for my anger has turned from them" (Hosea 14:4).

For all the interest in the politics of marriage and the many analogies to married life, the Jewish Bible has few descriptions of weddings. We find only glimpses of various elements. Genesis 29:22 mentions a wedding feast for Jacob and his wife, Rachel. Isaiah 61:10 describes the wedding clothes: "as a bridegroom bedecks himself with a garland, and as a bride adorns herself with her jewels." Jeremiah 7:34 refers to the "mirth and gladness" of a wedding. Psalm 45:10–15 describes a princess bride clothed in "many-colored robes" and accompanied by an escort of "virgin companions." Psalm 78:63 refers to the loss of a "marriage song" as a result of God's rejection of the Israelites, who "did not observe his decrees, but turned away and were faithless like their ancestors."

The Jewish Bible wholeheartedly takes sexuality as a normal and natural part of life. Throughout the Jewish Bible, marriage provides the couple with pleasure, as well as children. Love between a man and woman comes through especially strongly in the Song of Songs (in Christian Bibles, the Song of Solomon), which celebrates erotic love and is frequently cited at weddings. The inscription on a Jewish wedding ring often reads, "I am my beloved's and my beloved is mine; he pastures his flock among the lilies" (Song of Solomon 6:3). One of the songs (3:6–11) describes the wedding procession of Solomon:

> What is that coming up from the wilderness, like a column of smoke, perfumed with myrrh and frankincense, with all the fragrant powders of the merchant? . . . King Solomon made himself a palanquin from the wood of Lebanon. He made its posts of silver, its back of gold, its seat of purple, its interior was inlaid with love. Daughters of Jerusalem, come out. Look, O daughters of Zion, at King Solomon, at the crown with which his mother crowned him on the day of his wedding, on the day of the gladness of his heart.

At Passover, Jews recite many parts of the Song of Songs as testimony to God's close relationship to his people. From the fourth chapter:

> Come with me from Lebanon, my bride;
> Come with me from Lebanon,
> Depart from the peak of Amana,
> From the peak of Senir and Hermon,
> From the dens of lions,
> From the mountains of leopards.
> You have ravished my heart, my sister, my bride,
> You have ravished my heart with a glance of your eyes,
> With one jewel of your necklace. . . .
> Your lips distill nectar, my bride;
> Honey and milk are under your tongue;
> The scent of your garments is like the scent of Lebanon. . . .
> Your channel is an orchard of pomegranates
> With all the choicest fruits, henna with nard,
> Nard and saffron, calamus and cinnamon,
> With all trees of frankincense, myrrh and aloes,
> With all chief spices—
> A garden fountain, a well of living water,
> And flowing streams from Lebanon.

THE BOOK OF TOBIT

For a specific mention of a Jewish marriage contract and wedding night, we have to look outside the Jewish Bible to a cluster of Jewish texts that are part of the Christian Bible's Apocrypha. These books, composed in the two centuries before the Romans destroyed the temple in 70 C.E., include Judith, in which the pious widow lures the Assyrian general Holofernes to his death by her hand; Maccabees I–IV, which describes the revolts of the Jews against their Hellenizing rulers; Susanna, whom some elders falsely accuse of adultery but who is rescued by Daniel, who proves her innocence and the guilt of the elders; additions to the book of Esther, who saves Mordecai and the Jews from the evil Haman; and the lesser known but dramatic Tobit. Even though these texts are not included in the Jewish Bible, the stories were well known and much discussed in the rabbinical literature, and they describe in wonderful detail the life of Jews after they returned from the Babylonian exile in 538 B.C.E.

Tobit, a "Jewish novella"[3] set in eighth-century B.C.E. Nineveh, the Assyrian capital, is full of strange events. Tobit is blinded by bird droppings: Tobit's son, Tobias, captures a magic fish that bites his ankle: and a demon lurks in the nuptial bedchamber. Overall, the book asserts the responsibility of Jews to live righteously in exile and to marry each other rather than foreign women and men. Sarah and Tobias live in distant parts of the Assyrian empire. Sarah has married seven men, but, on each wedding night, the demon Asmodeus kills the groom before the newlyweds can consummate the marriage. Sarah's maid blames her, and, in despair, Sarah longs for death. She prays: "Already seven husbands of mine have died. Why should I still live? But if it is not pleasing to you, O Lord, to take my life, hear my disgrace" (Tobit 3:15).

In faraway Nineveh, Tobit has lost favor with the Assyrian king, who has removed him from his official post. As a consequence, Tobit loses not only his possessions but also his sight when he is blinded by bird droppings. He, too, longs for death. Both Sarah and Tobit are righteous Jews, undeserving of their hardships. The angel Raphael, in human disguise, comes to rescue both sufferers. He guides Tobias, Tobit's son, on a long journey to Sarah's home. En route, a magical fish attaches itself to Tobias's foot, and the angel Raphael instructs Tobias to kill the fish and harvest its liver, gall bladder, and heart. When Tobias arrives at Sarah's home, he asks her father for her hand in marriage. The father happily consents and draws up a marriage contract that bequeaths his wealth to his new son-in-law. After a wedding feast, Tobias and Sarah retire to the nuptial chamber to face the terrible demon. Tobias places the fish liver and heart on the incense burner in the bedchamber, and the smoke drives the demon Asmodeus to Egypt, where Raphael follows and binds him, that the demon might not return.

Before consummating their marriage, Tobias asks Sarah to leave the bed and give thanks to their Lord: "You made Adam, and for him you made his wife Eve as a helper and support. From the two of them the human race has sprung. You said, 'It is not good that the man should be alone; let us make helper for him like himself.' I am now taking this kins-woman of mine, not because of lust, but with sincerity. Grant that she and I may find mercy and that we may grow old together" (Tobit 8:6–7).

THE STORY OF TOBIAS

Following the example of Jacob and Leah, rabbis encouraged Jews to con-summate their marriage within seven days of the marriage unless the bride was menstruating.[4] But Jews did not delay consummation as a religious practice. However, the brief delay in Tobit inspired a Christian tradition of Tobias Nights in which newlyweds replaced immediate sexual union with a day or more of abstinence. This practice was well enough estab-lished that at the Fourth Council of Carthage, in 398 C.E., the Church codified it, encouraging the faithful to wait two to three days to receive the blessings bestowed by the priest. To some Christians, Tobias Nights served as a sacrifice of immediate sexual pleasure for the greater plea-sure of God. For others, this practice also heightened the possibility of conception.

In his monumental *The History of Human Marriage*,[5] Edward Wester-marck, a Finnish anthropologist who never married, describes many in-stances of delayed consummation. In some of these, the husband and wife simply remain apart, usually with their respective families. In Montene-gro, the new wife, fully clothed, spends one night with a bridesman and then passes several nights with her sisters-in-law before the husband's mother allows her to join her husband in bed. In Estonia, the bride and groom share a bed, but the groom may not loosen her girdle. Among the Serbs, the bride sleeps with a child on the first night. At multiday wed-dings that include large extended families and guests, the bride and groom stay with their families until everyone has left, a matter of a couple of days after the wedding ceremony. During Tobias Nights, Catholics usually di-rect their devotions to the Holy Virgin or St. Joseph.

Outside the Christian tradition, Westermarck gives many examples of other delays. In the Vedas, the oldest Hindu scripture, newlyweds are counseled to delay intercourse for three nights, to sleep on the ground, and to avoid salt and pungent food. Between them on the ground lies a staff "anointed with perfumes and wrapped round with a garment or thread."[6] For those couples wishing to give birth to a Vedic scholar, de-lays of 3 nights are rewarded with an ordinary pundit, delays of 12 nights with a first-class scholar, delays of 4 months with a "Brahman of more ex-alted rank," delays of 6 months with a *rishi* (saint), and delays of an entire year with a god. The staunch message is that abstinence bestows spiritual karma on the offspring.

Outside the major religious traditions, Westermarck alludes to examples of East African communities in which the bride and groom sleep in beds separated by a fire and abstain from food, as well as sex. In Southeast Asian societies, the bride stays with older women who protect her for a period of days from the naturally wildly desirous husband. Australian aborigine couples also sleep on opposite sides of a fire for several nights before their first intercourse.

Given the importance of consummation and its close tie to the wedding, why the delays? According to Westermarck, one reason is that the ritual delay reenacts the resistance of the bride to leaving her family, which figured in the ancient Greek weddings. It lengthens the rite of passage for the bride, honoring her loss of family and home. Another reason is that the delay accommodates sexual bashfulness. Instead of moving directly to the nuptial bed, the couple has a measure of time to prepare themselves. Some communities institute a delay in order to postpone childbirth, giving the couple some time to establish themselves. And, finally, among some groups, fear of evil spirits is especially high during the first intercourse. The first time entails risk and even danger. This fits the Tobias story well. The demon Asmodeus is a Jewish version of an Iranian Zoroastrian demon. The deaths of seven grooms highlight the vulnerabilities of the wedding night. Only through the guidance of an angel and the power of magic can the bride and groom vanquish a malevolent intruder and consummate a match made in heaven.

A VICTORIAN POSTPONEMENT

Charles Kingsley was a prominent Victorian clergyman, a prolific author, and an amateur scientist and defender of Charles Darwin. As a clergyman, he served as Queen Victoria's chaplain and Canon of Westminster. As an author, he wrote fairy tales (*The Water-babies*), novels (*Westward, Ho*), and popular poems, as well as sermons and moral treatises. As a theologian, he championed the Anglican Church against the high church theology of John Henry Newman and generally represented "muscular Christianity" as the British answer to the ascetic piety of the Roman Catholic Church. By "muscular Christianity," Kingsley legitimized competitive sports and hunting as part of a manly Christian life.

How merciful God has been in turning all the strength and hardihood I gained in snipe shooting, and hunting, and rowing, and jackfishing in these magnificent fens to His work. . . . It is all so full of God, that I see no inconsistency in making my sermons while I am cutting wood; and no "bizarrerie" in talking one moment to one man about the points of horses, and the next moment to another about the mercy of God to sinners.[7]

Kingsley saw England's expanding empire as an expression of a robust masculinity that brought American soccer (British football) and cricket, as well as the Christian faith, to the far corners of the world.

Charles met Frances ("Fanny") Grenfell in 1839 while on summer vacation from his studies at Cambridge University.[8] Though the son of a clergyman, Charles was religiously lackadaisical. Fanny was intellectual and attracted to the theology of John Henry Newman, who eventually left the Anglican Church for the Roman Catholic Church. Fanny's Catholic tendencies led to many spirited discussions about the relationship between the spirit and the flesh, for Newman and his followers found the separation of the two severe enough that clergy should not marry but rather devote themselves to matters of the spirit. And there existed a class divide between the clerical Kingsleys and the wealthy Grenfells. Still, it was love at first sight and Victorian passion of the first order. The first romantic stirrings of these two souls appear in their letters. In his love for Fanny, Charles regained his love of God: "I begin to love good for your sake. At length I will be able to love you for God's sake."[9] Charles's religious struggle ended with a kiss in January 1840. Soon after, he wrote Fanny, "I feel, Fanny, that I am under a heavy debt to God and how can I pay this better than by devoting myself to the religion I have scorned."

Fanny wrote in her diary about Charles's kisses: "My blood boils and bounds as I recall it."[10] Though still not engaged, soon they were signing their letters "Your own husband" and "Your own wife." Fanny's parents were deceased, and her older sisters opposed the match, forbidding Fanny to see Charles for more than a year. Charles, ever the moralist, took this forced separation as a test of their love and added his own constraint— they would not correspond during this time. Instead, they would share a practice of spending Thursday nights lying in bed imagining that they were in each other's embrace and Friday nights doing penance, prayers on Fanny's part and prayers plus sleeping on the floor on Charles's part. Fanny was sent abroad for two extended tours, but taking the baths in Germany and enjoying the landscapes in southern France did little to dampen her longing for Charles. In 1842, she wrote how she longed passionately for the man she called her husband and lay in bed imagining "delicious nightery" when they would lie in each other's arms "and I will ask you to explain my strange feelings."[11] Sometimes those feelings became so strong that she hardly knew what to do with herself. She longed to wring her hands, roll on the floor, scream, and run until she dropped. She consulted a doctor to learn why her heart "stops beating every five minutes in a strange way."[12]

During this year of separation, Charles, now graduated from Cambridge and ordained, drew a series of drawings of the two.[13] One shows Charles, fully dressed, absolving Fanny, kneeling and barefoot, of her sins; in another, the two of them sit by a river in the nude, Charles pulling a thorn from Fanny's foot; in another, the couple lies in a sexual embrace; in another, Charles is cutting grain in illustration of "The harvest is plenteous but the labourers are few," and Fanny sits with a baby on her lap, all three in the buff; yet another shows the couple ascending to heaven in a sexual embrace. At the time, Charles professed a belief that, if their spirits were pure, their afterlife would be perpetual copulation, the erotic made holy: "Do I undervalue earthly bliss? No! I enhance it when I make it the sacrament of a higher union!"

In 1843, Charles received a parish (a "living," in Victorian Anglican terms), and Fanny's sisters relented. A brief correspondence led to a proposal of marriage and Fanny's acceptance. They were married in January 1844. On their wedding night, Charles asked his bride to postpone their sexual union for a month. During the separation, they would prepare themselves for sexual intercourse as a sacrament. And so, during their first month after the wedding, the couple read devotions and said prayers before retiring to separate beds in the same bedroom. According to Fanny's memoir,[14] this delay was not a symptom of a physical problem or psychological inhibition and did not skew their sex life. Rather, after a month, they consummated their marriage easily and enjoyed a robust physical relationship. She bore her first child nine months after their first sexual wedding night, and she bore three more children in the next 14 years. Charles's drawings of the nude couple were more than a male fantasy. Throughout their lives, both of them believed that shedding their clothes was symbolic of closeness to God, a Victorian recapture of Adam and Eve's innocence before the Fall.

NOTES

1.   Quoted in Susan Chitty, *The Beast and the Monk: A Life of Charles Kingsley* (London: Hodder and Stoughton, 1974), 148.

2.   Unless otherwise noted, all Bible passages are from *The Oxford Annotated Bible with the Apocrypha Revised Standard Version* (New York: Oxford University Press, 1965).

3.   *New Oxford Annotated Bible*, 11 [Apocrypha].

4.   E-mail from Rabbi Howard S. Hoffman.

5.   Edward Westermarck, *The History of Human Marriage*, 5th ed., 3 vols. (New York: Allerton, 1922). The first edition was published in 1891. These examples, along with many non-European instances, are found in vol. 2, chapter 26.

6.   Ibid., vol. 2, 556.

7.   Charles Kingsley, *His Letters and Memories of His Life. Edited by his wife* (New York: Scribner, Armstrong, 1877), 61.

8.   Susan Chitty, *The Beast and the Monk: A Life of Charles Kingsley* (London: Hodder and Stoughton, 1974), ch. 3.

9.   Quoted in ibid., 58.

10.   Ibid., 66.

11.   Ibid., 74.

12.   Joan Perkin, *Victorian Women* (London: John Murray, 1993), 58.

13.   Reproduced in Chitty, *The Beast and the Monk*, immediately preceding pt. 11, ch.1.

14.   Kingsley, *His Letters*, 302.

CHAPTER 7

Early American Wedding Nights

Let me kiss you good buy to night oh if I could kiss you to night.
Yours Ever, Herbert

—Letter from Herbert Metcalf to Annie Hicks,
August 6, 1864[1]

My [Jane's] family is from New England, and if any of them ever stayed in a hotel for their wedding night, I'd be surprised. Weddings were quiet and mostly for family. My mother wore a dark suit with a gardenia corsage at her wedding, and her mother wore a dress of thin, crinkly georgette that would be reworn as a summer frock. The only photograph I saw growing up of a bride in a white confection with a train was a small picture of my maternal grandmother, making the best of marrying my grandfather Merrill, almost 40 years her senior; he treated her polio and was a rare catch in Castine, Maine, just after World War I.

I lived in many states as a child and sometimes saw big portrait photographs of my friends' mothers on their bureaus, arrayed in bridal gowns and veils. To me, the women in the photographs looked like glamorous stars, although, given the traditions of my family, I understood such displays to be of poor taste. Among the Methodists of my world, the newlyweds would "stand up" in church, and the two big religious occasions of Easter and Christmas greatly overshadowed weddings for pomp. Importantly, we never heard about "the honeymoon," if indeed the bride and groom went on one.

THE NATURAL EXPRESSION OF LOVE.

From *The Glory of Women* (1896), an illustration of "the natural expression of love." (Reproduced with permission of Duke University Libraries.)

This chapter looks at New England as a sample because it is one of the oldest clearly defined regions in the United States. However, as Carol Wallace wrote in *All Dressed in White*, "America's early history of weddings is as fragmented and various as the nature of the individual colonies."[2]

COLONIAL TIMES

In the early colonies, men and women married early and often. It was a great misfortune to have to live on one's own. The first bride in Plymouth was Susannah White, who had given birth to the first European child in Plymouth Colony just before she married Governor Edward Winslow. The two of them had been widow and widower for 7 and 12 weeks, respectively, when they united in matrimony. In many towns, house lots were given to men upon their marriage in order to encourage bachelors to enter wedlock. Betrothal was so public that a man who went through the motions of an engagement and then failed to follow through risked fines, imprisonment, or even the whipping post. By the same token, breach-of-promise cases were brought against women by men who had been jilted, or "shabbed," as it was also called.[3] There was even a "pre-contract," which Cotton Mather upheld—in his words, "a Solemnity called a Contraction a little before the Consummation of a Marriage was allowed of."[4] So the bridal couple could be united publicly and possibly privately even before the ceremony.

In the early days of New England, life was austere, yet the sexual urge and the power of physical intimacy to bind a couple were understood. To talk intimately, people used a "courting stick," which was an inch in diameter and six to eight feet long, fitted with an earpiece and a mouthpiece at either end. Essentially, the couple played the game of telephone in front of the large fireplace of the house, whispering to each other words that only they heard.

Frequently the couple drank a posset of spiced wine in the bridal chamber, but this was an occasion for psalm reading and prayer, not antic revelry. Sometimes the groom's friends scrambled for the bridal garter, with the winner supposed to have good luck and a speedy marriage. There are records in Marblehead, Massachusetts, of the bridesmaids and the groomsmen putting the wedding pair to bed. The groom might wear a brocaded nightgown, whereas the bride had just a nicer version of her usual attire.

There must have been some lively partying in the bridal chamber; indirectly that is what Judge Sewall meant when he wrote in his diary, of his own wedding night, that "none came to us." Both he and his wife were no longer young, and the wedding did not set the town afire.

AMONG THE COUNTRY FOLK

Martha Ballard, a midwife in colonial New England, kept a diary for 27 years. She lived along the Kennebec River, in what was then Massachusetts but later, a few years after her story ends in 1820, became Maine. This was the era of social childbirths, when relatives and neighbors attended births (and doctors tended the sick). Martha's position makes her a reliable source of information about who married whom, who (like her son) was subject to a paternity suit, and who had premarital relations.

At this time the local minister performed the marriage ceremony, and the town clerk issued the certificate. So far, so predictable. But the scholar who edited Martha's diary, Laurel Thatcher Ulrich, discovered that getting hitched in the early Republic was of scant import compared with setting up house. For example, in November 1792, Martha's daughter Hannah wed Moses Pollard, and Martha's daughter Parthenia was betrothed to a Mr. Pitt. It was as though the wedding was an afterthought compared to the significance of the young men's coming to dinner.

"Mr. Pollard and Pitt dined here. The latter was joined in the Bands of wedlock with Parthenia Ballard." Ulrich draws attention to a second and related curious fact: that neither bride would leave her childhood home with dispatch after the wedding. Instead, the husband and the husband-to-be came to and went from the ladies' home. The diary entry for the last day of November records that both men "took breakfast," meaning they had spent the night. The much bigger deal was "going to housekeeping," and Martha wrote about all what that entailed for Hannah. Buying basics like a pewter dish, six tablespoons, tea, a coffee pot, and the supplies to make several quilts kept the women exceedingly occupied for the first six weeks of Hannah's marriage—while she slept at home with or without the groom. For the women in Martha's family, Ulrich observes, the weddings were "surrounded by an intense productivity a gathering of resources that defined their meaning and purpose."[5]

Yet, there are many instances of a less sedate custom of colonial times, known as stealing the bride. It was only five years before, in 1783, that the last bride was recorded as stolen in Hadley, Massachusetts—Elizabeth Smith, who married Dr. Job Marsh. What this actually meant is described in the *History of Hadley*:

> Some young men who had not been invited to the wedding, seized the bride, in the street or house, and led her off, and kept her until they were invited to join the party. A Hadley tradition says they sometimes took her to a public house, and retained her until the groom ordered an entertainment for them. She was treated gently and kindly. These affairs seem to have produced no quarrels, but to have been sometimes an addition to the wedding frolic.[6]

The sport of stealing "Mistress Bride" existed in Connecticut apparently until after 1800. A bunch of young men, on the pretext that they had been slighted by not being invited to the wedding, rushed in after the marriage ceremony, seized the bride, carried her to a waiting carriage or lifted her onto the back of a horse, and took her to the nearest tavern. The last official record for such a rollicking beginning to a wedding night does seem to belong to Mrs. Job Marsh in Hadley, Massachusetts, but, in early-20th-century Rhode Island, men from the neighborhood sometimes invaded the bridal chamber and pulled the bride downstairs, sometimes taking her outdoors, and teasing the groom to come to her rescue. "If the room or house-door be locked against their invasion, the rough visitors break the lock."[7]

So much for our sedate forefathers.

TRANSCENDENTAL BLISS

Dually constrained by externals—sickness, peculiar families, and penury—and by the internal limit of being reclusive, Nathaniel Hawthorne and Sophia Peabody found each other and, after a five-year engagement, married in Boston on Saturday, July 9, 1842, when he was 38 and she was 31. In the last days before the marriage, it seemed that Sophia, who suffered migraines as a result of mercury in the medicine she was given as a teething baby, was in too delicate health to proceed. And, after the wedding in Boston, a big storm posed more uncertainty, as the couple had to stop in their carriage on the way to the Old Manse in Concord, which Ralph Waldo Emerson had lent them to begin their wedded life.

Nathaniel and Sophia each wrote a letter from their new home that first morning that discreetly proclaimed their happiness. (They did not, by the way, attend church.) Nathaniel's said he was exhilarated—"We are as happy as people can be, without making themselves ridiculous."[8] He would later refer to Sophia as "my dove." In Sophia's letter to her mother, she said she was extravagantly happy. Sophia made it clear that she wasn't misguided to suppose that life is a bowl of cherries. Rather, she saw the continuance of their loving rapport and expressed her belief that becoming physically intimate had led to an improved state of her overall health. In their reciprocal love, she found a core around which to build a new existence.

Sunday PM 5 o'clock July 10th, 1842

My dearest Mother,

I do not feel much like writing yet, but you must have a few words at all events. Just as we were thinking that the dust was rather inconvenient, though otherwise the surrounding weather was unexceptionable, down came a diamond-dropping, the outskirts of a strong shower farther before us. It was the most enchanting little bedewing of laughing tears that we ever saw. Then all the trees & shrubbery shone like polished emerald, & glancing shadows over the sun's face, an attempt at veiling himself modestly before far higher shining in our carriage, only made the aspect of nature more grateful. Within seven miles of Concord, our coachman stopped & we had no sooner entered & seated ourselves than a new & driving rain descended & low thunder seemed like celestial artillery greeting us, instead of earthly cannon which Mr Hawthorne suggested would announce our arrival to this good town. We were detained an hour &

then a silver gleaming in the west called us to proceed. We arrived at about five o'clock. Never was any fairy palace more exquisite that the house. Spirit-Elizabeth had filled all the vases with the loveliest flowers, & the smoke tree [?] & fine grass shrouding them in mist made them look more lovely still. The alabaster vase exceeded all— but it was hard to tell which to prefer. Mr Hawthorne was in perfect delight. Upstairs in his study the purpureal [sic] vase was standing on the centre table, brilliant with fairy flowers. In our chamber Elizabeth Derby's . . . [couldn't identify this word; looks like Groake or something] stood on the toilette with white lilies. It seemed as if some angel had come down from Paradise with the flowers of life & adorned our temple for us. Sarah was not in the house, but at the back door of the hall I stood & saw her down by the river. She ran up as fast as she could, & wished me joy with all her heart. Mr Hawthorne came forward & shook hands with her & him also she congratulated.

Dear, dear Mother, every step the horses took, I felt better, & not in the least tired. I was not tired at the house [?] [not sure of this word], & not tired when I arrived. My husband looked upon me as upon a mirage which would suddenly disappear. It seemed miraculous that I was so well. After dinner which was after six, I heard a voice in the kitchen & knew it must be our messenger from Paradise. I went out & met her in the hall. She embraced me & looked so happy for me, that one would have thought that she herself was this happiest bride since six thousand years. For has it not been six thousand years for my bloom of Time to flower? He is the result of the ages—the crown of the world! I carried her into the parlor where he . . . [probably "stood"—there is a hole in the paper here]. He smiled light upon her, & they [sh]ook hands, Elizabeth welcoming him most cordially to Concord. She took off her bonnet & staid [sic] a little while—all in harmony with the day. When I accompanied her to the door, she took hold of my bridal dress. "Let me see, said she, how this is. She lifted the same, & said "I am perfectly satisfied, I approve entirely—and glided down our stately avenue. She brought four pounds of butter from Rockwood & Carshire [?]! We had dined so late, we did not take any tea, even if Rose had given us the power. Mr Hawthorne was sure that today I should feel fatigued, but today I have been very well. Still & just now I have walked with him to the monument & home through the road. It is a perfect Eden round us. Everything is as fresh as in first June. We are Adam & Eve, & see no persons round. The birds saluted us this morning with such gushes of rapture that I thought they must know us & our happiness. My appetite is excellent & I feel a clear, new life which I think will be like the Phoenix's when it rises from the old ashes.

Dearest Mother, I have a letter to write to you about you & me— but not yet. I am going to keep quiet & find whether this wonderful revival be sound & real. I believe my father did not greet me after the ceremony, or did he. I did not know it, because I was in a trance? I am the happiest person on this earth. Fear not that I am tenderest keeping. Even your mother-heart would be satisfied, did it know my husband as he is—Goodbye now. Tell Bridget that Mr Hawthorne regretted he did not shake hands with her.

Your loving daughter.

Sophia A. Hawthorne

P.S. Would you send by the stage Sarah's tooth-brush & one pair of india rubbers if you can spare them. She left them at her mother's in Warren St. My love to all. James first called me Sophia Amelia *Hawthorne*. Goodbye.[9]

Sophia writes in rhapsodic prose, the lyricism a reminder of passages from the Transcendentalists, or from Romantics like Wordsworth or Goethe. Yet, she is not overwrought but sharply self-analytic. Elation makes her see the very light and colors intensified. The birds "saluted" them in the morning, yet she doesn't want to gush. Meanwhile, Sophia keeps private the use of her husband's name only to him—to her mother she calls him "Mr. Hawthorne." She uses the kind of signal phrase that was acceptable in 1842 for sexual intercourse—alluding to her state as "We are Adam & Eve." And she saves for the end telling her mother how much it meant to be called by her married name.

A CIVIL WAR SOLDIER LONGS FOR HIS WEDDING NIGHT

"I shall hug you tight" and "I wish I were a better man"—passionate longing and a desire to enter the nuptial chamber with a cleansed heart comes across in the original letters of a Civil War soldier, preserved in the house where I once lived. My host in Connecticut was looking through his family papers when I was writing this book and gave me love letters from an ancestor to peruse. A relative he can't easily locate on the family tree wrote these letters. But the old packet of them threw open a door for me—a door I thought would remain closed—about the wedding night. They suggest that American men long for affectionate union just as women do, and, while not perhaps inclined to disco dance or serenade their excitement, they expressed their nervousness and their eagerness for physical and emotional congress on the wedding night in reflections like these, full of expectancy and sent through the U.S. post as well as, today, by phone lines and e-mail.

The tender expression of the former Union soldier gives insight into one 19th-century man's mind about the intimacy he wishes for and then is promised in the course of the epistolary courtship. The packet of letters was sent by Herbert Metcalf in Meadsville, Pennsylvania, to Annie Hicks in Lafayetteville, New York.[10] Metcalf was seriously wounded during the Civil War, and he must have met Annie while recuperating at her family farm. In the packet of letters, he is writing to Annie after he has returned home to Pennsylvania.

Herbert wrote long letters in a handsome, ornamented, yet masculine script. He went into a romantic sphere to write them. Herbert chides Annie a little for writing shorter letters than he does. As the correspondence progresses over 1863 and 1864, he has taken a job in the railway office and is boarding with a family. He wants to tell her over and over he loves her and delights in hearing she loves him, but he doesn't want her to be bored. He tells her consistently that he is in good health and humor, how he likes the baby in the family who has her same name, Annie, that she should feel sad he is sewing on his own buttons, and that he is teaching Sunday school again. The letters are chatty, but there is an underlying intention to show that he is going to be a good husband.

Especially there is his readiness, once she has accepted the proposal in person and the ring he then sent her and they have settled on his coming to her and a wedding in October, to pour out love. On August 6, 1864, Herbert wrote: "I am quite busy nowdays at work but it seems to agree with me. Last Sunday I think I wrote you a love letter didn't I. I could write you another to night but in fact I could write one to you at any time but I guess I wont for fear it will make you sick of love." In the same letter he concludes that the Sunday school classroom is hot and then gushes in a sort of contrived incoherence: "I am rather tired to night to write much. I wish I could hold you in my arms to night wouldn't be happy? I think we would. Sundays especially Sunday evening. I do so long for you. After we are married Sundays will be the pleasantest day for we shall be together all day long. . . . If I don't get time to write tomorrow. Let me kiss you good buy to night oh if I could kiss you to night—Yours Ever, Herbert."

At the time of his September 19 letter, Herbert remains in Meadville and has not seen Annie over the summer, but, on the point of journeying to her for the wedding, he allows himself a more explicit expression of desire for their physical union. He underscores a word for the first time in any surviving letter and, no longer apologizing for his desire, suggests there is a standard of love letter etiquette where he may be faltering.

> I think I have made quite a business letter of this but I want to get thru with all business matters before I come if I can. I hope you will **not** be afraid of me and I will try not to be afraid of you. I shall hug you tight maybe for I feel now as tho if I once got my arms around you I would not want to let you go. As the time draws nearer for me to have you by my side I feel more and more my unworthiness. For your sake I could wish I was a better man and had been a better man. I wish I could come to you as pure as I believe you will come to me. But I cannot and maybe it is for the best. My wild oats are done I know the ways of the world pretty well I can shield you from many of its dangers teach you of its subtle ways and warn you against many of its temptations. You must keep me by your side make me nobler than I am and teach me to do my duty. I have thot all times & seriously of these things and I shall try to make you a good true husband and companion. . . . I shall write you each week until I leave for Prov[idence] try and write me every week. Let me close now [and] commence my work. Good night Annie & pleasant dreams Yours Ever, Herbert

Herbert becomes more avid and bolder as the wedding night approaches. It is as though it is permissible to think the thoughts as well as speak them.

By October 2, he is answering her letter of September 28 and will be leaving to go to her a week hence. Now he can make a little joke that he is working long hours "so you see I don't spend much time on the pretty girls." He tells her to wear whatever she and her cousin Lizzie decide, as it doesn't matter to him, and he will be satisfied, "but really I cant see the convenience in being married in any other than your traveling dress." For his part, presumably to take her after the wedding to his property in Providence, he is debating what kind of trunk to buy for Annie as he doesn't like the "immense Saratoga trunks" but doesn't want one too small.

What is on his mind vigorously now is sex—from kissing her in front of her family to embracing her in bed: "There is only one thing I am particular about in regard to the wedding and that is this I mean to kiss my wife before anyone else does."

Herbert has engaged a hired man and housekeeper whom he assures Annie she will like. Richard will do the heavy work around the house, such as bringing in the wood and coal and building the fire on winter nights, and Sarah is a good cook and housekeeper. And then back to sex:

> Give my love to sister Mary I guess you can spare a little of it for her for you have got it all. If you have a house full of people when I come to Milan [New York] I want them to understand that we have all of our courting yet to do. I never knew how much I needed you as I have these last few weeks. I get along very well day times when at work but when I come to go home and go to my bed room I feel lonesome. I am getting tired of sleeping alone. I used to think it was the best way but I don't think so now. I feel the want of some one to sympathize with me and I want to feel that there is someone by my side that loves me and that I love. . . . I shall try to be so kind to you that you won't want to leave me even to visit older friends and scenes of childhood. I must bid you good bye again. I wish I was with you this afternoon & evening but I will wait & hope kindest regards to cousin Lizzie and all. Yours Ever Herbert

BUNDLING

Bundling—sleeping together with clothes on—was practiced in two forms—with strangers, arising from the paucity of beds, and between lovers. Even in the finest plantation home in the American South, guests might all have to pile into the bedroom. As for the country folk who bundled as a kind of courtship, this too was for expediency and constituted many a wedding night *avant la lettre*.

The Arabic proverb "Trust in God but tie your camel" expresses the attitude of Scottish parents, who literally trussed (as opposed to trusted) their daughters for a bundling. A 1941 report about bundling among people in the Orkney Islands described girls' legs as tied by a special complex knot. Bundling in the British Isles was associated with varied customs, such as having the damsel put her legs in a large stocking, which was tied about her knees before her boyfriend came in and lay beside her.[11]

In theory, the couple wore clothing; and mothers and sisters of the girl being courted were in the vicinity to check up on the couple. Nevertheless, it was quite erotic, as described in 1904 by the Reverend Bingley while traveling in Wales but referring to America, as well:

> The lover steals, under the shadow of the night, to the bed of the fair one, into which (retaining an essential part of his dress) he is admitted without any shyness or reserve. Saturday or Sunday nights

are the principal times when this courtship takes place, and on these nights the men sometimes walk from a distance of ten miles or more to visit their favorite damsels. This strange custom seems to have originated in the scarcity of fuel, and in the unpleasantness of sitting together in the colder part of the year without a fire. Much has been said of the innocence with which these meetings are conducted, but it is a very common thing for the consequence of the interview to make its appearance in the world within two or three months after the marriage ceremony has taken place.[12]

Since bundling was often the cause of a birth of a child soon after the young people were united in matrimony, the church established a rule. A child born within seven months after the marriage of its parents should not be baptized unless the parents made a public confession of the "sin of fornication before marriage" and duly expressed penitence for their misdemeanor. The records of a Groton, Massachusetts, church list 66 couples that confessed to this lapse between 1761 and 1765.[13]

Bundling probably came to America from Wales or Holland, where it was called *questing*. The girl left the door or window open, and the young man, lying or sitting underneath, wooed her. Bundling was so common that Abigail Adams, sailing on a ship to Europe, wrote a letter to her sister Mary in which she described bundling in a completely offhand way:

Necessity has no law; but should I have thought on shore to have laid myself down in common with half a dozen gentlemen? We have curtains, it is true, and we only in part undress—about as much as the Yankee bundlers.[14]

During the heyday of bundling, in the 1700s, commentators debated whether bundling was a wholesome way for well-behaved young persons to get to know each other or an immoral ruse of lax individuals. According to the Reverend Samuel Peters, a Connecticut parson, "the modesty of the females is such that it would be accounted the greatest rudeness for a gentleman to speak before a lady of a garter, knee, or leg, yet it is thought but a piece of civility to ask her to *bundle*." He sensibly counseled that "people who are influenced more by lust, than a serious faith in God, who is too pure to behold iniquity with approbation, ought never to *bundle*."[15]

Another clergyman wrote "A Poem against Bundling, Dedicated to ye Youth of both Sexes" in 27 stanzas, ending with what would befall couples that bundled on Judgment Day:

Down deep in hell there let them dwell,
And bundle on that bed;
There burn and roll without control,
'Till all their lusts are fed.[16]

ROMANCE AND REALISM

After his 1927 trans-Atlantic flight, Charles Lindbergh was the most famous man in the world. He was every mother's darling and every girl's fantasy man. He met dozens of girls but didn't date any of them until he fell in love with Anne Morrow. From her time as a student at Smith College, well before they met, Anne had secretly been sweet on him. From her diaries, we know that Anne's idolization of Charles as a hero didn't turn instantly into real love. It took separation (while she was in Mexico, where her father was the U.S. ambassador) to transform admiration into love and acceptance of his proposal of marriage. For his part, he seemed to put her through an unconscious battery of tests of her fortitude, like putting her at the controls of the planes he flew before he proposed marriage.

Charles and Anne's family tricked the crazed media, not telling them where the wedding was going to be. The actual wedding was held on May 27, 1929, in Anne's parents' home on Palisades Avenue in Englewood, New Jersey, at 6:15 in the evening, although reporters had been led to think the affair was a mere party. After the wedding, Anne and Charles slipped out through the police cordon and the crowd of reporters, who heard about the ceremony from one of the guests at the small wedding, too late to follow the newlyweds. Charles had borrowed a motor yacht from a banker in St. Louis who was a backer of his transatlantic flight.

Few women's diaries and letters give a picture of the nuanced thoughts of a bride-to-be like Anne's. She would keep diaries and write poetry all her life until Charles's death. There is a description in one of Anne's letters home of how she was the chief cook and bottle washer, while the groom was the skipper on their honeymoon. As her biographer Susan Hertog writes:

Working in the hull of the boat in the heat of midday, Anne was not thinking about their public image. She was trying to make sense of Charles' notions of marine "housekeeping." She spent most of her time arranging cans and boxes of food in the ship's pantry. She could understand neither the purpose of her task nor the absurd amounts of gourmet food—shrimp pate de foie gras, even plum pudding.

Either Charles expected an impending disaster or a formal dinner party for twelve.[17]

Charles navigated while Anne played steward, cooking, cleaning, and mopping the decks. Writes Hertog, "Charles' demands were strange, and yet, at the same time 'natural.' Nonetheless, she didn't feel like a bride. In fact, she didn't feel female at all. She felt more like Charles's 'little boy.'"

It's a classic idyll—the just married couple borrowing somebody else's boat and sailing up the coast to the islands of Maine. The upper-class girl struggles to store provisions and clean, while trying to evoke poetic romantic feelings in her husband by reading aloud to him on deck. She said Charles, the epitome of manliness, was bored by her little library, but then he surprised her by paging through one anthology of poetry and reading aloud a love poem by A. E. Housman.[18]

A MATERIAL BRIDE

We have looked at bridegrooms who inclined to loving words and thoughts, because it is clear that brides become more emotional about the marriage rituals than do men. For balance, before leaving American wedding nights, we conclude with the following vignette of a couple who married soon after the Lindberghs, where the bride, instead of being starry-eyed, was a sheer material girl.

John Gellatly was an important early patron of the National Gallery of Art in Washington, D.C. He met his first wife, a beautiful heiress, Edith, in an art class. Edith died and left him a fortune. He amassed his important collection during and after Edith's life. Then he gave it as an *inter vivos* or lifetime gift to the National Gallery. In September of the next year (1930), John, 77 years of age, married for a second time; this time, his wife was a famously beautiful actress 42 years his junior. The new Mrs. Gellatly was unaware that he had run through his fortune until the wedding night, when he proposed giving her some shabby furniture he had in storage instead of a wedding present. They separated immediately, and, a year later, the estranged wife sued Gellatly for $660 in back rent on her apartment. He died two months later, leaving his wife $79, an umbrella, and an empty suitcase. His widow sued again to try to recover his art—a lawsuit that finally failed on appeal in 1948.[19] As one Victorian wit, Samuel Rogers, quipped, "It doesn't much signify whom one marries, for one is sure to find next morning that it was someone else."[20]

NOTES

1. Letter from Herbert Metcalf to Annie Hicks, August 6, 1864. Private papers of John Endicott, Litchfield, CT.

2. Carol Wallace, *All Dressed in White: The Irresistible Rise of the American Wedding* (New York: Penguin, 2004), 7.

3. The reference to "shabbed," meaning the same as "jilted," comes from Alfred Sereno Hudson, *The History of Concord Massachusetts* (Concord, MA: Erudite Press, 1904), 1: 218.

4. Cotton Mather, *Ratio Disciplina Fratrum Nov-Anglorum; a Faithful Account of the Discipline Professed and Practised in the Churches of New England . . .* (Boston: S. Gerrish, 1726), 112.

5. Laurel Thatcher Ulrich, *A Midwife's Tale: The Life of Martha Ballard, Based on her Diary, 1785–1812* (New York: Knopf, 1991), 138.

6. Sylvester Judd, *The History of Hadley, Massachusetts* (Somersworth, NH: New Hampshire, 1976), 237–38.

7. Alice Earle Morse, *Customs and Fashions in Old New England* (New York: Charles Scribner's Sons, 1893), 77.

8. Quoted in James R. Mellow, *Nathaniel Hawthorne in His Times* (Boston: Houghton Mifflin, 1980), 198.

9. This letter is in the Sophia Hawthorne Collection, Berg Collection, The New York Public Library.

10. John Endicott, private papers.

11. Mary Eden and Richard Carrington, *The Philosophy of the Bed* (London: Spring Books, 1961), 89.

12. Quoted in Henry Reed Stiles, *Bundling: Its Origins, Progress and Decline in America* (New York: Book Collectors Association, 1934), 29.

13. Mary Caroline Crawford, *Social Life in Old New England* (Boston: Little, Brown, 1914), 199.

14. Abigail Adams, *Letters of Mrs. Adams* (Boston: Little, Brown, 1841), 9.

15. Crawford, *Social Life in Old New England*, 199.

16. Stiles, *Bundling*, 53.

17. Susan Hertog, *Anne Morrow Lindbergh: Her Life* (New York: Doubleday, 1999), 108.

18. Anne Morrow Lindbergh, *Hour of Gold, Hour of Lead; Diaries and Letters, 1929–32* (New York: Harcourt Brace Jovanovich, 1980), 46–47.

19. Michael Gross, *Rogue's Gallery* (New York: Broadway, 2009), 144–45, 153–54.

20. Alexander Dyce, ed., *Table Talk of Samuel Rogers* (1860), in *The Concise Oxford Dictionary of Quotations* (Oxford University Press, 2008).

CHAPTER 8

The Spousals of Native Americans

May I hope it is
My young maiden
Sitting all alone
And awaiting me;
Will she come then?
Will she walk with me?
'Neath one blanket
We together be,
We—we two, we two,
We two, we two—
Will she come.

—"Lover's Wooing" or "Blanket Song," Zuni Love Song[1]

INFORMALITY

My grandfather's collection of books on the supernatural went up in flames upon his death. I [Jane] was three or four, and I recall the adults saying that burning books took much longer than they expected. But down the hill lived my great great-uncle, who had traveled the world, and he, or, later, his widow, allowed me to peruse such things as a headhunter's mace, the scenes on old cameos and choice pieces of black Wedgwood, and valuable, eclectic books. In his library I read at a table barely lit by the light

This 16th-century French manuscript, *Histoire Naturelle des Indes*, depicts "How the Indian, after satisfying and pleasing his fiancee, gets married." (The Pierpont Morgan Library/Art Resource, New York.)

through the stained-glass windows. The gilt edition of Longfellow's *Song of Hiawatha* before me, I would imagine walking and singing through a cornfield in the moonlight clothed in ankle-length tresses or how Hiawatha heard Minnehaha in the laughter of a waterfall, wooed her, and led her to his lodge. Hiawatha fashioned beds of tree boughs for his bride, and bluebirds chirped joyfully to them, and the sun blessed them, saying, "Love is sunshine, hate is shadow, Life is checkered shade and sunshine, rule by love."

From a glint in the eye to an electric touch or physical awareness of the other person, to gaining family approval, to making love and cohabitation, Hiawatha's courtship seemed to me like paddling a canoe down a swift stream and very preferable to the prospect of engraved invitations, stiff undergarments, and stockings with blue garters of the contemporary bridal scene. Later I learned that Longfellow made rather a mishmash of Indian language and myths. Yet, in 1988, the Morgan Library and Museum exhibited the Drake Manuscript, which made me think that Longfellow's romantic vision was not that far off course.

In the 1580s, Sir Francis Drake, who is associated with the manuscript and may have commissioned it, explored the waters and islands of the

Caribbean. The Huguenot artists on his expedition drew 199 separate images of West Indian plants, animals, and people. The final quarter of the drawings show the domestic life of America's original inhabitants, with a continuous narrative of their courtship. Probably, when the narrative mentions a mysterious locale called Loanbec, it is referring to one of South Carolina's barrier islands, which Drake visited on his way to rescue the Roanoke colony in 1586. The drawing that concludes the Drake manuscript depicts the culmination of a courtship after the man demonstrates to the girl's father, also present, that he will be a good provider.

That this manuscript came into public view for the first time in 400 years accentuates that it reveals to us a lost world. In the picture, the bride and groom wear fine loincloths, as well as a bead necklace for her and ankle bracelets for him. The groom holds a rabbit, indicating his skill at hunting, and the bride grinds corn in the basin, showing her own skill and connecting her with fertility and abundance. Behind her, a coconut tree grows, and baskets of food stand around the grass house. The groom has brought one of his oars, and a dinner cooks in the big iron pot. According to the narrative:

> Satisfied, the father says to his daughter, "You need this young man. He will feed you well; you see that he brings a lot of good things for us to eat, he works hard at fishing as well as hunting, he plants, gathers fruit in the wood, and, in short, does everything needed to feed the whole house." The father then turns to the young man and expounds on his daughter's skill at baking bread and dressing meat. After all the proper testaments of value have been made, the two are wed. "When they are married," our author says, "her parents no longer want to work and customarily their children feed them."[2]

Sherry G. Luttrell, director of education at the Berkeley Art Museum, commented on how the artist was viewing the subject:

> Given that we understand this as an image of a newly married couple that has just made love, the shapes and forms in the image are subtly supportive of that content. You have a proliferation of full and rounded receptacles on the one hand, and on the other, the exotic palm with its individual fronds and flowing forms, on some level suggestive of the male principle. And you see the aperture of all these receptacles, the open basins, the pot with steam rising. The artist has packed a large amount of natural and social information into this small scene. The variety of botanical things, and looking over the straw thatched roof he has even fit in a flock of birds. There is

natural information no matter where you look, setting the stage for the implicit natural lovemaking of the two people.[3]

The drawing dates from about the time when the real Hiawatha lived and bespeaks just as happy and uncomplicated a rite of passage. While highly structured and offering little individual choice, the Native American societies had in common relatively simple, relaxed marriage rituals. If a Native American marriage didn't work out, a woman could usually divorce her husband by the mere act of returning to her parents; when she died, she was often shrouded in her wedding dress. Some tribes allowed sexual exploration before marriage, whereas others required female chastity.[4] Overall, the relations of men and women were less regularized, as two stories of a man and a woman coming together as life partners indicate.

LOVE AT FIRST SIGHT: THE PATRIARCHAL FAMILY STRUCTURE AT WORK

There was room for romance, even though family structure was strong. For the Chipewyan, a hunting tribe in the wilderness of northwest Canada, a match was made for economic reasons; yet coexisting with this custom were both romance and a casual approach to finding a consort. The following story holds particular interest because the Chipewyan kept to the old ways so long; hunting caribou was their primary means of subsistence as recently as the 1970s.

Essentially, a Chipewyan woman was "given away" by her family, and that was that. If she dissented, she could delay and hope that her parents would lose interest in the marriage; otherwise, her fate was sealed, often by a betrothal as an infant. However, there was room for romance. An anthropologist who did fieldwork among the Chipewyan tells about a "love at first sight" courtship that an elderly man told him of in 1970.

> Eventually my informant, old David, began to tell me how he was traveling from Discho Lake to Lake End in the company of his father. He was then still a young man in his teens. As they rounded an island in the Discha River they saw another canoe. In this canoe was a young girl whom he decided to marry as soon as he saw her. His wife said little during this description except a few side comments to my interpreter (a woman in her fifties) verifying the incident. I was surprised that such a sudden decision to marry would be made, carried out, and remembered over half a century later. . . . I had the interpreter ask David why he wanted to marry that particular girl.

His response, to the amusement of all but the egg-faced anthropologist, was "because I was horny."[5]

Another romantic story was told by the person who lived it. A Sioux named Fools Crow, a competition rider and dancer, recalled July 4, 1916, as the date of his surprise engagement and marriage.

Fools Crow was working with racehorses in Kyle, South Dakota, when he went to have dinner with his family. They were about to sit down when a girl named Fannie, the youngest daughter of friends of his parents, entered the camp. She said her family wanted to speak with Fools Crow, so he followed her without guessing the reason. At Fannie's camp, her parents served him a good dinner and communicated that Fannie had fallen in love with him and that they approved. Fools Crow replied that he would discuss the matter with his father, and, when he got back to his camp, his father said he and Fannie's parents had already decided upon the match.

Fools Crow reflected and liked the idea. Then he went to get Fannie and a few of her things, which he moved to his camp. "As simply as that we were wed," he said. "I feel it was one of the best decisions of my life, for we had a wonderful marriage."[6]

MUSIC, DANCE, AND COURTSHIP

Most Indian societies provided some socially acceptable ways for young persons to meet. Often this meeting ground was a dance. During the Night Dances of the Sioux, girls clustered on one side of the lodge, and boys congregated on the other. When the drumming started, each girl walked over to the boys' side and chose a partner by kicking the sole of his moccasin. The couples, holding each other by the belt, formed a line and danced in a two-step motion around the fire. The next dance, it was the boys' turn to choose partners. The Hopi young people mingled at picnics after the sacred kachina dances; this was often the time that private visits were arranged for later. In hunting and gathering tribes the young women had the task of getting water and firewood. Thus the nearby spring or stream and the woods around the camp were places a young man might hope to catch a word with the girl he fancied. The young Omaha brave would get dressed up and hide in the bushes near a spot he knew the object of his desire would pass. There he would whisper a few words to her or play a tune on his flute. The tune was original, and, when a girl heard her boy's special tune, she knew he was near.

A young man would wait until the village was quiet and everybody was asleep; then, he would stealthily enter the lodge or tipi of the girl he admired. If she accepted him, he lay with her until just before daybreak, when he would silently return to his home. If a girl awakened to find a hand signaling under her tipi, she might either let the young man slip under the blanket with her or rebuff him. Among the Hopi, when the boy shook the girl awake, she would ask, "Who is it?," and he would reply "It is I," as she would be able to identify him by the sound of his voice if he had won her heart.[7]

When a Penobscot man proposed marriage, he would toss something near the girl he liked. If she picked it up, it was a sign of acceptance. A man would also pick another male relative as a go-between and have him deliver a message or item to the girl (usually using wampum). If the message was kept, the proposal was accepted and celebrated with a big dance. If the wampum was returned, the proposal was rejected. Married Penobscot couples did not live together for a period of two weeks after marriage. If they lived together before that time had elapsed, then the groom would have to host another dance![8]

JOINING BLANKETS

Marriage rites varied greatly among Native American societies. The wealthier families tended to insist on lavish celebrations, whereas poorer people were content to have their daughter announce her marriage by simply taking up residence with the bridegroom. In either case, the marriage rite was not a religious sacrament but a contract between the two people and, sometimes, their families. The public ceremony publicized the union to the entire village, much like today's newspaper announcements.

Among the Cherokee, the whole village gathered to enact a ceremony heavy in symbolism regarding the newlyweds' roles as mature members of society. On the day of the wedding, the bridegroom feasted with his male peers in one dwelling. Later, the couple met with the rest of the community in the council house, where the groom's mother gave him a leg of venison and a blanket and the bride received from her mother an ear of corn and a blanket. Then the couple exchanged the gifts of food and enclosed themselves together in the blankets. The Cherokee called divorce the "dividing of the blankets."[9]

AT HIS LODGE, THEN THEIR PLACE

A couple often did not spend the wedding night at the place where they would live. Among the Plains societies, a young man who fell in love told his parents of his intentions when he thought the girl reciprocated his interest. If his parents approved, they helped him assemble presents and load them on horses. One of the young man's relatives led the horses to the tipi of the girl's father or brother and tied them up outside the lodge while he went inside to smoke, make small talk, and finally state the purpose of his mission. The family council had a day to decide on the proposal. If they rejected it, the messenger took the gifts back to the young man's lodge. But, if the girl's family wished for the match, they unloaded the gifts and distributed them among themselves. Within a day or two, the bride, dressed in new clothes, rode off to his family on the best of the horses he had brought, loaded up with gifts from her family. The newly married couple stayed that night and the days after with the bridegroom's family, until the two mothers and their relatives, with the bride's help, had accumulated enough household goods for the couple to live alone in a tipi that the bride's mother pitched near her own.[10]

LEAVING BEFORE DAWN

The Tohono O'odman, also known as the Papago, of the southern Arizona desert, arranged matches outside the village, because people living in the same village were too closely related to marry.

The couple spent their first four nights together at the bride's home, so the bride could have her mother near. The mother told the daughter not to fear the young man, saying, "If he wants anything, don't be afraid of him," adding that the bride should accede to her husband's wishes without restraint. The bridegroom would come in after the family had gone to bed, sleep with his new wife, and leave before dawn. He would have been ashamed to leave in the daylight. The morning after the fourth of the bridegroom's nighttime visits, the bride's mother led her to her new home, taking along a little present. Having arrived, the bride worked for a month for her mother-in-law.[11]

WITH FRIENDS ON THE WEDDING NIGHT

Western Apache parents simply sent a maiden to the camp of a young man they admired. This brought honor to him and his family but was anxiety-provoking for the girl, because there was no assurance she would be accepted. To lessen the chance of her being embarrassed, a companion—a sister or good friend—went with her. When the two girls arrived at the youth's camp, they stood in the doorway of the youth's home, and the companion told his mother they had come to spend the night. If they were not welcome, they left at once for home. If they were accepted, they spent the night sleeping with the youth's sister or mother. When it was time for the newlyweds to move into their own dwelling, sometimes a companion couple was sent along for a few days to help break the ice. The bride slept next to the wall, her companion beside her, the groom's companion next, and then the groom, next to the fire.

Among the Hopi of northern Arizona, either the young man or woman could initiate the proposal. The bride had to show her bread-making skill by grinding a quantity of cornmeal, making bread at her own home, and then going to her future mother-in-law's to grind more cornmeal. For three days, from dawn until late at night, she ground cornmeal. She did the feat not only to show her ability but to compensate the boy's mother for the loss of his presence around the house and in the fields. When her work was presented, women kin washed the heads of the newlyweds in one basin. The women twisted the hair of the couple into one strand to unite them for life. After the wedding breakfast, the bridegroom and his close relatives descended into a kiva, or chamber of the pueblo, and wove the bride's wedding garments: two white wedding robes, one large and one small, a long wide belt, white buckskin leggings, and moccasins. The cornmeal the bride had ground was her payment for the finery. Sometimes, her husband had to raise a crop corn before she could have her garments. When the weaving was finished, the bride, wearing the finery, including the larger robe, went back to her mother's house, and her new husband joined her. Later, he would add a new room to the pueblo-style home. The smaller robe was put into a reed case and tied with the wedding belt. The robe served as wings to carry her soul to the afterlife, and the belt guided her in her spiritual flight.[12]

A COLONIAL DESCRIPTION

By the mid-17th century, among the Eastern tribes, church weddings began to replace spousals, or common-law marriages, in areas where Europeans had settled. Some Indians were married by an English official. Nonetheless, the tradition of spousals had carried over to the colonies, as well, through the 1700s. A description of an Indian wedding from a colonial source is presented in *Colonial Intimates* as customary for 18th-century native couples:

> In 1761 the Reverend Ezra Stiles spoke with John Paul, a Narragansett man, about old marriage customs. The thirty-year-old informant remembered seeing a wedding "according to [the] old Indian Way" when he was a "little Boy." The couple was, Stiles recorded, "shut up together a fortnight in a Wigwaum by themselves, the parents only bringing them Victuals. Then the old Indians bro't a Blanket to the young Squaw, which she receivg., the Peage [wampum] was mutually

given & exchanged, wc. [which] was to be kept in perpetuum. Then they made a feast, & the old Indians talkt to the couple, rejoiced & made merry & so the Wedding concluded."[13]

NOTES

1.   Nellie Barnes, *American Indian Love Lyrics and Other Verse* (New York: Macmillan, 1925), 35.

2.   Vera Klingenborg, "Introduction," in *Histoire Naturelle des Indes: The Drake Manuscript in the Pierpont Morgan Library* (New York: Norton, 1996).

3.   Interview with Sherry G. Luttrell, June 10, 2010.

4.   James Axtell, *The Indian Peoples of Eastern America: A Documentary History of the Sexes* (New York: Oxford University Press, 1981), passim.

5.   Henry S. Sharp, *Chipewyan Marriage* (Ottawa: National Museum of Man, 1979), 55.

6.   Thomas E. Mails, "Fools Crow," in *Native American Courtship and Marriage Traditions,* ed. Leslie Gourse (Summertown, TN: Native Voices, 2004), 51–52.

7.   Personal correspondence with Carolyn J. Niethammer in the late winter of 2010. This and the following citations from her cover much of the same content contained in her *Daughters of the Earth, the Lives and Legends of Indian Women* (New York: Simon and Schuster, 1977).

8.   Frank G. Speck, *Penobscot Man: The Life History of a Forest Tribe in Maine* (Orono: University of Maine Press, 1997), 254–57.

9.   Niethammer, personal correspondence.

10.   Ibid.

11.   Ibid.

12.   Ibid.

13.   Ezra Stiles, *Extracts from the Itineraries and Other Miscellanies of Ezra Stiles . . . 1755–1794,* ed. Franklin B. Dexter (New Haven: Yale University Press, 1916), 141–42.

CHAPTER 9

Presidential Wedding Nights

"Colossal impertinence!"

—Grover Cleveland (alluding to the
reporters, after his wedding night)

LOVE BY NIGHT, POLITICS BY DAY

All but one U.S. president married, and only one divorced—James Buchanan and Ronald Reagan, respectively. For the most part, these were unions where the wife gave the husband loving support and domestic harmony, buoying his performance of public duties. Because much luck comes into play in gaining the highest public office, few of the wives could have banked on achieving fame, wealth, or social position. It does not counterfeit George Washington's love for Martha Dandridge Custis that the widow was a wealthy Virginian planter—so was he. In our society, back to the first settlers, attraction and love have ruled the choice of a spouse, with a wish for security and a helpmeet coming in second and third. The desire for a helpmeet in the nation's early years is the reason that so many men and women had multiple marriages. Thus, strikingly, the presidents and their wives have been couples in love. And their wedding nights run the gamut.

Although only one marriage, that of Florence Kling to Warren Harding, flew in the face of strong parental opposition—her banker father boycotted Harding's marriage to a mere journalist—many of the First

George and Martha Washington's bed in their home at Mt. Vernon. Though both the bride and groom owned good furnishings, this bed for their married life was ordered from Philadelphia. (Courtesy of Mount Vernon Ladies' Association.)

Ladies were criticized for marrying beneath them, including Julia Dent Grant and Mary Todd Lincoln. It is amply documented that the wife of a future president recognized in an ambitious go-getter the making of great success. Some, like Sarah Childress Polk, propelled her husband's political career. When James Polk proposed, Sarah accepted on the condition that he run for the Tennessee state legislature before the wedding. Along the same lines, Mamie Eisenhower helped Ike write her husband's speeches. Other wives, like Jane Pierce and Bess Truman, complied with the basic program, even if they did not care for public life, but shunned the limelight. Naturally, the women who nixed the presidential gambit, such as General Colin Powell's wife, Alma, or turned down a suitor who ultimately attained the highest political office, are not famous. The First Ladies girded up and accepted or enjoyed their position.

Many couples, including the Thomas Jeffersons, spent their wedding nights at the bride's home. The most scandalous wedding night was Andrew Jackson's; he and his wife seem to have ignored the fact that she was still married to someone else. When her divorce finally went through, they had a second ceremony and wedding night, two years after the first.

John and Julia Tyler's wedding was held in secrecy, and John Kennedy's to Jacqueline Bouvier had 14 ushers and 10 bridesmaids. Ronald Reagan met Dr. and Mrs. Davis, Nancy's mother and stepfather, on the newly married couple's honeymoon, and they all got along. The Coolidges went to Montreal for their honeymoon, and the Lyndon Baines Johnsons went to Mexico. The John Quincy Adamses didn't have to go abroad because they were already in England, where the father of Louisa, born in England, was the American consul. Jimmy and Rosalynn Carter, only 21 and 18 at their wedding (on July 7, 1946), drove from Plains, Georgia, to a friend's summer place in Chimney Rock, North Carolina. The Hoovers can't have got much sleep on their wedding night, as early the next morning they took a train to San Francisco and boarded a ship to China, where together they surveyed geology for a mining project. Finally, it is certain that several of the First Ladies were not blushing brides when they married the future presidents. Martha Washington, Dolley Madison, Rachel Jackson, Florence Harding, and Nancy Reagan were previously married. Dolley, widowed for only a year after the death of a man she loved, admired James Madison but had mixed feelings about her new marriage. In a postscript to a letter she wrote on her wedding night to her best friend, Eliza Lee: "Evening. Dolley Madison! Alas!"

TWO DIFFERENT WEDDING NIGHTS

Rachel Jackson's first husband was a hot-tempered and unfaithful Revolutionary War hero. She left him when he had relations with one of his mother's servants and returned to her home, near Nashville. There she met Andrew Jackson, who was starting up his law practice, when he rented one of her mother's cabins.

Andrew and Rachel were married in 1792 when news came that the Virginia legislature had granted Rachel a bill of divorcement. Two years went by, and then the first husband challenged the marriage. It emerged that the report that the legislature had granted a divorce was untrue. It merely gave the right to plead a divorce case. However, in the meantime, the husband had obtained a divorce in Kentucky, so Andrew and Rachel were able to secure a new license in 1794. Thus, the Jacksons spent their legal wedding night where they had lived as a married couple. Later, in 1804, Jackson built The Hermitage (now open to the public) in Natchez, where the bedroom is preserved as when they lived in it.

No other presidential wedding night holds a candle to the Jacksons' for romantic mystique. According to Marsha Mullin, chief curator of The Hermitage, the place where they spent their (first legal) wedding night is uncertain.

They claimed that they were married in Natchez, Mississippi in 1791, and there is a house in that area named Springfield which the owners claim is the site of the wedding. But there is no record of this marriage being performed in either American or Spanish records. (Natchez was Spanish territory at the time.) However, the Jacksons were known as man and wife after this time. They were legally married in Davidson County, Tennessee, in January 1794 after Rachel's divorce from her first husband Lewis Robards was finalized. By that time they had their own home on the Cumberland River, Poplar Grove, and presumably spent that wedding night in their home.[1]

JOHN TYLER'S THIRD FIRST LADY

After the March 4, 1841, inauguration of William Henry Harrison, his vice president, John Tyler, returned home to Williamsburg, Virginia, to be with his wife, Letitia, and their eight children. Tyler had little interest in furthering his national career. But President Harrison caught a cold and died of pneumonia a month after his inauguration, and Tyler was called back to Washington to become the country's 10th president.

Tyler's presidential term saw three First Ladies. The first, Letitia, his wife of 29 years, suffered paralysis after a stroke, in 1839, and spent most of her time in the private quarters of the White House caring for her large brood. She descended to the rooms of state only for the occasion of the marriage of her daughter Elizabeth to William N. Waller, on February 7, 1842. The Tylers' son, Robert, was his father's secretary, and Robert's wife, Priscilla, and the president's eldest daughter, Letitia, served as hostesses for state affairs in the White House. Priscilla, Tyler's daughter-in-law, took on First Lady status after Letitia's death, in September 1842.

Julia Gardiner hailed from a wealthy New York family and was cut from more assertive cloth than Letitia. In 1839, she secretly posed for an engraving that was used in an advertisement for a New York clothing and dry goods emporium. It showed her strolling in front of the store with a promotion on her handbag urging readers to shop there. The picture of a rose on the handbag gave rise to Julia's nickname—"the rose of Long Island." Given the prominence of the Gardiner family on Long Island, this very early commercial endorsement by a well-known woman shocked society. In reaction to it, Julia's parents took her and her sister to Washington, D.C., in 1840, where President Van Buren received them at the White House. From there, Julia went on a European Grand Tour, during which she carried on brief romances with a German baron and a Belgian count.

In January and February of 1842, the Gardiners took up residence in Washington for the social season. In a letter, Julia said that a married congressman, Millard Fillmore, the future president, had openly flirted with her. She and her parents were guests in the White House of President Tyler. The next year, the Gardiners returned to the capital for the winter social season. Julia and her parents were again guests of President Tyler at the White House on February 7, 1843, and Julia became friends with the president's two oldest sons, Robert and John. John Tyler, widowed five months, was attentive to Julia, 30 years younger than he, and proposed to her at a masked ball celebrating the birthday of George Washington. Julia turned him down, but they began a romantic correspondence and were seen together publicly. The Gardiners went off to Europe again in 1843. Julia, her sister, and her father returned for a third consecutive winter social season in Washington, and, six days later, on February 28, 1844, a tragedy on the Potomac River prompted Julia to take a more serious look at the older, powerful man.

It was the last year of Tyler's presidency. During a ceremonial cruise down the Potomac River, the main gun of the steam-driven naval cutter, the USS *Princeton*, blew up during a demonstration firing, killing the sec-retary of the navy and five other people. Julia had accompanied her father on the boat, and Dolley Madison was aboard, as well; nobody had an in-kling that anything was wrong with the gun. And among those killed in the explosion was Julia's father. Apparently, Julia fainted into the arms of the president when she heard the news. Tyler comforted her in her grief. Four months later, the two were married, in New York City.

The quiet ceremony took place in the Episcopal Church of the Ascen-sion. The Gardiner family was in mourning for Julia's father, and there were only 12 guests, including the president's son John. After the cer-emony, they attended a breakfast in the Gardiner home on Lafayette Street. A ferryboat cruise, with naval salutes, in New York harbor fol-lowed. Two hours later, the Tylers, part of a party of four that included the newlyweds, Julia's 22-year-old sister, Margaret, and a maid—debarked at Jersey City. They took a train to Philadelphia, where they spent their first night as man and wife, then went on to Baltimore and Washington. Julia exclaimed, "Wherever we stopped, wherever we went, crowds of people, outstripping one another, came to gaze at the President's bride; *the secrecy of the affair* is on the tongue and admiration of everyone. *Everyone* says it was the best managed thing they ever heard of. The President says I am the best of diplomatists."[2]

Tyler invited Margaret to continue with them on the next leg of the honeymoon. Indeed, it was not unusual in Victorian times for a sister or mother to go along, but Margaret declined. The American public ate up the news of the fairy-tale marriage, and thousands turned out to glimpse the bride. A two-hour White House wedding reception was held on June 28, with wine and wedding cake displayed in the Blue Room. On the Fourth of July, the couple went on their honeymoon, first for two nights to a cottage prepared for them at the federal Fortress Monroe near Norfolk, Virginia, and then south to the president's plantation, Sherwood Forest, on the James River, in Charles City County. The matter of the bed at the cottage, prepared for them by the fort's commanding officer, was important enough that Julia described it to her mother, Juliana:

> A richly covered high post bedstead hung with white lace curtains looped up with blue ribbon and the cover at the top of the bedstead lined also with blue—new matting which emitted its sweet fragrance, two handsome mahogany dressing tables, writing table, and sofa, the room was papered to match, and the whole establishment brand new—True love in a cottage—and quite a contrast to my dirty establishment in Washington. It seemed quite as if I had stepped into paradise.[3]

Within a few days of their return to the White House, Julia's sister Margaret reported President Tyler's mild complaint that Julia's demand for his constant attention prevented him from working. Also, he had difficulty getting his sleepy wife out of bed in the morning, and he observed that in other ways she was a "spoilt child."

Juliana's advice to her daughter came as an order that she heeded without complaint:

> Help him with the re-election and tone down the lovemaking! . . . Let your husband work during all business hours. Business should take the precedence of caressing—reserve your caressing for private leisure and be sure you let no one see it unless you wish to be laughed at.[4]

As for more on the romance, Julia told her mother in July that "The P. bids me tell you the honeymoon is likely to last *forever,* for he finds himself *falling in love* with me every day." To this her mother replied: "You must not believe all the President says about the honeymoon lasting always, for he has found out that you in common with the rest of Eve's daughters are fond of flattery."[5]

FILLMORES: MORE LOVE THAN MONEY

Millard Fillmore was a New York State farm boy and woodchopper who apprenticed as a clothier. Abigail Powers, daughter of a Baptist minister, worked as a schoolteacher. The Fillmores had a five- or six-year engagement because they were too poor to marry. After the wedding, on February 26, 1826, in East Aurora, New York, they returned immediately to East Aurora, perhaps residing with Millard's father in East Aurora for a time before moving, in the course of the year, to their pretty house at 24 Shearer Avenue, which Millard built himself with help the year before. That is, he is the only president to have built his own "honeymoon cottage" (which is now open to the public from June to October). One of the trustees of the Aurora Historical Society stated that the dwelling has "a sense of peace and simplicity. In many respects, Abigail and Millard were true partners, and she was no doubt the most significant contributor to her husband's successes." The house has some of the Fillmores' belongings, including some items taken by them to the White House, and also a scrub table, original to the house, which was used for food preparation and meals and by Abigail for her students.

Abigail was the first wife of a future president to continue to work after her marriage. She taught school and at night tutored her husband, who completed his law studies, secured clients, and made friends. Their son Millard Powers was born in 1828 in the East Aurora house, where they lived for four years. In 1830, the Fillmores moved to Buffalo, and Abigail did not seek another teaching job. In 1832, Millard was elected to Congress, and in that same year their second child was born. Millard became president in 1850 and served one term.

HOW THE LINCOLNS' FAMOUSLY
UNHAPPY MARRIAGE BEGAN

What about the wedding night of a great president who became an inspiring legend, Abraham Lincoln? Easy to guess it wasn't at a four-star hotel with a month's honeymoon on a loop to Montreal! James M. Cornelius, the curator of the Abraham Lincoln Presidential Library and Museum, in Springfield, Illinois, sketches a picture with affecting details:

> Mary and he had been engaged in 1840 but broke it off on the first of January 1841—"the fatal first" as Lincoln referred to it later, lumping it in with the day the State technically went bankrupt (le plus ça change). They were later reunited by mutual friend Simeon Francis, editor of the Whig newspaper in town, for which both of them had written anonymous satires about Democrat state auditor James Shields. Mary wrote the harsher anonymous satire, so when Shields demanded to know who wrote it, Lincoln stepped forward to protect her anonymity. Shields challenged Lincoln to a duel; it was settled

up only when they got to the dueling ground. Abe and Mary were married about six weeks later, on November 4th, 1842, and he swore never to speak of anonymous writing or duels again.

The date was hastily chosen. Ignoring the duel episode, some alleged in centuries after that it was a shotgun wedding. No evidence at all for this—except that son Robert was born eight months and 27 days later. Who can say which night he was conceived?

Mary wore her sister Fannie's (Frances's) wedding skirt of white silk, from three and a half years earlier. We own it now—a lovely item. A new bodice was hastily made.

They were married in the evening at home of Mary's eldest sister, Elizabeth and Ninian W. Edwards, by the Episcopal clergyman Reverend Charles Dresser. A year later Lincoln bought Dresser's home, and that is the only home they ever owned. Mary had two bridesmaids (a sister and a friend), some accounts say there were three; Lincoln had only a best man, James Matheny, brother of the county clerk who signed the marriage license. The couple then went to the Globe Tavern, a few blocks away, and took up room & boarding for four dollars a week. It had about fifteen rooms, and was a big step down for Mary, who had lived four years at the Edwardses.

The wedding breakfast the next morning was at the Edwardses again. It was held on a tablecloth which Ninian Edwards senior, the first territorial governor of Illinois, and later governor of the state, bought in 1824 from the Spanish minister in Washington, D.C. when he was leaving the country and did not want his linens. The tablecloth was said at the time to be much more elegant than things made in the U.S. The Edwardses used it for decades, and now half of it is here in our collection—stained and tattered. We know they ate gingerbread at least.[6]

Coincidentally, the only letter Lincoln wrote as president to a child was written two weeks after he was sworn in, March 1861. It is addressed to Master George Evans Patton, 8 West 9th Street, New York, a house that still stands, facing the front door of the Church of the Ascension, where John Tyler and Julia Gardiner were married in 1843.

THE CLEVELANDS: WHITE HOUSE WEDDING AND GETAWAY

Grover Cleveland has the unique distinction of being the only U.S. president to marry in the White House. He brought both a romance and a suspect past into the office, for it was rumored that, as a young man in

Buffalo, New York, he had sired an illegitimate son. Cleveland was a sociable bachelor who liked saloons and beer halls. But, in fact, Cleveland's friend and law partner, Oscar Folsom, a married man, was the father. The mother, a prominent citizen in Buffalo, went ahead and named the baby Oscar Folsom Halpin, after her lover. Folsom fell from a wagon just after the baby was born, putting the natural father out of the picture. Named executor in Folsom's will, Cleveland was further involved as the ward of Folsom's 11-year-old daughter, Frances, who was originally called Frank. Eager to protect his friend's reputation, Cleveland also arranged for the adoption of the infant Oscar Halpin, in 1874, and provided ongoing financial support during his childhood. This noble act fanned the flames of gossip later in his career.

Henry F. Graff, the eminent biographer of Grover Cleveland, reveals more about this president's eventual marriage:

> Cleveland was an avuncular figure for Frank; he had bought her first baby carriage. . . . No one could have made up a scenario like this! When she went to Wells College he wrote and sent flowers once a week from the governor's mansion. Then, with Emma Folsom's permission, he courted Frank—she was named for an uncle and liked her name, but went with Francis.
>
> The President proposed, Frank accepted, and before the wedding she attended her college graduation: she was 27 years younger.
>
> Their expectation to hold the wedding at the home of Frank's grandfather was dashed as the grandfather died while she was on the high seas. Cleveland wanted to have his wedding in the White House, not in a hotel, so he became the first president married there, in an elegant room that was made into the most beautiful flower shop in the world. Since most of the Cabinet ministers were very wealthy men, Frank received a mountain of diamond jewelry—but Frank wore only the necklace her husband gave her. Queen Victoria sent a message of congratulations. They were married by a local minister and given a blessing by Cleveland's brother, a minister.[7]

The wedding was held in the Blue Room, and the reception and a light supper took place in the State Dining Room. In the middle of the evening, the bride and groom slipped away and took a train to a honeymoon retreat in western Maryland. According to biographer Graff, Frances Cleveland proved "a golden asset" who conducted herself "with uncommon aplomb and propriety." But, like many a wedding night, theirs witnessed an unplanned turn of events.

Cleveland and his new bride went to Deer Park, Maryland in very wet weather. He had arranged to rent a cottage in the woods on land facing the Blue Ridge Mountains. However, he had been mistaken that he was getting away from it all. The hounds of the media discovered the location and, the morning after, a crowd of newspaper reporters arrived with pencils in hand ready to sniff out anything they could.

"Colossal impertinence," fumed Cleveland. This intrusion infuriated him. He had bad relations with the newsmen, because they had damaged him during his 1884 campaign, when it was said he had an illegitimate child.

This was the beginning of having a president's private life ferreted out to supply an onslaught of yellow journalism. Prying newsmen who teemed to that honeymoon cottage and invaded the newlywed couple's privacy opened a window on the president's every move, which has never been closed. The press would not be denied access and would eventually argue that the right to know was an inalienable right they must defend.

FRANKLIN ROOSEVELTS: A WEDDING NIGHT IN LUXURY'S LAP

During his last year at Harvard, Franklin Delano Roosevelt proposed to his fifth cousin once removed, Eleanor Roosevelt, and she accepted. Franklin was raised as the only child of socially prominent parents who owned 1,500 acres of livestock, dairy, crops, and trees for lumber in Hyde Park, on the Hudson River. Eleanor was born into an equally posh family but lost both parents by the time she was 10 and was raised by her maternal grandmother. Franklin and Eleanor initially met as children and then reconnected as young adults when Eleanor, a serious girl, was working in a New York City settlement house. Franklin's mother thought her son too young to wed. She insisted that the engagement be kept secret for a year and took him and his roommate on a six-week Caribbean cruise. But Franklin and Eleanor would not wait a year, and they married on March 17, 1905. She was 20, and he was 23. The date was chosen so that "Uncle Ted," the president of the United States, could give away his favorite niece. The ushers received diamond stickpins of Franklin's own design—this was the Gilded Age!

The first week they spent alone at Hyde Park. Their bedroom on the second floor, across the hall from Franklin's boyhood room, had two bay windows overlooking the Hudson River. The Roosevelt mansion, now a historic house and museum, still has the walnut bed from that bedroom, with its heavy scrollwork of carved drapery on the headboard and the footboard and its urn-shaped finials. It would be moved around, as beds tend to be, and, when it was in the Chintz Room in the White House, the visiting Queen Elizabeth II slept in it.

An amateur photographer, Franklin may have had one of the servants snap the photograph of himself and Eleanor in their first photo at Hyde Park. It shows Eleanor with an elaborately trimmed broad-brimmed hat and a very long mink fur piece over her white dress. Next to her, Franklin wears a dapper three-piece suit with a flower from the estate's greenhouse as his boutonniere. After a quiet week, they returned to New York City so that Franklin could resume his studies at Columbia Law School.

In June, they began a three-month sweep of Europe, sailing first on the British liner *Oceanic* to England. This was Franklin's 11th trip to Europe. At Brown's Hotel, in London, the management mistook Franklin for the president and gave them an extravagant suite. Eleanor may have cast herself as an "ugly duckling," but in July 1905, in Venice, she so charmed the gondolier that he gave her a volume of poetry by the Renaissance poet Tasso, which he said he had owned for 30 years.

EISENHOWERS: A WEDDING NIGHT ON THE LAM

Mamie's father, John Doud, made a fortune in the meatpacking business and retired at 36. The Douds had two homes, one in San Antonio, where Mamie met Dwight (called "Ike" from boyhood), and the other in Denver, a spacious home in town, with gardens on a hill, that served as their primary residence. A wedding was in the air in the spring of 1916, but, in late June, Ike called Mamie and said, "Let's get married *now*."[8]

Ordinary furloughs were canceled because of the war, but Lieutenant Eisenhower was granted a 10-day leave. It took him two and a half days to travel by train from San Antonio to Denver.

Mamie, 21, and Ike, 25, were married in the music room of the Douds' house at noon on July 1. The family pastor wasn't available on short notice, so a visiting English clergyman officiated. The music room was filled with pink gladioli. A harpist played as Mamie descended the staircase with her father. Both bride and groom were in white—she in Chantilly lace and he in his starched dress uniform. Ike had remained standing two hours before the ceremony in order not to wrinkle his trousers. After a meal, Mamie changed into a silk dress and Ike into a gray suit, and they took a train to Eldorado Springs, 32 miles outside Denver. They stayed at the New Eldorado, the new resort's most sumptuous hotel. It had ballrooms, an orchestra, a pool and an artificial beach, picnic pavilions, burro rides, fine dining, hikes, and thermal waters. A photo from 1910 shows elegant ladies in fashionable hats and men in suits and ties, lounging on the veranda—no children. The children came later as, after World War I, the Springs became more of a family destination.

After a romantic wedding night, the next day the young Eisenhowers were lunching when Mamie's family showed up—her father thought the couple would be more comfortable riding back in the family Packard. So Mr. Doud brought the newlyweds home, and, at midnight, the Eisenhowers boarded the eastbound train for Mamie to meet her in-laws. The couple went to Abilene to meet Ike's parents and then on to Kansas City to visit his brother Arthur before returning to San Antonio, where Lieutenant Eisenhower was stationed.[9]

THE CLINTONS' BEDS

Newlyweds nest and sequester, and part of that involves outfitting their new home or living quarters. Martha and George Washington both inherited plantations and furnishings, which meant that they did not lack for beds, but the first piece of furniture Martha bought in her life was probably their conjugal bed. After George's death, Martha moved upstairs and never entered their bedroom again.[10]

A modern version of the nuptial bed of a president is the Clintons'. Being their age and background (I [Jane] dined with Hillary at least once at college), I think of it as "the way we were." This personal story comes from an article titled "Hillary Slept Here and There: Her Life at Yale," from the first issue of the *Hillary Clinton Quarterly*. It was written by Carolyn Wyman, who freelanced for the *Quarterly* and who also wrote features for the *New Haven Register*. She included several quotes from Gregory Craig, a 1972 law school graduate who had previously rented the apartment that Hillary and Bill, classmates at Yale Law School, shared. Wyman quotes Craig as saying that the place came with two pieces of student-issue furniture: a wooden picnic-like table and "a huge hunk of foam rubber" that served as a platform bed.

Bill proposed to Hillary after buying and furnishing a cottage in Fayetteville, Arkansas, where they both had jobs to teach law at the university. Several biographies mention that the cottage contained an antique bed covered with flowered sheets from Walmart. Since the newlyweds did not take a honeymoon right away, presumably they went back to the cottage after the wedding.[11]

Gregory "Greg" Craig went on to defend Bill Clinton in his impeachment trial in the Senate and served as the first White House Counsel in the Barack Obama administration.

NOTES

1.   Letter from Marsha Mullin, March 31, 2010.

2.   Robert Seager, *And Tyler Too: A Biography of John and Julia Tyler* (New York: McGraw-Hill, 1963), 8.

3.   Ibid., 11.

4.   Ibid.

5.   Ibid.

6.   Interview with James Cornelius, Curator, Abraham Lincoln Presidential Library and Museum, May 1, 2010.

7.   Interview with Henry Graff, March 14, 2010.

8.   Mamie Eisenhower, "My Memories of Ike," *Reader's Digest* (February 7, 1970), 72.

9.   Lester and Irene David, *Ike and Mamie: The Story of the General and His Lady* (New York: G. P. Putnam's Sons, 1980), 12.

10.   This bedstead is considered to be the "bed mattress etc." George Washington records purchase of from Philadelphia upholsterer George Bertault, in his household accounts on March 16, 1797 for $362.08. Although it is the only piece of Washington furniture for which documentation exists detailing Martha Washington's involvement in its manufacture, by the terms of her will, George Washington, as was common for the gentleman of the house, kept the household finances, making it difficult for us to know Martha's role in the purchasing process and her taste in furnishings. Based on an interview with Laura B. Simo, Associate Curator, George Washington's Mount Vernon Estate, Museum & Gardens.

11.   Letter from Frank Marafiote, ed., *The Hillary Clinton Quarterly*.

CHAPTER 10

Elopement

Spread thy close curtain, love-performing night,
That runaways' eyes may wink, and Romeo
Leap to these arms, untalk'd of and unseen.

—Juliet, in *Romeo and Juliet*[1]

As a child, I [Jane] fantasized about eloping. The man who sought me for his own would lean a tall ladder against the house and risk the ire of my elders to climb up and tap on my window. Or I might be the one to tiptoe down when the rest of the family was asleep and position a ladder there, knowing he was coming—like leaving milk and cookies for Santa. Perforce, light footsteps would rouse me from half-sleep, the window would be flung open, and we'd embrace. I'd see his face? Not at all. The essence was escape from my sheltered world to freedom and adventure—that was the climax of the oft-repeated daydream. I was concerned, when we lived in one particular house where I had a first-floor bedroom, that this would kill my chances of an elopement.

I confess I did have a bride doll. Mine was of molded hard plastic, with rosebud lips, wide painted eyes, and a cloud of wavy hair. The dress was glued on. To change her into another outfit, you had to untack the dress she came in and stitch it on for her to be the bride doll again. She had a fancy satin gown with lovely detail, so who would want to take it off anyway, as she was the bride doll? It was fine for the bride doll to have a formal wedding with my other toys and dolls, because that was her destiny, if not mine.

The Elopement, Thomas Rowlandson, 1792. Yale Center for British Art, Paul Mellon Collection, B1977.14.346.

When Juliet longs for Romeo's embrace, was I the only one in the audience thinking the young couple should run away from their families and Verona together? A happy ending? Not on the Bard's life. Shakespeare had written several comedies, plays with happy endings like *As You Like It*, which climaxes in betrothals, and *Much Ado about Nothing*, which ends in a wedding. In *Romeo and Juliet* the full weight of opposing families bears down on the lovers and the only escape is death.

When my son Burton was marrying, he created a spreadsheet for where to hold the wedding and reception. His fiancée was doing fieldwork in Asia, so he was the principal wedding planner. I told him to consider elopement, appealing to his sense of logic and frugality. Instead, he and his wife had a wedding that they mostly paid for, which brought disparate people together and was an exciting party for everybody.

GRETNA GREEN, SCOTLAND

But many have chosen to make an end run around the confines of formal marriage and especially around opposing parents. From 1754 until 1970, you had to be 18 to marry in England, at a time when 21 was the age of maturity in most of Europe. The town of Gretna Green lies just over the border from England, in Scotland, where anyone over the age of 16 could marry without parental consent. The village saw a steady stream of marriages and some sensational elopements. These were called "anvil marriages" because, from the 18th century, the proverbial place to get hitched was a blacksmith's shop, evidence that it was best to strike while the romantic urge was hot.

Since marriage in Scotland was a matter of signing a contract before witnesses, the officiants were not pastors of the church but any enterprising folk, mostly men, who saw a commercial opportunity. Preceding them historically were the "Fleet Parsons" in England, ordained clergymen of the established church, who performed, for a fee, quick marriages for all comers in the vicinity of London's Fleet Prison. Tavern keepers advertised that they kept a parson in order to bring runaway couples to their tawdry accommodations. The Marriage Act, passed in 1753, ended the traffic of couples to Fleet Street. Thereafter, a couple had to travel 300 miles to the Scottish border, where "irregular" marriages stayed within the law until 1940.

The most famous of the Gretna Green marriage officiants was Joseph Pasley, a giant of the trade, also known for drinking one Scots pint of brandy (equaling 2¼ pints U.S.) every day for the last 40 years of his life. Robert Elliott, who wed Pasley's great-granddaughter and took over Pasley's business, wrote a memoir of the Gretna Green elopements. He describes the pattern: a secret departure of the girl from her house, a harrowing carriage ride, a quick ceremony, and then the arrival of the father, usually having had obstacles and feints thrown in his way by sympathetic persons as he pursued the young couple. One father stood guard for weeks thinking his daughter and her swain had not yet arrived; another shot the groom in the bedroom with his daughter, not only murdering him but causing his daughter to die of grief. One story of a famous aristocratic pair had a curious sequel two generations later when the granddaughter had to elope because her mother, par for the course, didn't approve of the financial means of her choice of a husband.

As the marriage ceremony evolved, it was very simple. The runaway pair were asked their names and addresses and whether each was single. If each was, each was next asked, "Did you come here of your own free will and accord?" If the replies were affirmative, the officiant began filling in the form and proceeded with the familiar "Do you take this to be your lawful . . . as long as you both shall live?" exchange, and the bride then gave the groom a ring; the groom handed it to the priest, who returned it to the groom, and so on.

Most of the marriage trade went to two inns in Springfield, just to the south of Gretna Green: the Maxwell Arms and the Queen's Head, the latter known as "The Marriage House." People wrote with diamond rings on the windowpanes at the Queen's Head; someone etched the following:

Transporting hope to clasp the charming Miss,
In her fair arms, to what unequalled bliss;
What joys I tasted, when, from Gretna's shrine,
I drew the maid and swore she should be mine.[2]

John Linton, a former valet and innkeeper, was the landlord of the upscale hostelry Gretna Hall Hotel, a kind of runaways' resort, from 1835. In his previous job, he had been gentleman's gentleman to the lord of Netherby Hall, which is associated with a very popular poem by Sir Walter Scott. In the poem, "Young Lochinvar" comes out of the west to rescue fair Ellen, who is being married forcibly to "a laggard in love and a dastard in war." But, when he alights, the bride has just made her consent, so he sweeps his lady up and away on his fiery steed.

Linton married many of the wealthy at Gretna Hall. The hotel had several stacks of chimneys (token of the warmth within), extensive landscaping, and a 200-yard carriage drive. Adjoining were long shady walks where lovers could saunter and lose themselves in each other's company. There was a parlor set apart for the ceremonies, whose door was locked. If someone came in pursuit during the vows, the couple could get through them without being pulled asunder. Linton would rush the newlyweds through his private apartment and into a secret chamber. They hid there while he told the relatives, "You came too late—the couple is married and gone."

Linton's son Richard followed in his father's footsteps, and they provided 24-hour service.

These stories come down to us because they entertained listeners in their time. The trope of the furious father was slightly ridiculous because he had no power to impede or cancel the union and could only drag the girl away by brute force. The unexpected was the rule. For instance, in 1735, "country people and very well dressed came to be married, but before the minister had half performed the ceremony the woman was delivered of a daughter . . . out of wedlock or within was the unanswerable question"[3]

The public view was generally to let love reign, as exemplified by one of the cases Elliott recalled.

On June 5th, 1815, there arrived a chaise at Springfield, with a lady and gentleman, who sent for me and told me they wished to be married; but inquired what the fees were, and thinking them too high pretended to be quite easy about the business; he, however, bid me something less than the usual charge, and I, thinking he might be short of cash, agreed to take it; but when about half the ceremony was got through, a chaise and four horses drove up to the Inn containing the lady's father and another gentleman who inquired of the hostler if two young people had been there during the day to get married, and being told that there were a gentleman and lady up stairs at present about being united; but he thought the ceremony would be over by this time as Mr. Elliott was very sharp about the business, he rushed up stairs, but getting to a wrong room, I advised the young couple, for they had heard the chaise stop, to retreat to a bed-room, which is contiguous to the marriage-room, which they soon entered and closed the door after them, the gentleman having the presence of mind to put off his coat and pull the lady after him. The father and his friend entering the marriage-room, demanded of me where the villain and his daughter were; to this I coolly answer that I had married them, and that they had gone to bed in the next room to consummate [*sic*] the marriage, fearing pursuit. Not satisfied with my reply, he entered the bedroom in a great fury and forcibly pulled them both out of bed, handling the poor gentleman in a very rough manner, tearing his vest to pieces and part of his trousers, exclaiming, "How durst you run away with my daughter and go to bed with her, you villain." However, the gentleman persisting that they were married, as did also the young lady, who being pulled into the marriage-room by her father's friend, was closely questioned upon the point, but she still held that they were married, which had the desired effect; for the gentleman went to the father and reasoned with him, so that in a little time he cooled, and clasping his daughter in his arms, said that he forgave her, but that her fortune would be reduced for uniting herself to a man who had nothing but good looks to recommend him. However, Mr. C. got his vest and trousers mended, and pocketed as great a fortune as any of the rest of the family: after which he paid me more than my charge, for my seasonable advice, and departed.[4]

In the mid-19th century, a railroad was built that let couples off at Gretna Junction, just on the English side of the border, from which point they walked under the railroad bridge and followed a footpath to Springfield and Gretna Green; scouts appeared along the path and encouraged them to go to this or that "priest."

In 1857, it became compulsory to reside 21 days in the area before a couple could marry. This actually helped trade because the fleeing lovers would stay in local lodgings. The coup de grace for the blacksmith parsons came when Parliament ruled that only a minister of an established religion or a official of the state could conduct a marriage.

ELOPING *AVANT LA LETTRE*

In one of the most romantic elopements in history, the bride and groom spent their first night apart. A semi-invalid spinster of 40 is an unlikely candidate for a marriage founded on hot passion, but so it was, which is why—the whole world loving a lover—we love the story of the two poetic geniuses Elizabeth Barrett and Robert Browning.

They exchanged hundreds of letters before they met. She was an established poet, critic, and translator from the Greek, and he was an obscure poet who sent her his work. She praised his poetry, and at last he persuaded her to let him visit her. Elizabeth's home on Wimpole Street, in London, was ruled by a tyrannical father who forbade his children to marry. Elizabeth, however, did not seem to be an attraction, so the father let the young poet pay his call of homage.

Robert made successive visits under the pretext of highbrow discussions, until the father decided he was a fortune hunter and forbade him to return. Then the visits became more secret until the pair were sure of their love for each other. On September 12, 1846, they eloped. Elizabeth sneaked out of the house and met Robert at St. Marylebone Church. After the ceremony, she went home, which is where she spent the first night and the first week of the secret marriage, before the newlyweds fled to Italy. Elizabeth never saw her father again, and the Brownings lived happily in Florence for 15 years. Elizabeth's health improved, possibly related to her having given up laudanum, and at age 43 she gave birth to a son, Robert ("Pen"), who would become a painter and sculptor.

In their expatriate years, Robert's work gained recognition, and Elizabeth wrote numerous works, of which *Sonnets from the Portuguese* immortalized their courtship. She lived until 1861, and Robert survived her by a quarter-century, lionized in the United States at Browning Societies across the nation.

Two popular movies have been made from the same script by the same director, both with title *The Barretts of Wimpole Street*. The roles of Elizabeth and Robert were played in the 1937 version by Norma Shearer and Frederic March and in the 1954 version by Jennifer Jones and Bill Travers. The action of each of these films stops with the scene at the church, with Elizabeth's cocker spaniel waiting by the church door. The terrible father, played by Charles Laughton in the first film and John Gielgud in the second, threatens to kill Elizabeth's dog when he hears she's left home for good—but the dog goes along with the honeymooners, thus foiling his insane plan.

The Barretts lived at 50 Wimpole Street. The fictive home of Henry Higgins (from the Broadway musical comedy My Fair Lady) was at the nonexistent 27a. John Lennon and Paul McCartney wrote "I Want to Hold Your Hand" at number 57. When I was in college, I often went through the door of 50 Wimpole Street, placed at the entrance to the rare books room of Wellesley College, but this piece of the Brownings' house was returned to England several years ago.

In the Sonnets are celebrated the sensual as well as the romantic aspects of the courtship. Here is Sonnet 26:

> I lived with visions for my company
> Instead of men and women, years ago,
> And found them gentle mates, nor thought to know
> A sweeter music than they played to me.
> But soon their trailing purple was not free
> Of this world's dust, their lutes did silent grow,
> And I myself grew faint and blind below
> Their vanishing eyes. Then THOU didst come—to be,
> Beloved, what they seemed. Their shining fronts,
> Their songs, their splendors (better, yet the same,
> As river-water hallowed into fonts),
> Met in thee, and from out thee overcame
> My soul with satisfaction of all wants:
> Because God's gifts put man's best dreams to shame.

Sonnet 26 palpitates with both the poet's immediate sensations and her lofty idea of love, both romantic yearning and fulfillment—just what their wedding night and elopement epitomized to Elizabeth Barrett Browning.

AMERICA'S GRETNA GREENS

In the United States, long before people went to Nevada for quickie divorces, similar circumstances created a marriage-go-round in two otherwise sleepy towns—both of which have born the epithet "America's Gretna Green."

Elkton, Maryland

Elkton, Maryland, was a sleepy Eastern Shore town until the northern states passed increasingly restrictive laws about marriage in the early 20th century but Maryland did not. Elkton is two miles over the Mason-Dixon

Line, and many couples would marry on a day trip, but others stayed in a small cluster of hotels like the New Central and the Ritz, which were usually full and which did a brisk room service business from their restaurants. And, in Elkton, all through the 1920s and the Great Depression, the neon signs glowed, illuminating the night as the hotels, restaurants, and bars in the business section of the small Eastern Shore town stayed busy.

Elkton, Maryland's heyday for the quick marriage trade was in the 1920s and 1930s, when couples came from at least a dozen states to this marriage haven. They usually hopped back on the train north, but many local people opened their homes and rented rooms, putting large painted signs in their front yards that advertised their willingness to help couples get a license and to furnish overnight lodging. Among the famous people who got hitched in Elkton were Babe Ruth, Joan Fontaine (to her third husband), Bert Lahr, and former Attorney General John Mitchell and his famously outspoken wife, Martha. This was where the underage could elope or a debutante elope with her chauffeur.

At their peak, between 36,000 and 38,000 weddings were performed each year in Elkton, a town that, according to the director of the Elkton Historical Society, "should have married 250 given its size." The busiest year saw nearly 40,000 ceremonies. Explains Mike Dixon, Cecil County historian:

> This was the first state to the south of population centers to the North, especially Pennsylvania, Delaware, and New Jersey. In 1916 Delaware permitted instant marriages but that changed to a three-day waiting period so couples were sent over to Maryland. So several cab companies in Elkton went out and hired ministers, and set up vertically integrated businesses, so the cabbie took you to get a license, flowers, jewelry, and sometimes a hotel room for the night.
>
> The town was lined with competing wedding shops. A portion of the town looked distastefully on the instant weddings and periodically would try to stop them with local referenda to have a waiting period, or limit the signage to shut down the storefronts and houses that the marrying ministers worked out of, but they were defeated.
>
> In 1939 when Maryland went to a 48-hour waiting period, a hotel owner told the Associated Press that business was off 75 percent six months later, but they still came. People still come here to get married. The reason is a sentimental feeling about the place, or if their grandparents married in Elkton they come as a romantic legacy.[5]

In 1935, an international incident ensued when the prime minister of Iran, on an official visit, sped into town on his way to New York City from the nation's capital. Despite the flags flying on the diplomatic car, the prime minister, sitting in the back seat with his poodle, was mistaken for a self-promoting "marrying minister" and was arrested. The police chief was basically a farmer who had been called from his plough and didn't know the "minister of Persia" from Adam. Some in town said the poodle bit the sheriff, at which point he said, "Oh, hell, lock him up." According to historian Dixon, it is not an established fact but it is widely believed that President Roosevelt himself called looking for the minister.

The Wellsburg, West Virginia, Alternative

America's second "American Gretna Green" lies in West Virginia, on the bank of the Ohio River. Wellsburg, the seat of Brooke County, is an industrial town with paper mills and glass plants. Described in *A Guide to the Mountain State* in 1941 as "a town of narrow streets and smoke-begrimed old buildings,"[6] Wellsburg thrived as an American Gretna Green for many years. Most states had a three- to five-day residency period for a marriage license; West Virginia had none. Its ministers and county clerk married thousands of couples a year in the early part of the 20th century. A trickle of marriage licenses was recorded up until 1900, but the flurry turned into a blizzard after other states shored up their laws regulating marriages. In 1933, more than 4,000 marriages were performed before Christmas Day, and Wellsburg's Cupid role had become the subject of fiction and screwball comedies. Thousands a year crossed the river by ferry, riding the train from Pittsburgh or coming from the South. This lasted up until 1937, when the legislature enacted a law requiring three-day notice by a couple intending to wed. According to the same Writers Project guide, after that law was enacted, the taxicab companies that worked with the parsons on commission tried to salvage the business by offering to make advance arrangements for the brides and grooms.

A mayor of Wellsburg named Anthony J. Cipriani described the marriage mill in precise terms of dollars and cents. It went roughly like this: taxi drivers met the "out-of-towners" at the train station, coming in on the 12 o'clock from Pittsburgh, and offered them a package deal—the trip to the courthouse for the license and to the minister's for the ceremony—usually asking $10. Then, while waiting for the next northbound train at 4 P.M., the couple went to a restaurant for a little celebration. Cab drivers would coach the couple as necessary in the law, reminding them, for example, that they had to be at least 21 years of age. Cabbies also provided other services, including serving as witnesses and taking the newlyweds to Scott's drugstore for rings (which could be fine jewelry). Some of the drivers owned their cabs, whereas other cabs belonged to the glass company or were part of a town cab service—in either case, they were luxury cars like Cadillacs and Buicks. According to Mayor Cipriani, a cab driver could earn as much as $200 or more a week in the 1930s, at a time when factory workers expected to make $20 a week.[7]

When a girl accompanied by male friends rode out to meet the bride-groom and get hitched against her parents' wishes, this was known in New Hampshire as a "Flagg marriage," named after Parson Flagg of Chester, Vermont, whose house was a kind of Gretna Green. Ministers like Parson Flagg kept a stock of state licenses on hand, ready to issue at a somewhat inflated price to eloping couples. However, such marriages were "unpub-lished" and therefore improper.[8]

WOOING LADDERS

In plays, farces, jokes, and romance novels, elopements begin as follows: the young man climbs up an outside wall to his beloved's bedroom win-dow. She throws on a cape or a few clothes, and they descend very qui-etly so as not to alert her parents. Sometimes she has to grasp the vines of wisteria or ivy and find her footing in the stones or brickwork as he has done while climbing up, but often she clutches her intended's body as they descend. The ladder itself takes on a sexual meaning in, for instance, old cartoons. Life imitates fiction, and many a bride has escaped by this means in the face of parental opposition to her lover. In an outstanding and witty variation on the symbolism of the elopement ladder, two mem-bers of a Long Island, New York, volunteer fire department, Mary Carl-son and David Paganini, exchanged their vows in buckets atop the tower ladders, with 50 fellow firefighters and emergency medical technicians in attendance.[9] It seems outlandish; then again, in the province of La Man-cha, in Spain, according to a custom observed as recently as the 1960s, boys wandered village streets carrying a "wooing ladder" on their backs, which they used to climb up to the bedroom of the young lady they were courting.[10]

Because the modern wedding is our society's most extravagant cel-ebration (we sometimes think it should be the 25th anniversary!), sex is probably the last thing on the mind of many couples who have ex-pended insane, astronomical amounts of time, money, and effort creating the "perfect" day that, as it takes shape, has to live up to ever-rising ex-pectations. What the newlyweds probably want more than each other is oblivion and three days of sleep, as well as assurances that they will never have to see another wedding planner again. Except, of course, that they are now expected to produce photographs of their perfect vacation; you have to be surprised that these marriages actually outlast the honeymoon.

And to think they could have eloped and actually had enough energy left for wholehearted sex! Yet, according to Jane's focused talks with married couples of all ages, they rate as the most important aspect of their wedding that it brought friends and family together for a joyous celebration. Go figure!

NOTES

1.   Act III, scene 2.

2.   Olga Sinclair, *Gretna Green: A Romantic History* (London: Unwin Hyman, 1989), 42.

3.   Ibid., 25.

4.   Robert Elliott, *The Gretna Green Memoirs* (London: Gretna Green Parson, 1842), 35–36.

5.   Interviews with Mike Dixon, Cecil County (Maryland) historian, February 28 and March 15, 2010.

6.   *West Virginia; A Guide to the Mountain State* (New York: Oxford University Press, 1941), 489.

7.   Anthony J. Cipriani, *Wellsburg, West Virginia, 1791–1991* (Wellsburg, WV: A. J. Cipriani, 1991), 106–7.

8.   E-mail from Chester (Vermont) Historical Society, April 18, 2010.

9.   "N.Y. Firefighters Tie Knot atop Ladder," UPI News Track, September 27, 2009.

10.   Nina Upton, *Love and the Spanish* (London: Cassell, 1961), 90ff.

CHAPTER 11

The Honeymoon

There seems to be an unwritten law that going on honeymoons is like joining the Masons . . . secret and mysterious, and the fewer questions asked the less embarrassing for everybody.
—Martha Byrd Porter, *Straight Down a Crooked Lane*[1]

In historical romance novels, the breathtaking lovemaking generally ends with the wedding night. What of the protective seclusion after the wedding that is intended to usher the newlyweds into married life? According to Anne Monsarrat's *And the Bride Wore . . .*, in the Regency period, during which so many books of the genre are set, the seclusion was brief: "Social duty soon called society couples back to town to receive and return the calls of well-wishers, and any girl who had the entrée at court, was expected to be presented anew, as a married woman, within a few days of the wedding."[2] The correspondence of a Mrs. Delany gives details of numerous weddings over much of the 17th century. She describes the goings-on that surrounded a brilliant match made by her cousin, Georgiana, with a grandson the Duchess of Marlborough: "They were married on Thursday between eight and nine o' the clock at night. After they were married they played a pool at commerce, supped at ten, went to bed between twelve and one, and went to Windsor Lodge the next day at noon, and are to return on Monday."[3]

Gambling at cards and billiards were typical ways for high society to pass the time between the wedding and supper and the time alone. There was no sequestering for weeks of intimacy or fabulous getaways to tell your friends and family about.

The word "honeymoon" first appears in Thomas Blount's *Glossographia* (1656), in which he defined the honeymoon as the waxing and waning of the emotions of the newlyweds. "Married persons . . . love well at first, and decline in affection afterwards: it is honey now, but will change as the moon."

The first wedding trips as we know them were the privilege of the English upper class. As far back as the time of the Tudors, royals and aristocrats took extended wedding trips. Called bridal tours, they often lasted several weeks or months. Like the Grand Tour of a young man who finished up at Oxford or Cambridge, the bridal tour could extend as far as the Alps, Pompeii, or the Pyramids. Couples of more modest means, as in Jane Austen's milieu, made a round of visits with friends and family the morning after the wedding. In the 19th century, the middle class also wanted to get away from familiar scenes; English writer John Cordy Jeaffreson quipped, "It was very unusual for a bride, having the slightest claim to gentility, to pass the evening of her wedding day under her father's roof."[4] In France, honeymoons gained popularity in the 1830s as a way to ensure privacy, that is, that the couple could stay snug in a hotel room rather in the midst of family.[5]

Charlotte Bronte and her husband, the Reverend Arthur Nicholls, went on a month-long tour of Wales and Ireland immediately after their marriage. They were married before breakfast on June 29, 1854, and immediately hit the road, she in her white embroidered muslin dress and white bonnet. They spent their first night at an inn in Conway, North Wales, 130 miles away from where they were wed—effectively a honeymoon abroad. It would have taken at least a half-day to get there. Charlotte was already suffering from a cold before they set off, and the weather in Wales was wet and wild. They spent their first night in a "comfortable inn" where Charlotte wrote to her friend Ellen and presumably to her father, too. The first few days were spent exploring the North Wales coast from Conway to Bangor.[6]

When Herman Melville's literary prospects made him a reasonably good catch, he married Elizabeth ("Lizzie") Shaw, a young lady from a proper Bostonian family. The wedding took place on August 4, 1847, in Boston, after which they went by steamboat on a bridal tour through the Erie Canal to Niagara Falls and then on to Montreal. Lizzie had not visited New York City—the orientation of the American upper crust was Europe, for which they might sail without ever having seen points of interest in the United States—and was delighted by Canada's French culture.[7] It may have given Melville some peace of mind, as well, to get away from New York City, where the "fair forsaken Fayaway" put a notice in the *Daily Tribune* three days after the Melvilles said their vows in which she threatened to file a breach of promise suit against the writer.

Barbara Penner, a Canadian architectural historian living in London, retraces the typical 19th-century honeymoon in America in a fascinating book, *Newlyweds on Tour*.[8] She concludes that the American bridal tour, while modeled on the British, had a distinct and civic character. The couple was to marvel at American vistas while they gave a sentimental uplift to their fellow travelers by the rice on their clothes, their shy silence, and even their overtly affectionate behavior.[9]

A typical honeymoon was a northern tour, over the waterways to Niagara Falls. This site was an evolving allegory—from a manifesto of nature's flow and passion to the need to control great forces. The rush of sexual initiation no longer was an irresistible force but was something to be tamed in a man by the improving influence of the bride: "The idea was that, if passion was like a destructive stream, one needed to control it, so as not to end up crashing and destroying oneself. Marriage was seen as an essential way to regulate one's life and passions."[10]

The pattern of tourism was that adventurers paved the way for the well-heeled. Then middle-class Americans arrived, and the rich went elsewhere. Thus it went with the wedding journey. Affluent Americans emulated the bridal tour, and the middle class scaled it down so that it was within their means. Once there were trains, newlyweds could go much farther afield, and they sought out and popularized new destinations across the land.

Penner paints a broad picture of the American honeymoon in the first half of the 19th century. According to Penner, the honeymoon's rise in the 1820s coincided with the growth in America's market economy. The opening of New York State's Erie Canal, in 1825, gave impetus to the first honeymoon suites, featuring flying cupids, rose-colored windows, and oversized beds on Hudson River steamboats. Honeymooning ensured that the first few days of married life played out not in the familiar home but in the impersonal, commercial world of railroads, steamboats, and hotels. In this sense, the honeymoon—like many of the other elements of the white wedding that emerged at the time—helped to legitimize consumerism in society.

The early honeymoons usually lasted a month, the traditional "honey-lunacy" period. There were two aspects of early honeymoons that seem almost inconceivable today. First, honeymooners often traveled in a party that included friends and relatives (including the bride's mother). Second, in addition to spots of natural beauty like Niagara Falls, honeymooners enthusiastically visited places like prisons, battlefields, insane asylums, schools for the deaf and dumb, Shaker villages, cemeteries, factories, and orphanages. The early tour was much more social, civic, and patriotic than today's honeymoons.

Honeymoon suites first appeared in the 1840s on Hudson River palace steamboats. From there, they were adopted by palace hotels in big urban centers, particularly those constructed in New York City in advance of the 1853 Crystal Palace exhibition. Known as bridal chambers, the suites were lavishly decorated, and subject to endless public scrutiny. Thousands of visitors toured them in person, thanks to captain's tours and hotel opening days, and virtually, in media articles that microscopically noted every feature, from carpets to bedspreads, and breathlessly quoted the amounts lavished on their décor. When the Metropolitan Hotel opened, in 1852, the *New York Herald* reported that the bridal suite, consisting of a parlor, a large bedroom, and a servant's anteroom, "claimed the attention of all the ladies yesterday, and was filled with visitors till a late hour."

Even for those who no longer believe that the Victorians were sexually repressed, the sheer publicness and exuberance of these rooms still comes as a surprise. These suites, along with other emerging sentimental rituals like Christmas, made it seem right and proper that significant life events be celebrated with extravagant acts of consumerism and be promoted as an idealized image of conjugal love in which sex and goods intermingled. The feminized appearance of the chamber also underscores that this vision of love and luxury was highly gendered. These were bridal chambers, after all: their elaborately layered white interiors resembled nothing so much as a bride's gown and served to remind spectators of the act of bridal "unwrapping" that would later take place.

But it would be wrong to suggest that bridal chambers simply represented the triumph of consumerism, for their glory days were short-lived. By the 1860s, they had fallen out of fashion. Leading sensation writers of the day compared these luxurious suites to upper-class brothels. In George Lippard's *The Quaker City* (1845) and George Thompson's *The Bridal Chamber and Its Mysteries* (1855), bridal chambers emerge as places where sentiment was faked, love deceived, and virtue lost.[11]

The departure of the newlyweds immediately after the wedding reception was proper and expected once honeymoons became significant trips. Kate Chopin (nee O'Flaherty), author of *The Awakening*, married Oscar Chopin on Friday, June 9, 1870, in St. Louis. Bound for New York, the port of departure for their honeymoon in Europe, they took a train at once, arriving in Cincinnati at six o'clock the next morning. On the train, they were not long on their own and interacted in the civic spirit that Barbara Penner identified: "We met several acquaintances on the cars who congratulated us very extensively, and who could not be brought to realize that they must call me Mrs. Chopin and not Miss Katy. They joined us however in consuming a few champagne bottles that had escaped the dire destruction of their companions to meet with a more honorable consummation by the bride and groom."[12]

By Sunday afternoon, June 12, they had arrived in Philadelphia, after a "long, dusty, tedious trip!"

Once the exciting honeymoon was in fashion, a bride might reasonably expect one, as is seen in the case of Queen Marie of Romania, the popular queen at the end of a dynasty.

Crown Prince Ferdinand of Romania was an eager bridegroom to the beautiful Marie, granddaughter of both Queen Victoria and Czar Alexander II of Russia. The wedding (in 1893) was held up; the reason was that Victoria was against the match because it was between a Catholic prince and a Protestant princess. While this was being sorted out, Ferdinand and Marie met for a second time at one of the ancestral homes of Kaiser Wilhelm II. The king of Romania, Ferdinand's uncle, made the toast: "Let me drink to your 'honey day.'" Ferdinand raised his glass politely, but his hand was trembling, and, after the meal, he drew Marie aside in a pet. "Did she hear?" "Hear what?" Said the Prince:

> Don't you understand what he means? He means that instead of a honeymoon he will only allow us a honey day! That's just how he is—he does not care for or understand other people's feelings. With Uncle it is all work and no play, year in and year out, all through the seasons. He never cared about a honeymoon for himself . . . he is all duty and no weakness and expects everybody to be the same. It's always like that, everything has to be sacrificed. He has no feeling nor understanding for the wants and desires of the young. When it is a question of state he is absolutely pitiless![13]

The honeymoon was in fact a brief sojourn at a dreary hunting lodge. No wonder the next heir to the throne shocked his mother by choosing to elope with a commoner named Zizi Lambrino, in September 1918.

The keynote of the modern wedding night is the impending departure, a stepping stone to the honeymoon. Take, for example, Winston and Clementine Churchill, who married in 1908. They left the reception early in the afternoon to go to Blenheim Palace, where Winston had proposed. Clementine was wearing a tailored going-away dress, and, according to a critique in a men's fashion review, Winston wore his wedding suit, which made him look like "a glorified coachman." They drove to Paddington Station, boarded a specially reserved coach, and changed at Oxford to reach Blenheim. From there, they left right away to spend a week of their honeymoon at Lake Maggiore in Italy—energetic newlyweds on a traveling honeymoon.[14]

NOTES

1.   Martha Byrd Porter, *Straight Down a Crooked Path* (Richmond, VA: Dietz Press, 1945), 69.

2.   Ann Monsarrat, *And the Bride Wore . . . . : The Story of the White Wedding* (New York: Dodd, Mead, 1974), 75.

3.   Ibid., 75–76.

4.   John Cordy Jeaffreson, *Brides and Bridals* (London: Hurst and Blackett, 1987), 2:273.

5.   Michelle Perrot, ed., *A History of Private Life: From the Fires of Revolution to the Great War* (Cambridge, MA: Harvard University Press, 1990), 318–19.

6.   Lyndall Gordon, *Charlotte Bronte: A Passionate Life* (New York: Norton, 1994), 305. Also e-mail from Sarah Laycock, Library and Collections Officer, Bronte Parsonage Museum, Haworth, England, May 1, 2010.

7.   Andrew Delbanco, *Melville: His World and Work* (New York: Knopf, 2003), 92–93.

8.   Barbara Penner, *Newlyweds on Tour: Honeymooning in Nineteenth-Century America* (Durham, N.H.: University of New Hampshire Press, 2009).

9.   E-mail correspondence with Barbara Penner, February-March, 2010.

10.   Ibid.

11.   Ibid.

12.   Emily Toth, *Kate Chopin* (New York: William Morris, 1990), 101.

13.   Hannah Pakula, *The Last Romantic: A Biography of Queen Marie of Roumania* (New York: Simon and Schuster, 1984), 63.

14.   Jack Fishman, *My Darling Clementine: The Story of Lady Churchill* (New York: David McKay, 1963), 19.

CHAPTER 12

Guide for the Perplexed

Loves mysteries in soules doe grow
But yet the body is his booke

—John Donne[1]

A young man was looking for books on ice fishing. The reference librarian borrowed several for him from another library. Weeks later, when the young man's father returned the books, the librarian commented that she hoped they weren't too basic. "We have been ice fishing for many years," said the father. "We wanted to read books on the subject not for new information but because we love thinking about ice fishing." Through the ages, the authors of self-help books have taken the stance of instructing the ignorant. Sometimes they even impart the instruction in tones of "It's my way or the highway." But, as readers, we read for our own devices.

In Cole Porter's 1928 song, "Let's Do It (Let's Fall in Love)," the "it" is suggestive of sexual intercourse: "Penguins in flocks on the rocks do it. Even little cuckoos in their clocks do it" because sex is a natural act, requiring no instruction, only celebration. But copulation is one thing, and lovemaking is another, more complicated thing. For this reason, self-help books on marital sex have a long history and still claim large readerships (and detractors for any graphic content). Alex Comfort's *Joy of Sex* sold millions of copies, has had a sequel and new editions, and still sizzles enough that, as late as 2008, an Idaho public library removed copies from the shelves and squirreled them away in the director's office. Only the threat of ACLU litigation returned *Joy* to the shelves.

If sexual intercourse is natural, as old as the emergence of hominids millions of years ago, why do we read sex guides? To borrow from Francis Bacon's 1625 essay *Of Studies,* they serve "for delight, for ornament, and for ability." Few couples have grasped a sex guide and followed its directions to the letter or even felt they had to agree with the prescriptions the author gives. Yet, untold couples have weighed expert advice over the past 400 years. Why?

Two reasons stand out. The first is that these books give us permission to think about sex in an impersonal setting. Reading them differs radically from talking to a parent or a friend. Sex is laden with taboos, so it is not surprising that historically parents have said little to their children about its mechanics or techniques, especially since the devil's in the details. For many parents, giving a child a book is not just easier, but better for the details. A book delivers information in a format that can be studied at any speed, almost anywhere, and internalized to each person's capacity. The reader does not have to satisfy the demands of a personal authority figure such as a parent or clergyman. As an experience, books fit the privacy of sexual exploration to a tee.

Illustration from *The Glory of Women,* from the chapter "Truths for the Newly Married." The text reads: "A normally sexed woman loves to be loved and caressed by him who has her heart." (Reproduced with permission of Duke University Libraries.)

A WIFE'S DEVOTION

The second reason is that sex advice books give men and women the opportunity to compare their thinking on the mysteries of sexual love to what experts have concluded from wide experience and with the voices of authority. Whether they are like the ice-fishing enthusiasts or novices, the new bride or groom may pick up actual pointers or just develop a generalized inner script; either way, they gain a perspective on the beginning of conjugal sex.

SEXUAL CURIOSITY

In the classical world, men and women did it. In the Middle Ages, they did it. In the Renaissance, they did it. But only in the Enlightenment of the 1700s did important Western thinkers see sex as something to be studied and not merely judged or celebrated. Enlightenment thinkers discussed sex outside the church and the tavern. In their view, sex, like other human activities, could be improved through instruction. Sex manuals belong to this Enlightenment tradition.[2]

This is not to say that religious and social values did not impinge on the study of sex. As we will see, they did and do. But the Enlightenment's curiosity about the empirical world reached out to all human activities. In very popular ways, sex manuals, for all their prejudices, slowly opened the door to sexual knowledge in language that the average reader could understand. Over the centuries, these guides helped men and women, in the privacy of their reading space, to think for themselves about their intimate lives. With the advent of sex advice books, knowledge of sex broke out of the limits of personal experience and, in return, enriched it.

Until the late 19th century, marriage manuals were written primarily by men, and they conveyed particularly male views of women. They continued an age-old split between viewing women as sexually passive vehicles for men's pleasure and viewing women as unfathomable and (if sexually aroused) dangerous. Until the 20th century, the guides wavered between arousing the woman and controlling her. The manuals endorsed pleasure with one foot on the brake.

ON THE FRENCH SCHOOL BUS

As a student at a military dependents' school near Paris, I [Jane] had a long bus ride home. The driver was a GI who disliked his job (or us), and a hush of fear reigned. What I particularly remember is the boy whose popularity derived from bringing on board some sort of home medical encyclopedia that he could read in French. A bunch of us would huddle around, the boys in the first circle and around them the girls, listening to him read about conjugal sex—luxuriant details describing arousal, penetration, and orgasm. Way before *The Joy of Sex*, the French had books about sexual technique, and, whether out of prudence or sincerity, the author focused on the wedding night.

Self-appointed experts on sex were part of French literature from the 17th century on, often using a nom de plume. Nicholas Venette's *Tableau de l'Amour Conjugal* was published in 1668, when the rest of Europe had not yet dwelt in print on amatory relations between the bride and groom. It brought the wedding night into the homes of literate French people.

How to seduce a woman and how to keep her from straying were two sides of the same coin in works on marriage and adultery in 19th-century France. The proper launch of a marriage was the preoccupation of the self-help mentors, who decided that for the honeymoon to last required deftness on the part of the man. These manuals came down hard on the majority of new husbands. A bride's physical pleasure had to be drawn out; she had a nature that welled up with emotion and had to be calmed. Her tender emotions needed sensitive handling.

More than a century later, the prolific storyteller Honoré de Balzac (1799–1850) admonished the groom to initiate the bride slowly so that she served his needs and stayed faithful. In the 1826 edition of his *Physiologie d'Amour*, Balzac posited women as sly and wayward creatures whose husbands' job it was to keep them from going on a rampage. Three years later, Balzac's perspective had evolved. In the 1829 edition, Balzac added a new appendix to the section called "The Conjugal Catechism." It begins with a parable of the monkey that wants to play a violin—the symbol of the awkward lover. Being unable to make the notes it wished, the monkey took the bow in both hands and struck blow after blow to the instrument, then sat on the broken pieces and wrapped his hair around the broken bow.

Balzac was expressing the opinion that it is always the man who is foolish because he does not learn the art of love. He concluded the comparison by saying that, when he looked at the inept husbands, he couldn't help picturing that monkey he once saw trying to play the violin. According to Balzac, the woman is a "delicious instrument of pleasure," and the man "breaks the heart he doesn't understand." If the bride turned into a peevish or unfaithful wife, this was the result of her husband's blindness, egotism, and insouciance in the bedroom. The smart husband combined "caresses of the soul" with an effort to give the bride physical pleasure. Moreover, keeping his bride happy required that the new husband devote time and energy to fine-tuning her sensuality. Balzac compared this to how a novelist, sculptor, or musician learns to love his art:

Woman is a charming instrument of pleasure, but we must understand the quivery strings, we must study the setting, the modest
key-board, the ever-changing and capricious fingering. How many
orangutangs—I should say, men—marry without the least knowledge of what a woman is?[3]

Men, he concluded, sully and despise the jewels of the new bride "by
breaking open the door of a strange house, fully expecting to be well received in the charming room."

All sex manuals indirectly or directly deal with the physiological differences between the male and female sex drives. In *An Intimate History
of Humanity*, Theodore Zeldin notes that "the belief that sexual energy
needs to be discharged, like ammunition that will explode in one's own
face if not shot into his target," has prevented generalized sexual expression beyond tumbling in the bedroom, including "sensations of various
degrees of mildness, most of which go to waste."[4] This disconnect between a husband's copulative fire and his ability to please his wife outside
the bedroom lay at the heart of the marital problem of France's most important 19th-century writer, Victor Hugo, the author of such passionate
novels as *Les Misérables* and *The Hunchback of Notre Dame*.

By his own account a virgin when he married, at 20, Hugo had been
saving himself for Adèle, his age-mate and childhood friend. The two were
secretly engaged, but Victor, out of respect for his mother, who opposed
the match, waited until she died to marry Adèle. Still a teenager, he wrote
to Adèle to tell her that he loved her with all his heart and was resisting
his impulses on her account: "How great is your power over me since the
mere image of you is stronger that all the effervescence of my age."[5]

In old age, Hugo described his wedding night, avowing that he had
had nine orgasms during their first night of love, October 13, 1822. His
friend, the poet Lamartine, described Hugo in the first days of his marriage
as being "like an inebriated grape-picker" who harvested his wife's virginity.[6] There followed seven years of outward marital happiness and, for
Adèle, almost constant childbearing. Victor worked hard at writing—some
50 books over 50 years—and enjoyed sex with Adèle as a regular nightly
indulgence. While wife to her priapic husband, Adèle began an affair with
Victor's best friend, Charles Sainte-Beuve. After giving birth to her fifth
child, Adèle, 27, announced to her husband that it was Saint-Beuve, not
Victor, whom she loved and that she would bear no more children by Victor. They never shared a bed again. Too late, Hugo seemed to realize that
bedding a wife with intercourse galore wasn't the be-all of a love relationship. He was alone when he wrote her on July 17, 1831:

This bed where you could be (although you don't wish it anymore, *méchante*), this room where I could see your dresses, stockings, and scarves draped on armchairs, this table where you would come and disturb me with a kiss, all that is mournful and poignant. I didn't sleep last night. I was thinking of you as you were at 18; I was dreaming of you as if I'd never slept with you.[7]

By the end of the 19th century, nuptial advice books in France were acknowledging the sexual pleasure of the bride. In 1909, Dr. Rhazis (a nom de plume) published *L'Initiation Amoureuse, ou l'Art de Se Faire Aimer et de Plaire* (*Love's Initiation, or the Art of Being Loved and Giving Pleasure*). This book looked at marriage as the locus of sexual intimacy, not as a social requirement. The wedding night was a singular sexual occasion, and the groom had serious work to do, not in consummation per se but in bringing about his wife's transformation from girlhood to womanhood. Dr. Rhazis underlined and elaborated on Balzac's view that the new husband was often sadly lacking in finesse:

> Picture an ardent young husband. Scarcely inside the marriage bed, he hastens without any preparation to achieve his own end. But how many miscalculate their own energy and find that their flame dies before they have reached their desired goal? He has hardly had time to knock on the door, and has done so in such a clumsy and brutal manner that it will be a long time again before he sees it so ready to open. That is because he has caused pain without having had the time or opportunity to bring about the contrary feeling which ought to efface the memory of pain.[8]

The wedding night could be a traumatic event or a loving memory. Either way, writes Rhazis, the bride will bear the psychological imprint. The wedding night wasn't solely about proving the girl's virginity, marking an alliance, or beginning a procreative endeavor; it was about providing a chance to bring joy and delight to the conjugal bed.

RUSSIA: THE NEW HUSBAND WHO SHOWED OFF

We turn to the wedding night of the great writer Leo Tolstoy (1828–1910), whose young wife could have benefited from a published guide to marriage, especially marriage to a famous writer. Instead, what Tolstoy put his wife Sofya "Sonya" through exemplifies what a husband should not do. An obsessive gambler with a history of debauchery and 16 years her senior, Tolstoy insisted Sonya read all about his sexual past in his auto-biography. This permanently unsettled her and caused a first, deep rift in the couple's long, tumultuous marriage.

In 1856, when the 28-year-old Count Leo Tolstoy visited Sonya's family's country villa near Moscow, he had freed his serfs before Czar Alexander II abolished serfdom, and he had written *Childhood,* which was Sonya's favorite book.

Sonya waited on the colorful guest at dinner, carrying some pages of his second book, *Boyhood,* inside her dress near her heart. The count became a frequent visitor again in 1860. He liked the way Sonya and her sisters were being educated—to sew, keep house, and educate their younger siblings—and he told his own sister that, if ever he married, it would be to one of the Behr girls. He proposed in a love letter that he thrust into Sonya's hand as they played together a song called *Il Bacio* (The Kiss) on her parents' piano.

Once Sonya accepted the proposal, Tolstoy imperiously demanded that the wedding take place in one week. He brushed off all talk of what was in those days the all-important trousseau. But he did make time for Sonya to read his diary, which described his extensive sexual experience and his ideas of women as a necessary evil.

On the morning of the wedding, September 23, 1862, the bridegroom burst in and interrogated Sonya about the quality of her affection and the degree of her passion for him, to the point that Sophie wept. After the wedding reception's champagne toasts, the sleeping coach (called a "dormeuse"), with six horses, a coachman, and a valet stationed at the back, pulled up at the front door. According to custom, the family sat in silence before the newlyweds' departure. Then the bridal couple took a 130-mile drive to Yasnaya Polyana (Sunlit Meadows). The trip took 48 hours, so are we presumptuous if we suppose that they consummated their marriage in the coach? At Yasnaya Polyana, the housekeeper, Auntie Tatyana, welcomed them with an icon of the virgin, and Tolstoy's brother offered the traditional bread and salt. Leo and Sonya bowed, crossed themselves, and kissed the housekeeper. Tolstoy's entry the next day and Sonya's letter to her sister a week later were happy in tone, but the bridegroom had sown the seeds of jealousy and self-doubt in his young bride.[9]

The parallel between Effie Ruskin and Sonya Tolstoy is unnerving. Both Ruskin and Tolstoy fell in love with their wives when they were pubertal girls of 11 (Sonya) and 12 (Effie). Both men were about 34 when they married them. Both brides changed their names for their husband, becoming Sonya and Euphemia. On the surface, it would seem a great gulf that the Ruskin marriage was never consummated, whereas the Tolstoys produced nine children in the first 15 years. Nevertheless, just as

Ruskin was disturbed that his naked wife looked different from a marble statue and furthermore made her feel ugly as a sexual woman, Tolstoy was revolted by pregnancy and childbirth and made Sonya matter-of-factly accept his history of escapades. And he pulled the sexual strings: when Sonya was pregnant and nursing (pretty much nonstop), he would not have sexual relations with her and moved his bed out of their room to avoid temptation.

ENGLAND: TAMING THE SEX DRIVE

A bride knew that marriage was supposed to be calming and edifying for a man as it gave her a sanctioned place in her community. She was supposed to be pure in the sense of sweetness and light and also in the sense of being a virgin at her marriage. As Victorian ideals replaced the more earthly values of the previous century, men wished to match the bride's purity.

Although mid-19th-century Victorians read avidly and bridal guides to weddings sold well, these books were silent on the wedding night. This silence reflected the Victorian conviction that sexual innocence was virtuous. In an age of "muscular Christianity," men and women contrasted the eager male and the gentle woman. Those who read poetry considered the thoughts of Oliver Goldsmith, of the previous century:

> Need we expose to vulgar sight
> The raptures of the bridal night? . . .
> Let it suffice that each had charms;
> He clasp'd a goddess in his arms;
> And, though she felt his usage rough
> Yet in a man, 'twas well enough.

Many Victorian women loved the poetry of John Keats (1795–1821), who died, at age 26, in Rome, before he could return to England to consummate his passion for Fanny Brawne. Here is a poem to his love:

> This living hand, now warm and capable
> Of earnest grasping, would, if it were cold
> And in the icy silence of the tomb,
> So haunt thy days and chill thy dreaming nights
> That thou wouldst wish thine own heart dry of blood
> So in my veins red life might stream again,
> And thou be conscience-calmed—see here it is—
> I hold it towards you.

The 1852 *Complete Guide to Forms of a Wedding* gave detailed suggestions for the time of the ceremony but became hush-hush as the wedding night approached. The short section on etiquette after the wedding meticulously informed on the couple's dressing for dinner, while hinting at a deferral of sexual intimacy: "The lady, at the proper period, retires to her apartment, and having taken sufficient time for her evening toilette, directs the chambermaid to inform her husband that his apartments are ready."[10] Reading this must have made a bride practically hear dramatic chords of music. She was spared the specifics because the advice was largely allegorical.

At the end of the 19th century, Dr. Sylvanus Stall emerged as an early voice for medically based sex education. He wrote a series of "Ought to Know" books that delivered the medical lowdown for popular consumption. The popularity of these books is an example of the power of advice coming from outside the family circle to an expanding readership. The 1897 edition of Dr. Stall's *What a Young Husband Ought to Know* claimed that the author had sold more than a million copies of his advice books in England alone and an unspecified (but presumably vast) number in America; editions were issued in six other languages.[11] Some of his hints are those a father might say to a son today: to relax, not to sleep around and catch disease, and to be gentle and take it easy with the bride. He goes so far in his graphic information as to explain why the breaking of the hymen can be painful and why some virgins do not come to wedlock with this barrier intact.

According to Stall, male potency is iffy on the wedding night. Even if the young man exercises and lifts barbells and neither smokes or drinks for several months before the wedding, he may experience erectile dysfunction on the big night. It will only be temporary, but Stall commends that the bridegroom wait for some time after the wedding to consummate the marriage so that he wouldn't be feeble and the bride will be assured that his affections are of the spiritual nature. Should he hasten into the performance of his conjugal duty while his energy is at the ebb, likely as not, Stall warns, he will have feeble children. According to Stall, sexual indulgence at the outset of marriage on the part of either of the nuptial pair was the chief cause of the high mortality rate among first-born children. Here we see that medical knowledge of the physiology of conception was so limited that the physician confused actual conception with the physicality of the sex act.

Concerning the bride, the doctor counsels:

> In Greece the custom prevails of allowing three days to intervene between the marriage ceremony and the consummation of marriage. It

would be well if such a custom prevailed everywhere. It would allow the exhausted, nervous, timid bride to bring to the consummation of the marriage relation renewed vigor and mental composure.[12]

Stall held that most women have much less sexual desire than do men; indeed, "of the great majority of women it would be true to say that they are largely devoid of sexual pleasure." A little interest in sex among females is a good thing, Stall concluded, contrasting this with the attitude of women who are "proud of their deficiency" and "speak of their coldness and indifference as though it were a virtue." He offered multiple explanations for the bride totally devoid of passion:

In some it is the result of ill health, produced by lack of sufficient exercise and outdoor recreation; because of excessive social demands, late hours, indigestible food, the enervating and exhaustive effects of novel-reading, and especially also of tight lacing, with all of its sad effects in debilitating and displacing the sexual and vital organs which are located in the pelvic and abdominal cavities.[13]

According to Stall, the main reason for marital indifference was constipation, "which is so prevalent among women."

By 1918, in her bestselling *Married Love*, Marie Stopes gave ample cases of the collision between ideal and real in discussing the ignorance of the bridal pair.[14] There was the phenomenon of the bride traumatized by the physical part of married life: "I know of one pair of which the husband, chivalrous and loving, had to wait years before his bride recovered from the shock of the discovery of the meaning of marriage and was able to allow him a natural relation. There have been not a few brides whom the horror of the first night of marriage with a man less considerate has driven to suicide or insanity."[15] In 1919, one man told her he didn't read about sex before marriage so that neither he nor his wife would know anything in advance: "We should just be a couple of innocents walking into our Garden of Eden."[16] Stopes also warned that, while men were more often ignorant than debauchers, if they had experience only with prostitutes, they would find the wife frigid and unresponsive by comparison.

Sigmund Freud theorized that sexual desire, though largely subterranean, is the primary motivation of human beings, and Charles Darwin proved that we have ancestors in common with apes and lower animals. The large reading class in England, and especially writers and artists, started to express primal, if partially tamed, sexual needs and appetites. Isadora Duncan's dance and Maurice Ravel's music threw off constraints and demonstrated that sex could be healthy even if it wasn't connected with making babies. Thus, we saw in chapter 3 how the precursor of surrealism, Lautréamont, wrote a book, as disconnected as a dream, in which he became Maldoror the way Eminem became Slim Shady, a wicked shadow, and fantasized about a wedding night in the ocean with a luminous lady shark.

In this continuing mood of self-exploration of sexual motives, Robert Sermaise (a pseudonym for no one knows whom) wrote *The Fleshly Prelude*, published in 1938; it harkens back to Rousseau's ideal that going natural is better than going civilized. In *The Fleshly Prelude*, a jocular uncle advises his nephew on initiating his beautiful but repressed fiancée into conjugal sex. The "prelude" refers specifically to sexual foreplay, where time and again the narrator, following his uncle's instructions, coaxes the bride and divests her of fears about the act, his member, and feeling passions, until she is "vibrating with joyous impatience, similar to a child who, on coming to the end of an unknown road, suddenly discovers the blue expanse of the sea, glittering in the morning sun."[17] At times, the new husband thinks he should just forget delicacy and leap on his bride, but ultimately he is rewarded for his restraint by her boundless lust. The uncle has the last word after praising his nephew's "experiment":

> Many times when, during the War, we were "in the blues," young officers confided their amorous exploits to me,—and often with splendid vigour. But, in almost every case, what a lack of light and shade there was!—what lamentable ignorance as regards the reflexes of a virgin!—what brutality on the occasion of the initiation! And when I reproached one of them for having celebrated the first night of his marriage cavalierly, without waiting for a few days necessary for his young wife's fleshly awakening, he looked at me nonplussed and exclaimed: "Well that's a good joke! We were absolutely alone in my bachelor's quarters, and I was bursting to have her. Wait a few days before possessing my wife! What should we have done all that time!"[18]

AMERICA

America's founding fathers drank deeply of Enlightenment politics. They believed reasonable men—no, not women—could govern themselves. Our founding fathers came on the first wave of mostly British immigrants, and, after independence, many waves of immigrants from all over Europe and, to a lesser extent, from Asia arrived, seeking political freedom and economic opportunity. These immigrants brought a robust diversity of religious beliefs and practices. This led to a wide variety of books of marital instruction.

As more and more people flocked to jobs in American cities and towns, they shopped for food, rather than growing it for themselves. They no longer took food for granted but tried to discern which foods were healthy and which were not. Sylvester Graham, eponymous for the graham cracker and a powerful Christian voice, preached that a vegetarian diet curbed sexual urges. In an 1834 tract, Graham counseled sexual restraint for men before marriage and temperance after. In accordance with the New Testament equation of adulterous thoughts and the act of adultery itself (Matthew 5:27–28), Graham sought to restrain the mind as well as the body.

Those LASCHIVIOUS DAY-DREAMS, and amorous reveries, in which young people too generally,—and especially the idle, and the voluptuous, and the sedentary, and the nervous,—are exceedingly apt to indulge, are often the sources of general debility, effeminacy, disordered functions, and permanent disease, and even premature death, without the actually exercise of the genital organs! Indeed! this unchastity of thought—this adultery of the mind, is the beginning of immeasurable evil to the human family.[19]

A practitioner of water cures (hydrology) and health educator, Thomas Low Nichols, advocated that women should choose whether or not to have children and who the father should be. His *Esoteric Anthropology* (1853), a sexually explicit textbook of physiology, was widely read. Arguing against a male-determined sex regime, Nichols recognized women's sexual desire but held that "once a month is the natural period in which a woman requires sexual union; and it may be doubted whether any greater frequency is not a violation of natural law."[20] The goings-on in the bridal chamber evoked a warning about excessive sex. Nichols continues:

The exercise of abnormal amativeness is known in all its positive intensity by those newly married. The honeymoon is one nightly repetition of legalized prostitution, sinking the pure, high and holy into the low, debasing and animal. Think you, oh! New-made husband and wife, that in this you do right?—that in this you elevate your better natures?—that in this you find peace, strength and happiness?

As the 19th century concluded, advice books approached sex on the wedding night in three ways. Some suggested that it was a physical necessity for men only; some suggested that sex was a rapport of love, as distinct from procreation; and others suggested that intercourse should be avoided except for procreation. In her 1883 *Tokology: A Book for Every Woman*, Dr. Alice Bunker Stockham asserted that the first interpretation was given most credence: "Physicians and physiologists teach, and most men and women believe: that sexual union is a necessity to man, while it is not to women."[21]

The Enlightenment confidence that dispassionate discussion leads to better understanding notwithstanding, many guides suffered from a strong Christian distaste for sex as pleasure. An extreme example is Ruth Smythers's *Instruction and Advice for the Young Bride* (1894). The wife of a Methodist minister, Mrs. Smythers advised brides to bear the pain of sex in order to enjoy the pleasures of marital stability:

> To the sensitive young woman who has the benefits of proper up-bringing, the wedding day is, ironically, both the happiest and most terrifying day of her life. On the positive side, there is the wedding itself, in which the bride is the central attraction in a beautiful and inspiring ceremony, symbolizing her triumph in securing a male to provide for all her needs for the rest of her life. On the negative side, there is the wedding night, during which the bride must pay the piper, so to speak, by facing for the first time the terrible experience of sex.[22]

Mainstream sex guides by Henry Hanchett and John Kellogg assumed that only men had a sex drive, making women the passive receptacles. Physiologists did not understand how sperm was produced. They believed that men had a fixed supply, which they should not waste by masturbating or having sexual intercourse too often. For example, Kellogg counseled married men to have intercourse just once a month lest they exhaust their supply early in their married life.

As public discussion of sex became more acceptable, women became more outspoken about their sexuality, and their tracts found an avid readership. Ida Craddock (1857–1902) pioneered in openly providing sex counseling to men and women in Chicago and New York. She was an outspoken critic of censorship and openly published tracts of sexual advice clothed in mystical language. In her 1900 pamphlet, *The Wedding Night*, Craddock gave explicit, take-it-slow advice on "genital union" to both bride and groom. She posited that the bride was likely inexperienced and slow to arouse. It was the man's responsibility to make sure her first intercourse was pleasurable. This meant no intercourse on the wedding night, just sweet caresses of the neck and bosom. To deal with the impulsive male sex drive, Craddock, who identified herself as "Priestess and Pastor" of the Church of Yoga on 137th Street in Harlem, resorted to yoga, an Indian discipline barely known to Americans.

> To the average uninstructed man or woman, there is no apparent relation between the honeymoon and that philosophy which I prefer to call "yoga." And yet, if yoga were properly understood and practiced in the marital embrace by every newly married couple, their sex life would be, from the start, so holy, so healthy, so happy, that they would never care to descend to the methods commonly practiced among married people today—methods which involve loss of sexual self-control, tigerish brutality, persistent rape of the wife's person, and uncleanness.[23]

Instead of viewing masturbation as sinful, she saw it as a dissipation of essential energy. She urged men to ejaculate only during penetration and assured both man and woman that sexual union would enhance their spiritual understanding and eventually lead to "union with the Divine during the act."

Craddock inveighed against manual stimulation of the clitoris, which gives a woman a "male" orgasm. "As to the clitoris, this should be simply saluted, at most, in passing, and afterwards ignored as far as possible, for the reason that it is a rudimentary male organ." Instead, she urged the man to engage in lengthy intercourse of 30 to 60 minutes to stimulate the bride to a true vaginal orgasm. Craddock was drawing on a classical tantric yoga technique of prolonging sexual pleasure by delaying ejaculation. In the slowness of the sex act, the couple enters a meditative and ultimately transformative state.

According to Craddock, there was no substitute for the penis: "There is but one lawful finger of love." She described in some detail the "finger-glove" fit of penis and vagina and advised a man with an abnormally large or small penis or a woman with an abnormally tight or slack vagina to confer with the partner before marriage and to seek medical advice. Craddock dismissed hymeneal bleeding as an indication of virginity and advised women who had a thick hymen to have a physician snip it before the wedding night.

Craddock brought to the sex advice forum a new sensibility. She described male and female genitalia in graphic terms. Though still beholden to the notion that sex should be restricted to genital penetration, she shifted the framework from traditional Judeo-Christian terms to the yogic tradition, which saw sex, properly performed, as a form of meditation and spiritual realization: "Only that wedding night, only that honeymoon in which spiritual communion with the Ultimate Force of the universe forms part and parcel of the sexual act, is truly best."

A target of Anthony Comstock, who persuaded the U.S. Congress to pass a law forbidding the distribution of "obscene, lewd, or lascivious" material, including writing on birth control, Craddock was thrice charged with violating the law.[24] For the first offense, she received a suspended sentence. For the second, she spent three months in prison. For the third, the result of distributing *The Wedding Night* through the mail, she received a five-year sentence. Rather than face the long imprisonment, she committed suicide.

After Freud's visit to America in 1909, the number of articles about sex exploded, and discussions of sex became more descriptive of reality than prescriptive of what people should and should not do. Marriage manuals took a distinctly more positive stance toward sex as expressive, emotional, and even recreational. Sherwood Anderson looked back on the period following the First World War and said that "A kind of healthy new frankness was in the talk between men and women, at least an admission that we were all at times torn and harried by the same lusts."[25]

Also in Comstock's crosshairs was Margaret Sanger (1879–1966), who in 1916 burst on the scene with the publication of *What Every Girl Should Know* and the establishment, in Brooklyn, of America's first birth control clinic. For the latter, she went to prison for 30 days. In her books for adults and her extensive lectures, Sanger separated sex from procreation. Marital affection was a higher form of love than the desire for children. She felt that true love did not depend on the production of a family. Even if a couple desired children, Sanger advocated that they delay procreation for two years in order to settle into a rich sexual relationship. She saw women in sexual slavery as long as sex carried the risk of pregnancy.

> We maintain that a woman possessing adequate knowledge of her reproductive functions is the best judge of the time and conditions under which her child should be brought into the world. We further maintain that is her right . . . to determine whether she shall bear children or not, and how many children she shall bear if she chooses to become a mother.[26]

Sanger devoted a long life to providing birth control—she coined the phrase—to women and helped finance the research that produced the contraceptive pill, which the FDA approved in 1960, and that improved over time it so that women could take it without serious side effects. Fairly quickly, the pill allowed women to enjoy sex without risk of pregnancy. In the early 1960s, Mary Quant, designer of the miniskirt, asked, "Am

I the only woman who has ever wanted to go to bed with a man in the afternoon? Any law-abiding female, it used to be thought, waits until dark. Well, there are lots of girls who don't want to wait."[27] David Reuben's *Everything You Wanted to Know about Sex but Were Afraid to Ask,* published in 1969, embraced sex as recreation as well as the foundation of life-long commitment and means of reproduction.

In the 1970s, significant numbers of unmarried couples began living together, and by the end of the 1980s cohabitation had lost its association with a decadent youth culture. It had become a normal part of the courtship process. The current meaning of the wedding night rarely involves the bride's losing her virginity. It shifts the focus from an intact body to an intact commitment to trust each other and to grow in each other's love. Without watchful eyes and warnings to trim their passionate feelings, newlyweds can delight in being the "one" the other has chosen. Today's brides still feel wonder and delight, and bridegrooms exhibit tact and delicacy on this special night.

NOTES

1.   Thomas N. Corns, ed., *Cambridge Companion to English Literature: Donne to Marvell* (New York: Cambridge University Press, 1993), 137.

2.   Roy Porter and Lesley Hall, *The Facts of Life: The Creation of Sexual Knowledge in Britain, 1650–1950* (New Haven: Yale University Press, 1995), 21.

3.   Honoré de Balzac, *Physiologie du mariage,* trans. by the authors (Paris: Charpentier, 1829), 59.

4.   Theodore Zeldin, *An Intimate History of Humanity* (New York: Harper-Collins, 1994), 102.

5.   Henri Guillemin, *Victor Hugo par Lui-même,* trans. by the authors (Paris: Écrivains de Toujours aux Éditions du Seuil, 1975), 50.

6.   Quoted in Graham Robb, *Victor Hugo; A Biography* (New York: Norton, 1997), 97.

7.   Henri Guillemin, *Hugo et la Sexualité,* trans. by the authors (Paris: Gallimard, 1951), 14.

8.   Dr. Rhazis (pseudonym), *L'Initiation Amoureuse* (Paris: De Porter, 1909), 80–83.

9.   Cynthia Asquith, *Married to Tolstoy* (Boston: Houghton Mifflin, 1961), 17–37.

10.   Quoted in Helena Michie, *Victorian Honeymoon: Journey to the Conjugal* (New York: Cambridge University Press, 2006), 34.

11.   Sylvanus Stall, *What a Young Husband Ought to Know* (Philadelphia: Vir, 1897).

12.   Ibid., 128.

13.   Ibid., 124–25.

14.   Marie Stopes, *Married Love* (London: s.n., 1918).

15. Ibid., 112.

16. Quoted in Michie, *Victorian Honeymoon*, 114.

17. Robert Sermaise, *The Fleshly Prelude* (Paris?: Vendome Press, 1938), 119.

18. Ibid., 196–97.

19. Quoted in Helen Horowitz, *Attitudes toward Sex in Antebellum America* (Boston: St. Martin's Press, 2006), 71.

20. Quoted in Michie, *Victorian Honeymoon*, 134.

21. Quoted in Ellen K. Rothman, *Hands and Hearts: A History of Courtship in America* (New York: Basic Books, 1984), 255.

22. Ruth Smythers, *Instruction and Advice for the Young Bride: On the Conduct and Procedure of the Intimate and Personal Relationships of the Marriage State for the Greater Spiritual Sanctity of This Blessed Sacrament and the Glory of God* (New York: Spiritual Guidance Press, 1894), http://www.squaredancecd.com/Bride/brides/htm.

23. Ida Craddock, *The Wedding Night* (New York: Ida Craddock, 1900), 19–20, http://www.idacraddock.org/.

24. Vere Chappell, "Ida Craddock: Sexual Mystic and Martyr for Freedom," www.idacraddock.org.

25. Sherwood Anderson, *Memoirs* (Chapel Hill: University of North Carolina Press, 1969), 143.

26. Margaret Sanger, "The Child Who Was Mother to a Woman," *The New Yorker*, April 11, 1925, 11.

27. Quoted in John D'Amelio and Estelle Freedman, *Intimate Matters: A History of Sexuality in America* (New York: Harper and Row, 1988), 306.

CHAPTER 13

Between the Sheets

The deep, deep peace of the double bed after the hurly-burly of the chaise-longue.

—Mrs. Patrick Campbell[1]

After two failed marriages, I [Jane] met a former attorney, who had recently bought a vineyard in northwest Connecticut, torn out the vines, and cleared it. I was prepared to live almost anywhere for the right match. In no time, the fates turned up your classic prince—beautiful, six foot two, ninth-generation Harvard, intellectual, with pewter curls.

John and I were both born in 1946; 40-some years ago, we might have met crossing Harvard Yard. He would have been running from class to varsity or pick-up soccer, ice hockey, tennis, or basketball—you name it, he still plays it—and I would have been heading for the library.

When two people come together late in life, they come with beds, a certain kind of baggage. With John's background came a lot of antique furniture, such as coasters with hunting scenes, 18th-century highboys, tables, and chairs, silver sugar tongs, and so forth. Moreover, his father, after retiring from editing parts of the *Herald Tribune* and *Family Circle*, owned an antiques shop that, tragically, an arsonist burned to the ground. Among the antiques in John's house is a massive walnut four-poster. To get into John's bed, I, although of middle height, had to take a running leap. And, in my mind, it said "matrimonial bed in master bedroom" so loudly that I could only be surprised that my consort had no interest in wedding bells and wanted to live in sin.

John liked to sleep under heavy covers and to keep the windows closed for three out of the four seasons. John Adams, another Harvard man, kept his windows closed lest the mephitic nighttime air affect his health. Ben Franklin, not a Harvard graduate, celebrated opened windows at night and slept in the nude. When John, two years after my moving in, bought a new bed, it went (sigh) to a spare room to be used by our overnight guests, "The bed thy centre be, the walls thy sphere," John Donne declared, and this new furniture seemed the Taj Mahal of beds to me. Made by a local furniture maker, the bed was so harmonious in its lines, so fine in its design and cherry wood, and so elegant in its workmanship that I loved to rest on it for an afternoon. It's a pencil bed, so the four corners have posts, slender beveled posts that you can ring with your hand only at the uppermost part. Joining the posts at their tips are slender wooden horizontal rods. This allows for a canopy. But I, who already wondered aloud where the air was to come from during the three seasons when we slumbered with closed windows, expressed sufficient enthusiasm for the pristine canopy-free cherry bed that it remained an imaginary framed space without walls—pleasing and aesthetic—so long as I lived in that house of John's.

As a girl, I imagined being in bed in Snow White's glass box in a clearing in the woods surrounded by a carpet of white wildflowers. I'd lie in bed without appearing to breathe, as that seemed to be the state of Snow White that conjured up the prince. I also fantasized that I was the girl in *The Princess and the Pea,* whose manly host was willing to wait for me to grow up (and not complain of awakening sore from those peas in the mattress pile).

When my grandmother Emma remarried after being widowed, she took over a house furnished with her mother-in-law's beds. The suggestion that the sleigh bed in the back room was too dark for a small bedroom with a northern exposure astonished my grandmother. The sleigh bed had been my grandmother's second marriage bed, as well as her mother-in-law's; it had been there for 100 years, like the painting of King Richard II of England, who, my grandmother used to remark, had been an attractive child but turned out to be a terrible grown-up. Only remodeling would alter the long-standing spell of the grim Victorian furnishings she inherited.

I married Chris in the late 1960s. He rode out from Cambridge to Wellesley on a motorcycle. We studied together, and my grades soared to straight As. When my brother died, I needed a boon companion with whom to go forth into the world. So, one evening at the Union Oyster House, I asked Chris to marry me. I dreamed of being a marionettist, sold some puppets in a crafts store in Harvard Square, and hung our marionettes in the bay window of our first-floor apartment north of Harvard Square.

Bed? My parents offered one, but we examined the idea as objectively as we would have anything else and decided beds were too bourgeois and hard to move. When you were ready to go some new exciting place to live, you had to deal with the bed. We imagined our life as an endless path. So we slept in the bedroom on a mattress. The floor was not insulated, and we suffered a deep cold, not only the first chilly night but the whole year we lived there. In a few years, we moved to the Middle East and then to a series of Manhattan addresses—57th Street, sleeping on a mattress; then 114th Street, still on a mattress; and, finally, Columbia University's Butler Hall, on 120th Street. There we graduated to a Marimekko-covered pull-out couch, which, while suited for a small apartment, was inadequate for a tall man and me. He can have been comfortable in it only after I left to go live in Europe.

When Chris and I divorced, a decade later, we were living outside the city, and I left behind a marital double bed for another mattress in Manhattan. I learned to support myself, finally to stand on my own two feet. Our two children went back and forth from Bronxville to the Upper West Side.

At 40, I met a Romanian-born engineer, who had learned English from Shakespeare and spoke with a delightful accent and had been on the Romanian national chess team as a teenager. I was living on another mattress, a single one this time, because this was all that would fit into my tiny Manhattan office/apartment share, with my third child's standard crib alongside. It had been a year and a half since I'd been intimate with a man, and I recall pinning the engineer to the wall in my zeal, while at the same time, because of the prolonged chastity, thinking that this was like a wedding bed, myself being virginal, all things considered. We married, and I conceived immediately our daughter, a Columbia College graduate, Class of 2010, who has the best of both of her now divorced parents.

I felt rather chaste in my bed, as one may when re-singled. The male I shared it with, Mickey, had rich fur and an expressive tail and took up only a far corner of the bed. As mentioned earlier, I moved to the country to be with John who had looked me up on an Internet dating site; John would acquire the lovely pencil bed, providing us with the symbol and trappings but, significantly, never the reality of nuptials. For my part, I purchased a vacation home for my family in Maine, and to furnish it I moved my own bed, which had provided slumber in the years when I was alone with a cat in bed. This bed John transported in his SUV to Maine where he reassembled it a year prior to handing me a pink slip: "I love you but want you to leave." Thankfully I had my house readied when calamity struck—a place of my own to go.

I could sleep under the stars shining through the window at the head of the bed, as the carpenter who used to live there planned it, and regain equilibrium. I could dream maybe there was a man who would value me and express love for me enough to embark on matrimony; and after swimming in the Penobscot Bay and solo walks on the rocky beach I felt ready to recognize such a prince. Soon I met a handsome, self-possessed man, another attorney, David, who is trustworthy, openhearted, and loving to me and my children, who offered me his hand in marriage. I was given an opulent engagement ring (my first), tourmaline from Maine, and diamonds. We live outside of Boston and on the peninsula in Maine, where from the windows in the late spring we see wild madder (also known as bed straw) in its pale green bloom, enough to fill 200 mattresses.

Meanwhile, in the converted servants quarters of an historic mansion where David was living when we met was a squeaky 19th-century four-poster. Sleeping on it reminded me of the lumberjacks in logging camps, sleeping in their underclothes and packed (several dozen under the same cover) atop hemlock branches: one man would wake up and shout "Flop!" and then all the men turned over. On the bright side, David and I learned to cooperate by a simultaneous flipping over without really waking. For a time we slept half the night on a stack of quilts in the living room and the rest on the bed (going from too hard to too soft), but soon we dismantled the bed and stored it and the sagging link springs under the eaves, and slept and communed like graduate students on the horsehair mattress!

This palpable return to our graduate student days, too, seems to be about wedding nights! And while I still believe in daydreams—indeed, "love-thoughts lie rich when canopied with bowers"[2]—I think a bed shared with one's own declared spouse most conducive for passion.

A SIGNATURE BED

A flourish of praise to the nuptial bed appeared in 1882 in *Le Lit* (*The Bed*), a short story by the French writer Guy de Maupassant. The narrator happens upon a pack of letters tucked in the lining of a Louis XV upholstered chair, one of which is someone's reverie about his bed: "the bed, my friend, is our whole life." Perplexed by those who buy new beds, beds "without memories," he thinks back first on a birthing and then on a wedding night that took place in his same bed:

> Here are two lovers who find themselves flesh pressing against flesh for the first time in this tabernacle of life. They tremble but are transported by joy as they feel each other's nearness. Then, slowly, their lips meet. They are mingled in a divine kiss—a kiss that is the portal

to heaven on earth, which sings of human pleasure, promising it forever and heralding the ecstasy to come. And this bed heaves like a
rolling sea, swaying and whispering as if it were itself alive and joyful
because of the rapturous mystery of a love's consummation. What is
sweeter or more exquisite in the world than these embraces which
make of two beings one entity, giving both in the same moment the
same thought, expectation, and boundless joy that fills them with a
raging and celestial fire?[3]

For those who want their first wedded night to be in a signature bed,
there are fine furniture makers, like Daniel Gugnoni, who will realize their
vision. He and one woodworker assistant at Troy Brook Visions create
museum-quality tables, chairs, desks, and—their most intimate product—
beds, about a dozen a year in their workshop in Litchfield, Connecticut.
Couples tell Daniel and his wife, Barbara, "We want a bed to start our
lives together."[4]

Barbara observes, "These beds are a marriage of strong wood and color
with very swaying lines—femininity and strength. Men and women have
different ideas. A bed is a big oasis to the bride: it defines space and blocks
out the rest or the world. Women like tall posts and sleigh beds with their
enclosed feeling—the bed is a space. To the groom, it's an object and
mainly utilitarian."

Daniel, a trained sculptor whose knowledge of wood fibers and grains
informs his functional pieces, rarely repeats himself: "My ideal is something that I want to make, the result of a recurrent doodle over time."
Made of sustainable woods like cherry from the Alleghenies, tiger maple
from New England, or African mahogany, with magnificent finishes of oil
and varnish or a green water base, his beds last a lifetime.

The beds have individual characters. "You impose your will on metal,
but you work with wood," says Daniel. Some couples ask him to use wood
from the property of the home where they grew up or to reuse wood sal-
vaged from something else. The wedding bed he made for himself and
Barbara in 1992 he describes as a compromise—"where Barbara wanted
a sleigh bed with solid headboard and footboard, I used slats"—whereas
Michael and Rosemary Buntin, as an engaged couple, devised their dream
bed together. "We came into the shop because we wanted a new bed. We
had each been married before and wanted a fresh start, not mine or hers
but ours. All the pieces are one of a kind because they are handmade, but
he asked what we liked and came up with a bed with a low headboard,
and feet that come out and arch a little. I fall asleep in the bed as soon as
my head hits the pillow, yet I now take work to bed, because I'd rather be
there than at my desk."[5]

A BRIEF HISTORY OF BEDS

The Old English word for bedstead and bedding are "baence" and "streow," bench and straw. The bedding itself was constant for many centuries: pillow and or bolster, light coverlet, and a warmer cover of fur or goatskin, wool or quilt on top. Medieval beds were constructed of massive timbers nailed together, with either a raised headboard or footboard but not both. Bedding wasn't listed in early wills or inventories because it was normally inherited by servants.

Testers (from the Latin *testa*, meaning "head"), or canopies, arrived in the 14th century. Square canopies hung on rods or chains. The full tester covered the entire bed, and the half-tester covered only the area over the upper portion of the body. Some of these beds were large enough to enclose a chair, and a lamp might be hung inside, making it in effect a little room. A simple cupboard called an aumbry, where drink and food could be stored, stood next to the bed. By this time, the bedstead and the bedding were becoming important furnishings in the house. The 16th century saw the advent of the oak four-poster, a raised wooden box carried on four tall posts—the traditional style of the bed as we know it today. Either the bed was placed against the wall, or there was a little *ruelle*, a space between the bed and the wall. The *ruelle*, just large enough to conceal a lover, was a feature in many bawdy farces.

In the 1500s, the screw-cutting lathe changed the design and decoration of the bedstead. Metal screws replaced permanent wood joints, making the bed moveable. Royal beds traveled with their owners. Such a bed traveled with Henry IV of France in December 1600, when he first met Marie de Medici. That it arrived late gave the king an excuse to anticipate the wedding night with the princess. Nine months later, the first of their six children, the future Louis XIII, was born.

> With metal screws instead of permanent tendon joints, the bedstead could now be dismantled at will and need not be left at home. This made it more worth while to decorate it, and the cabinet-maker began to divert some business from the upholsterer. It is significant that at the time of this change—about the mid-sixteenth century the chalet is first called a lit and the bedstead called a bed. With woodwork to be carried too, there is even more packing and carting and unpacking and assembling of beds in the accounts of royal journeys, and much bad temper when the beds travel more slowly than their fortune, when he goes to a first meeting at Lyons with his bride-to-be Marie de Medici. His bed fails to arrive providing a neat excuse for anticipating the wedding night.[6]

Aristocrats in Renaissance Italy commissioned beds and bedchambers for newlyweds. The prospective bride brought a rich dowry of money, precious jewels, and clothes. The prospective groom provided an appropriate setting for the wedding night. In 1515, Salvi Borgherini commissioned a lavish bed and bedchamber furnishings for his son, Pierfrancesco, and his new daughter-in-law, Margherita Accaiuouli. Described at great length by Borgherini's contemporary Giorgio Vasari, the nuptial setting included a walnut bed, wedding chests, and 14 painted panels depicting the biblical story of Joseph. Interior decorators hung the panels on the bedroom walls and placed them as an enclosure around the bed. However, the lavish bedchamber fell afoul of partisan politics. The Medici supporter Pierfrancesco was forced into exile by rival partisans supported by Frances I, the king of France. As tribute to their French ally, in 1529 the anti-Medici faction offered him the Borgherini bedroom furnishings. Vasari reports Margherita's reaction:

> This bed, which you want for your private interest and greed for money—although you cloak your malevolence in false piety—this is the bed of my nuptials in honor of which my father-in-law Salvi made all this magnificent and regal decoration, which I revere in memory of him and for the love of my husband, and which I intend to defend with my very blood and life.[7]

Fortunately for Margherita, the Medici returned to power the next year, leaving the grand bedchamber intact.

In Renaissance England, the bed also featured hangings and coverings. Canopies symbolized divine authority of the rulers. The bedstead was a simple, solid frame concealed by valences, possibly with fancy carving on the headboard. The bride might see a birthing rail around her bed—a reminder that fortunes depended on her producing an heir. The expression "being privy" to a secret comes from the fact that only high-ranking courtiers could enter the king's privy chamber. One custom in England and France was that, the day after the newlyweds slept in the bed the first time, the bed became the property of the head of the bedchamber. Architectural painter Lawrence Wright tells, in his history of the bed, how, when Princess Elizabeth, daughter of King Edward I (1239–1307), married, a nobleman claimed the once-used bed that required two great horses to carry it to their castle; since the nobleman and his wife wanted to repossess it, they had to negotiate with and pay the earl. By the same token, when Edward III married, the Earl of Oxford claimed not only the bed but also the basin in which the bride had washed on the wedding night, as well as her bedroom slippers.

Beds were so valuable that it is hard to believe that they were bequeathed outside the family. This rings true for me only because of something that happened one summer at a lifesaving station on the Bay of Fundy, where my relatives on my mother's side lived. Newcomers who had bought one of the old houses had been lent furniture to supplement what the old sea captain, the former owner, had possessed, and one item was a massive matrimonial bed that had belonged to my great-aunt and uncle but which nobody wanted anymore. The newcomers had added interest to the rather remote community and been treated as family. However, when they decided to draw a line that everyone had forgotten about and interfered with someone's garden or woodshed, my aunts and uncles and parents were outraged. People quickly took sides, the outward manifestation of which was that a massive carved walnut bed traveled out of the newcomers' house and down the gravel road to somebody else's house and, later that weekend (the comical part), traveled in the other direction to a third house. I can see my male relatives bearing the bed—of sudden value to those who had divested themselves of it—as stern-faced as pallbearers.

In England, beginning in medieval times, the Office of the Great Wardrobe provided furnishings, furniture, and garments for the royal palaces. A subdivision called Wardrobe of the Beds supplied the wedding night. The office was turned over to the Lord Chamberlain in 1782. He ran the palace affairs, and one of his perquisites consisted of taking the king's bed after his wedding night or his demise. Happily, this custom meant that state beds made their way into many great English homes. The king had one bed where he consummated his marriage and usually others for other big occasions. Why? Because the royals moved from one stately house to another on royal progress, keeping the subjects aware of their monarch and also, in practical terms, "sweetening" the court, since, before the advent of modern plumbing courtyards and gardens were used as latrines by hundreds of people.[8]

THE COUPLE ON SHOW

From the 14th century, upper-class Europeans slept in individual beds topped with coats of arms or even plumage; the accent was on the bedding and the tapestry over it, not the bedstead. For instance, a bed at Versailles would scarcely show any wood at all, being an array of velvet, satin and silk panels, canopy, and curtains. Moreover, a bed rarely belonged to a couple but rather was part of a room. The bedding used on royal beds was dazzlingly rich. The bedsteads were carved, painted and gilt with silver, and covered with velvet and taffeta clothes and silver and gold fringe. The tapestry curtains hung on long loops. Headpieces might have ostrich feathers, and the counterpanes were of satin quilting, and gold and silver threads.

In the time of Charles I of England (1600–1649), a spectator to the scene in the queen's chamber on the night of the wedding of the 14-year-old Prince of Orange to the 10-year-old Mary Stuart (not the Queen of Scots, who was executed in 1587 by order of Queen Elizabeth I but the daughter of Charles I) described the "state bed" of blue velvet, which was richly framed with gold and silver, with buttons and embroidery of gold and silver, surmounted with four grand white plumes."[9] The bride and sometimes the groom would receive guests in bed the morning after their wedding. The Duc de Saint-Simon about 1700 said that, the day of his marriage, his wife received "toute la France" while in her bed.[10]

The beds of the upper classes were curtained like a fortress. The sexual act was as private then as now, hidden from observers and scandalous when carried out during the day.[11]

As we saw in chapter 4, royal parents often tucked their newlywed children into the nuptial bed. Equally prevalent was the widespread custom of receiving in one's bed the morning after the wedding; the courtiers at Versailles would gather for news of l'epreuve (the proof).

Beds were single, not double, through most of history. This implies that it was customary for the husband and wife to have sexual intercourse and then for one to leave the bed for another in which to spend the night. The individual bed also explains the conundrum of highly regulated sex in the same societies where adults went naked to bed. The husband slipped into the wife's bed naked and vice versa, but they probably slept separately and were not generally entwined all night long. If compelled to share beds with people other than their spouses, adults would simply remove their boots or shoes and sleep dressed. Also, beds were moved around the house, so there was no matrimonial bed or master bedroom. Add to this that "bed" referred to the bedding, the textiles of which were worth much more than the bedstead, and the bed as a piece of furniture seems to have played a minor role on the wedding night. Even when the four-poster came into popularity, it was a public spot to lounge with friends, with multiple uses for all types of social interaction.

In France, the public bedroom was called the parade bedroom, and newlyweds received visitors there. (A woman also received compliments after childbirth, and a person who lost a close relative would also receive condolences on the parade bed.) Usually, it was a gigantic bed in an alcove framed by columns and separated from the rest of the room both by a balustrade and by its position atop a platform so that one had to mount the platform to reach the bed.

Toward the end of the 1600s, a time beautifully documented by Dutch paintings of domestic interiors, rooms began to be reserved for sleeping.[12] The rising middle class had sufficient income to build separate bedrooms. This class also had a modern sense of private space where one could complete the entire ritual of retiring to bed by oneself or with one's spouse. This middle-class sensibility is also seen in the popularity of reading a book in private. At this time, many painters captured women curled up with a book of poetry or fiction, reading silently to themselves rather than to an audience.

The Grand Trianon, built for Louis XIV's favorite mistress, Madame de Montespan, at the palace of Versailles and completed in 1708, had beds with testers (tops) wreathed with tassels, draped with fabrics, and topped with bouquets of plumes. The frames were now far from plain, with headboards carved as intricately as other prized furniture. Meanwhile, the bed stopped moving around the house and stayed put in a room designed for sleep.

Like the Dutch burghers, French aristocrats developed a new longing for privacy around this time. The Duc de Luynes, a courtier at Versailles, recalled the rapid decline of the show-type bed from the time of his wedding in 1710, when he and his bride endured all the public rituals lying in state on their formal bed, to 1738, "when people were opting out of these performances." The Duc de Croy, reporting on the marriage of Louis XV's son in 1747, opined that such rituals were "highly embarrassing"; when his own daughter was married, "there were no such ceremonies."[13]

The change to private bedrooms that excluded the public wasn't mere fashion. Marriage was becoming less a family contract than an affectionate union. The whole architecture of the upper-class house came to reflect the closeness of husband and wife, with features like corridors that linked the two master bedrooms or master suites with single beds in one room.

AMERICA

In colonial America, the bed was an important piece of furniture but one not especially identified with coupling. The most elegant beds were arguably those made by the Shakers, who were celibate and for whom there were no wedding nights at all. And, whereas Victorians came to love opulent furniture, the bed wasn't an object of as much attention as, say, a credenza, cheval-glass, or chair, because it wore a bed skirt all round. If a room had a bed, a trunk, and a stand on which to put a candle, it was furnished. Usually, beds were high to keep them far off the floor, so a stool or short set of stairs might also be required to help people get into them. Colonial documents indicate that the bedroom, especially in a drafty house on a cold day, was the place where the couple entertained. As Americans prospered, they too reserved the bedroom for sleeping and moved the social part of their lives to parlors.

THE POLITE BED

Victorian discomfort with sexuality on both sides of the Atlantic went to absurd lengths. The idea that it was necessary to cover furniture legs lest they excite the male seems to have started as a joke, but in America the joke became a reality in some homes. When middle-class ladies and gentlemen in proper society considered separating female-authored books on a shelf from those written by males or putting skirts on a curving leg, it comes as no surprise that our grandparents wouldn't shout out, "Darling, let's go to bed."

When Queen Victoria's sensibilities were offended, she was known to state, "We are not amused." The Victorian attitude extended to the polite bed and is satirized in the novel *Enchanted April*, published in 1922 and turned into a hit movie in 1992. In the novel, four English ladies, strangers to one another, share a month's rental of a medieval castle in Italy. To go on holiday without their husbands is a bold gesture. When they arrive, the ladies set out beds and bedrooms, and the commanding doyenne, played by Dame Joan Plowright in the movie, gives insight into how delicately a prudish Victorian would handle the subject of where beds might be placed.

> In the 'eighties, when she chiefly flourished, husbands were taken seriously as the only real obstacles to sin. Beds too, if they had to be mentioned were approached with caution; and a decent reserve prevented them and husbands ever being mentioned in the same breath.[14]

By contrast, Shirley Temple Black fondly remembers the twin beds of her second wedding night, in California, in December 1950. As Shirley Temple, the child actress cheered audiences during the Great Depression. Fans still remember the dimpled, curly-haired dancer as they drink Shirley Temple cocktails (nonalcoholic) and admire the Shirley Temple peony. As Shirley Temple Black, she served as ambassador to Ghana and Czechoslovakia, as U.S. representative to the United Nations, and as White House chief of protocol.

In a location kept secret by the owner, Shirley and her husband Charles's honeymoon began in a simple cottage:

The twin beds were separated unromantically by a stubby bureau, but a log fire snapped and crackled, a small dinner table was set for two with lacy white linens, wineglasses, and a single candlestick. . . . From a distance we could hear deep-mouthed barking of seals, plainly audible above the nearby sound of waves, that broke, slid, and hissed among the boulders in a darkened cove directly beyond our room.

At exactly half-past eight, I proposed a toast. We had been married exactly four hours.

"Most exciting thing that's happened since PT boats," Charles rejoined.

What a long meal. Bolting the door, we snuffed the candle, banked the fireplace logs, and pushed the two beds together.[15]

British actor Sir Michael Caine remembers with exasperation the wedding night he shared with the lovely former Miss World finalist Shakira Baksh in a more public venue. As he told *People* magazine:

Shakira and I got married in Las Vegas. Then we went to the Beverly Wilshire Hotel. They had done the traditional Indian thing of hanging a bell on the bed so you can hear if activity is going on or not. So the first half hour of my honeymoon was spent trying to prize a bell off a bed.[16]

SECOND BEST BED?

The paucity of biographical certainty about Shakespeare has drawn attention to his last will and testament, in which he bequeaths goods, property, and money to his sister, his daughter Susannah and her children, his one grandchild by a daughter who was deceased, the poor of Stratford, and several friends, specifying in one case the purchase of a memorial ring. His wife, Anne, receives only the "second best bed." It was usual for wills to specify beds, as they, along with silver and pewter, were the most prized objects in a home—but second best?

Scholars have pondered and written about Shakespeare's every word, including his will. They have wondered whether the will gives evidence of marital discord. But the answer may be simpler. According to Larry Danson, a Renaissance scholar:

A second best bed might have been more comfortable than the first best (one shudders to think about the third or fourth). First beds were sometimes more for show than use. Or Mrs. Shakespeare would have received whatever in the estate remained after the bequests, like the 36 pounds to Hamlett Sadler to buy a ring, or the whole of New Place to his daughter Susannah. Since Susannah was now going to be the lady of that house, maybe she would naturally get her pick of beds. Therefore to prevent squabbling between mother and daughter, the thoughtful Shakespeare made sure his wife would get to lie in the bed she had so often made.[17]

UNMADE BEDS

With the idealization of domestic bliss in the 18th century came a change from public to private in the symbolism of the bed. The unmade bed became a subject in art just when the bedroom was becoming more erotic.

A photographer friend of mine said that of all the subjects he has ever treated, none made him feel lonelier than a photograph he took of a lover's hairpins strewn on a bed sheet the morning after. Somehow shocking—the hairpins, the crumbled sheet contrasting with diffused sun from the open window—as if she had flown away!

Drawings of unmade beds entered art not only just when beds became private and sexualized but also in advance of the more quotidian association with the domestic delinquency of leaving one's bed unmade. Given the uncomfortable straw mattress, a poor person wasn't inclined to lie abed; also, it was the bed of whomever slept in it, not a bed of one's own. Contrastingly, a matrimonial bed was as stately as the word sounds, and for the upper class. Gradually, as *The Age of Comfort* points out, by the early 19th century, the private character of the bed replaced the public. There were linguistic changes that indicated the new sexiness; in English, for example, we say we are "going to bed" as a synonym for having sex. The bed began to look erotic yet also bespoke conjugality, whereas, we conjecture, a hayloft looked more like a place to seal a relationship with intercourse or to transgress and romp.

The Romantics were the first to explore the artistic potential of the unmade bed. Artists as eminent as Eugene Delacroix depicted this intimate subject. A 19th-century drawing by the German realist Adolph Mensel and a watercolor by the French salon painter Paul Delaroche show a mass of crumpled sheets which become a visual metaphor for a story of a consummation. Delaroche's watercolor, *An Unmade Bed*, exemplifies a type of studio drawing as "vicarious self-portrait," a representation of the artist's inner sanctum. The blocks of subdued color function like a collage as a record of a private, hidden night—a distinct contrast to the popular paintings Delaroche did of Napoleon and Marie Antoinette. The late contemporary artist Felix Gonzales-Torres took a close-up photo of rumpled bed sheets that became a popular poster image.[18]

NOTES

1. *Yale Book of Quotations* (New Haven: Yale University Press, 2006), 120.

2. *Twelfth Night*, Act I, scene 1, line 42.

3. Guy de Maupassant, *Le Lit*, trans. by the authors, http://www.bmlisieux.com/litterature/maupassant/lelit.htm.

4. Interview with Barbara and Daniel Gugnoni, February 26, 2010.

5. Interview with Michael Buntin, July 1, 2010.

6. Lawrence Wright, *Warm and Snug: The History of the Bed* (London: History Pres, 2004), 61.

7. Quoted in Andrea Bayer, ed. *Art and Love in Renaissance Italy* (New York: Metropolitan Museum of Art, 2008), 65.

8. Val Davies, *State Beds and Throne Canopies* (London: Archetype Books, 2007), 5.

9. Wright, *Warm and Snug*, 82.

10. Ibid., 82.

11. Pascale Dibie, *Ethnologie de la Chambre à Coucher* (Paris: Bernard Grasset, 1987), 79.

12. Joan DeJean, *The Age of Comfort: When Paris Discovered Casual—and the Modern Home Began* (New York: Bloomsburg USA, 2009), 166.

13. Ibid., 168.

14. Elizabeth von Arnim, *Enchanted April* (New York: Pocket Books, 1993), 87.

15. Shirley Temple Black, *Child Star: An Autobiography* (New York: McGraw-Hill, 1988), 475.

16. "My Life in Pictures," *People*, May 3, 2010, 84.

17. Interview with Larry Danson, April 6, 2010.

18. Matthew Hargraves, *The Varieties of Romantic Experience: Drawing from the Collection of Charles Ryskamp* (New Haven: Yale Center for British Art, 2010), 30–31.

CHAPTER 14

The Bride Wore . . . Lingerie

"Let me take that charming garment off, my dear," he told her, and before she could protest, he swiftly whisked it over her head, and deposited the nightgown by the side of the bed. "There, now we are equals."
—Bertrice Small, *The Duchess*[1]

Bridal lingerie has a suitably filmy history. Once upon a time, when I [Jane] was assigned a lingerie article for *Cosmopolitan* magazine, I was very excited. No, I thought heaven had rained down upon me. Although all I wanted from underwear was quantity and comfort, I had always loved beautiful apparel earmarked for the night. The magazine gave me a list of manufacturers, which I took as a help with research—until I handed in my feature and learned that these were *advertisers,* who would turn into a dozen or more bad fairies if they saw my article with no mention of them.

So it was killed, but not before the beautiful variety of lingerie had seduced me and created a new appetite to own these dreamy garments and start my own small (one sacheted drawer full) collection of the antique and retro, the little nothings and the bias-cut glamorous, for the occasional and sensual pick-me-up.

Men who are interested in wedding-night customs, please indulge those of us who love bridal lingerie. Also, be apprised that, no matter how chilly the season or sporty your lady, and even if she would wear something only to bed, not in it, what she dons on the wedding night will be of moment to her. If this was something left out of your wedding, there are always the anniversaries to suggest a special purchase.

American Victorian-era wedding nightgown. (Cincinnati Art Museum, Gift in memory of Mrs. William Leo Doepke [Ethel Page] by her granddaughter, Sara Doepke.)

A LONG LOOK

Romans slept in the underclothes of what they wore in the day—put on your sandals and you were good to go to the public bath. In medieval times, total nakedness was the everyday rule for bathing and sleeping; people slept cocooned in their sheets. Among a priest's list of vows in 1279 was that a wife might not sleep in her chemise without her husband's consent. (Similarly, it is said that, in imperial China, a woman remained supine and did not turn over during the night in case her husband wished to have intercourse with her.)

In hostelries and guestrooms, it is known that unrelated individuals slept akimbo and naked in a large bed, until the Church, reversing the causality of Genesis, insisted that the nakedness of Adam and Eve engendered sin; after that, people dressed (or didn't undress) for bed. Moreover, until the 17th century, people didn't have different clothes for day and night—there were no nightdresses, so the person who received in the bed was dressed quite like the visitor.

A lack of concern about nakedness disappeared slowly in the 16th and more rapidly in the 18th and 19th centuries. With more private space came special night attire, initially among people of means. Specific garments for the night came into use at about the same time as the fork and the handkerchief, the late 1500s.[2]

From the late Renaissance until Victorian times, girls wore smocks to bed. In Romance languages these garments had names like *chemise* in French and *camisa* in Spanish, which eventually came to mean only the day-shirt. Readers of Regency romances are well acquainted with night rails (loose smock worn as a nightgown) as the last barrier between the heroine and her inamorato, hiding yet revealing one's charms. The nomenclature is complex and overlapping. In the Elizabethan period, men wore nightshirts that were like their day shirts, and, while the sexes dressed very differently in the day, they dressed in similarly shapeless garments at night. Shakespeare's wife wore a cambric smock a little longer than the smock she wore in the day. Over this she put on a cape of the same fabric (wool or linen), and both these items were perfumed. William Shakespeare either slept unclothed or dressed for bed in a nightshirt—a little looser perhaps than his day shirt, and with a lower neck opening as well as lace at in the neck and sleeves and ruffles at the wrist. When searching for it under a pillow, Shakespeare might have inquired, "Wherever is my night-gown?"

The man's nightshirt eventually had a collar, but daywear did not influence nightwear for either sex. For instance, when the waist on ladies' dresses went up in 1814, this was not accompanied by a similar alteration in the dresses worn at night. The nightgowns that Elizabeth I ordered for herself and her favorite male courtiers served as dressing gowns to be worn when receiving company.

In the 1830s, the nightgown was a light garment worn exclusively by women and children. My grandmother from Maine told my brother and me when it was time to put on our nightgowns. By the mid-19th century, a nightgown was essentially a feminine garment. George Meredith, in his poem *Love in the Valley*, wrote, "When from bed she rises clothed from neck to ankle / In her long night gown sweet as boughs of May." An 1885 caption in the *Illustrated London News* advertised "A *happy bride supplied with a handsome lingerie*."

Once ready-made garments came on the market, innovations in lingerie for the bride made good advertising copy. Women's nightdresses gradually became prettier, with small standup collars, yokes with tucked fronts, and long pleats down the front. Gradually, in the 1880s, frills down a front slit and trimmings at the hem were added.

It was like decorating a cake. Whereas, for a millennium, chaste young women did not wear lacy apparel on their wedding nights, decoration being risqué, bridal lingerie now began to show off the bride's assets.

A combination nightgown and pantaloons became popular in the 1880s. With frills at the wrists and knees, it buttoned down the front and had lace ruffles. This garment was of calico or silk and looked more like something to wear riding a bicycle built for two than something for a wedding night. With fabrics and trimmings, whether cotton or silk, becoming flimsier, there was a fashion for the diaphanous and (at last) for the high Empire waist. The late 1880s also saw an explosion of ribbons (especially pink and blue), frills, lace, and ruffles. There may have been a good explanation for the prim attire in the bride's trousseau. As the authors of *The History of Underclothes* observe:

> The fact that (respectable) women began to wear "attractive" nightwear only after the introduction, in the early eighties of [the] last century, of the practice of birth-control, has an obvious implication. In the days of unlimited birth-rate the feminine nightdress was markedly unappealing: perhaps a calculated discretion.[3]

That Victorian women typically wore the plainest of gowns is seen in the one unadorned garment among all the elaborate, rich ones that Queen Victoria, played by Emily Blount in the movie *The Young Victoria*, wears for her first night with the Prince Consort. Sometimes a bowed ribbon encircled the bust line and the gown was bare at the arms. We may think of Scarlett O'Hara and saloon girls in cowboy movies in black or red racy numbers, but, throughout most of the Victorian era, brides wore garments that left their silhouettes vague. These nightgowns were traditionally not bought via mail order, as were the other trousseau items, but were sewn by a family member or by the bride-to-be herself. The bride might pretend she was planning to make lace curtains when she and her mother bought the fabric and trimmings at the dry goods store.

But a bride's wedding-night attire did have an erotic element that is missing today, and that is the barrier that the garment supplied to intimacy. Sometimes it was just a matter of getting the long gown up and off. Often the gown was fastened with "lover's knots." These prettily tied knots (not bows) have been a wedding custom since ancient times. The idea was for a husband to loosen the knots as the couple undressed. A mid-19th-century anthology gives us an earlier proverb first recorded in 1600: "He hath undone her virgins girdle; that is, of a mayde he hath made a woman."[4] The ribbons trailing from a bridal bouquet are reminiscent of the bygone lover's knots.

THE WEDDING SHEET

In Latin American countries, the bride sometimes slept under a special wedding sheet. Such a sheet plays a pivotal role in the plot of *Like Water for Chocolate*, Laura Esquivel's novel, which was made into a film of the same name. A matriarch in this Mexican family determines her daughters' fates—the older one, Rosaura, will marry the handsome young man who is in love with Tita, the younger daughter, while Tita will remain unmarried and take care of her mother as long as the mother lives. Forbidden love drives the plot. Tita, a gifted cook, concocts dishes with magical properties. As she is baking the wedding cake, she suddenly runs from the kitchen into the room where two of the women are embroidering the wedding sheet. "It was a white silk sheet, and they were embroidering a delicate pattern in the center of it. This opening was designed to reveal only the bride's essential parts while allowing marital intimacy." How lucky they had been to obtain French silk at that time of political instability. The revolution made it impossible to travel in safety, which is why, if it hadn't been for a Chinese man who dealt in smuggled goods, it would have been impossible to obtain the material, since Mama Elena would never have allowed one of her daughters to risk traveling to the capital to buy the things for Rosaura's dress and trousseau. But the sight of the whiteness of the sheet blinds Tita for a moment so that all she can see is whiteness everywhere: "When she looked at Rosaura, who was writing out some invitations, she saw only a snowy ghost. But she showed nothing, and no one noticed her condition." Her blinding whiteness persists that night, as that wedding sheet makes real the fact of her sister's marrying the man she herself loves and is loved by. It is months before Pedro carries through with his marital duty to the "wrong woman." In the movie version of the book, the image is of the nuptial sheet with its embroidered keyhole, spread over Rosaura, and Pedro kneeling by the bed in prayer.[5]

THE TROUSSEAU

With the wedding came the trousseau (from the French "trousser," to pack up or truss). Emma Roualt, soon to become the notorious Madame Bovary, "busied herself with her trousseau. Part of it was ordered from Rouen, and she made herself nightgowns and nightcaps with the help of fashion-plates which she borrowed."[6]

The fragrant chest with bridal and honeymoon items folded inside used to be a possession of most girls, whether poor or rich. The trunk smelled of fragrant wood, often cedar, when a mother opened the lid to examine the contents with a young daughter. The daughter felt she was glimpsing her future in the layers of linens and garments. On the society pages of newspapers of 100 years ago might have appeared an itemization of the trousseau of the wealthy bride, assembled for her honeymoon to Europe.

By 1900, the rule of the trousseau became "a dozen of everything." What to sew and purchase for the trousseau was a great topic of discussion in women's magazines like *Godey's Ladies Book*. The adviser in *The Lady's Realm of London* in 1903 described the various necessities and concluded as follows:

> There is nothing more charming dainty and comfortable than the robe de nuit of the moment. Surely a touch of illusion in such a matter as a robe de nuit with an underlying current of coquetry is permissible in a young and charming bride. Two or three dozen nightdresses are not too many. . . . Americans and other ultra-smart folk are very fond of black silk or gauze nightgowns; but I do not think they should have a place in bridal trousseaux; I confess to a predilection for the purest white. Silk, fine lawn, muslin and cambric are charming for night wear. . . . You should spend a large portion of your trousseau money on these important garments.[7]

TO DAZZLE AN EMPEROR

It seems that fashions peak in the direction of excess before beginning to wane. The trousseau, which began as a practical outfitting of the bride, a trunk of prettily sewn items that adumbrated the mysteries of one's future, became disproportionately huge at the upper echelons of society. One of the most extravagant trousseaus belonged to the Empress Elisabeth, known as "Sisi," of Austria, who married the Emperor Franz Joseph in Vienna in 1854.

Franz Joseph of Austria still had the acrid taste of the 1848 rebellion in his mouth when he went seeking a consort. His mother, Archduchess Sophie, who had seen to it that her husband abdicated in favor of their son, encouraged Franz Joseph to check out his Bavarian first cousin for a bride. As in many fairy tales, the younger sister, Elisabeth, 15 years of age and still wearing her hair in two braids down her back, rather than the older sister, caught his eye. The mothers and sisters quickly acceded to his wish.

Ferdinand and Elisabeth became engaged, and there followed cotillions and masques for the whole month of August 1853. Delighted by his future bride, Franz Joseph made three trips from Vienna in short order to see her, and he probably would have married her on the spot except for the need, on his side, to organize the wedding festivities and the necessity, on her side, for her to put together her trousseau.

The extravagant bridal trousseau filled 25 trunks, but nearly every piece in it was a gift from either the groom or his mother. It included a sable-trimmed velvet cloak and muff, 4 ball gowns, 17 fancy gowns with trains, 14 silk dresses, and 19 summer frocks, as well as crinolines, corsets, all manner of headdresses, hats, and shoes, fans, parasols, hairbrushes, ribbons and combs, and other objects. In the underwear category, the trousseau had 12 dozen camisoles, 14 dozen silk or cotton stockings, 10 bed jackets of muslin and silk, 12 embroidered nightcaps, 3 negligee caps of embroidered muslin, 24 night neckerchiefs, 6 dozen petticoats of pique, silk, and flannel, 5 dozen pantalets, 24 combing coats, and three bathing shirts.

Given its riches, it is surprising to learn that Franz Joseph fretted over the trousseau: "With the trousseau, it seems to me, things are not moving ahead well, and I have difficulty believing that it will be pretty."[8] Surprising only if we don't take seriously contemporary Viennese standards of fashion.

The wedding took place in Vienna on April 24, 1854, in monarchic splendor, in St. Augustine's Church, which was draped in red velvet and illuminated by more than 1,000 candles. Elisabeth's white bridal dress was embroidered with silver and gold and decorated with white roses and myrrh flowers. She wore the Hapsburg diadem in her hair. After the wedding mass, guests, enough to file a 19-page document, passed by and kissed her right hand, which rested on an embroidered cushion. This ritual, called a *baise-main*, was so enervating that it sent Elisabeth briefly into hiding to have a good cry.

After a gala banquet, the two mothers led the bride to her rooms; 12 pages holding gold candelabra stood along the way. Franz Joseph's mother, Sophie, stayed in the room next to the bedroom until Ludovika, Elisabeth's mother, and four maids undressed Elisabeth and put her to bed. Then Sophie fetched her son and brought him in and said a final goodnight to the bride, who, Sophie later wrote with pique, hid her face, surrounded by the masses of her hair, in her pillow, pretending to be asleep, "as a frightened bird hides in its nest."[9] Determined to turn this "Bavarian provincial" into a queen worthy of her son, Sophie accompanied the couple to their residence in the palace of Laxenburg, where she enforced an Austrian regime of numerous changes of lavish sets of clothes every day.[10]

THE LATE 19TH CENTURY

As the form of the nightgown became more subject to fashion beginning in the 1880s, examples became more revealing and playful, with satin ribbons and lacy ruffles. By the turn of the 20th century, "proper" wedding lingerie was becoming sexy. A French fashion maven gave this advice about outfitting the tremulous bride with a very suggestive sort of attire:

It would be distressing to pass over in silence the article of clothing that surpasses all others—the conjugal nightdress. You mustn't describe this sort of thing to a young lady—one has to respect the exquisite and slightly exaggerated modesty of seraphims, but you must place it in her wedding trousseau. The bride will not wear it right away, but after a while she will understand the value of this Oriental silk, or that batiste, cut with wide lace insets and aquiver with Valenciennes lace that rims it in flounces at the bottom. She will become accustomed to this transparent network which, in front, from throat to waist, reveals the charming assets of her young and supple bust.[11]

The outstanding fashion rag *La Vie Parisienne* frequently featured risqué fashion themes—"How They Go to Bed" dealt with nightgowns. In the late 1870s, government censorship relaxed, allowing displays of lingerie and even nudity. Some lingerie was downright erotic, featuring silky fabrics.[12] In 1903, the avant-garde French fashion maven the Comtesse de Tramar observed:

The elegant woman takes particular care concerning her undergarments. She may wear the simplest, most modest dress yet proclaim her femininity by her luxurious intimate toilette. . . . Intimate finery . . . is the veiled region evoking the most desired indiscretion. The man in love expects to make contact with shivering silks, satin caresses, and charming rustlings.[13]

Undergarments were becoming dainty, delicate, and even spicy things for gentlefolk, and seductive underwear was no longer exclusive to women of the night. The Comtesse de Tramar went on to encourage women to dress to seduce.

A husband has the right to see pretty things. As much as another man he has an eye for beauty . . . the nuptial chamber evokes luxury in its understated elegance—a pretty love-nest and the bird that inhabits it ought to give the same attention to what she appears to the husband in, as is done to making the interior of the room elegant and gay. Why stop halfway and leave a discordant note in the harmony of lines and colors? Light batiste and the rustling of silk stimulate desire, and within their darling promises hold the flight that palpitates at the feet of the dove.[14]

THE EDWARDIAN ERA

What the bride from a family of means wore was usually a part of a set, including petticoat, drawers, corset, and full-length nightgown. A former

staff member at the Metropolitan Museum of Art's Costume Institute who
now runs a wedding accessories business described the new look: "They
are gorgeous and have beautiful lace and hand embroidery. Often there is
a provenance like 'My great-grandmother wore this on her wedding night
at the Hotel Centrale in Cincinnati. The nightgown was quite plain but
had dainty embroidery.'" Presumably these garments would carry a bride
through the entire postwedding interlude until breakfast.

Although this may seem incredible to us, a woman of means in 1900
apparently might have worn a nightgown over a corset. Moreover, despite all the fine stitching in her trousseau, when she took off her crepe de
chine peignoir, she was likely to be wearing a shapeless long garment that
was almost an exact copy of the medieval nightshirt. A bride stored her
chemise in a flat satin bag that was way more frivolous than her virginal
nightgown, which came in a variety of fabrics, such as fine ecru or white
wool, muslin or batiste cotton, with tiny stitching and a few ribbons and
bows.

What did the groom wear? The male nightshirt was often elaborately
stitched, and, if lace was out of fashion in the Victorian era, there were
still ruffles on a placket down the front, and possibly discreetly at the
wrists. However, the nightshirt went into decline around 1900, when pajamas replaced nightshirts. Now there could be the amusing plays in the
French "théâtre de boulevard" in which the distraught bridegroom, faced
with some awful intrusion on the wedding night, traipses around the stage
in his pajamas (often with a dressing robe flying behind him). To some,
pajamas lacked the sex appeal of the night shirt:

> For 50 years these were manufactured almost exclusively in broad
> coloured stripes which reduced men's sexual attractiveness in the
> bedroom to that of multi-coloured zebras.[15]

To recap, in an unfolding drama that is almost Darwinian, the medieval bride and groom slept naked; later newlyweds slept in undergarments
that looked like their outerwear; still later, the outerwear changed but the
nightshirts/rails remained long and voluminous; then, in the Edwardian
period, women's and men's attire split off from each other and evolved
separately.

THE 20TH CENTURY

In the Roaring Twenties, women's nightwear choices included pajama
sets, sleeveless slip-like gowns, and long gowns with Empire waists. Women
copied men's pajamas, but fashioned in silk or another slinky fabric. Not

only were the styles innovative, but also the attitude shifted to "anything goes." Meanwhile, there was no longer a sliver of a chance that a bridegroom would come to bed in one of those handsome nightshirts that for certain brides surely awakened the same interest as a kilt.

And when both sexes traipsed around having breakfast the morning after, for instance, answering the door at the hotel, they wore what they were wearing in private during the night—pajamas and open dressing gown for the man, negligee or robe over the nightgown for the woman. The idea that this attire must never be seen out of the actual bed had disappeared. Moreover, the nightwear was crafted in a variety of fabrics, including silk, artificial silk and mercerized (polished) cotton, that were too comfortable to give up for one's day clothes until absolutely necessary.

The teasing numbers from the twenties have a dance hall look—swishy slips of white satin adorned with intricate lace and embroidery, the drawers now reduced to matching panties and quite like the satin boxers that are stylish today.

Edward and Wallis, the Duke and Duchess of Windsor, were the trendsetters of fashion in the thirties. The Duke, the former King Edward VIII, who gave up his crown to marry an American divorcee, inspired men's sports clothes in the United States by what he wore on yachts and the golf course when he visited our shores. The Duchess, the former Wallis Simpson, the ultimate tailored woman, naturally went off on her honeymoon with a big trousseau, some 40 pieces of luggage occupying a compartment on the Orient Express, in addition to Edward's things. The couple spent their first night in the train car surrounded by hundreds of yellow roses. Wallis, who was denied royal status and court privileges, had interlocking Ws mounted with crowns embroidered on her undergarments. She, of course, would have preferred "HRH" (for Her Royal Highness), but in the privacy of her undergarments she was Edward's queen.

We remember thirties movie stars because their evening clothes are imitated in the bias cut, gaping side slits, and slender straps of the glamorous nightgowns that a bride might chose to wear today. The skirt of the nightgown was lengthened and full (pleated) so that the bride could swirl around. Over the gown she might wear a bolero jacket, not merely to meet the codes for movie propriety.

LACE: AN ANCIENT SARTORIAL ART

True fancy lace, an openwork distinguished from embroidery and made of silk or cotton, started in Greece, where statues of goddesses often wore robes edged with lace. Handmade lace reached its height in the

16th century in Venice, where it became very intricate and was known, poetically, as "punto in aria," or "stitches in the air."

In the Middle Ages, centers for making a new type of lace by the use of bobbins developed in Flanders and France. Instead of being made by a needle that ties together the threads, the lace is fabricated by the use of numerous bobbins that twist the thread. Nearly all top-of-the-line lingerie was decorated with exquisite lace, and knowing something of the story of lace makes us appreciate and judge its quality. Valenciennes in France was renowned for its fine bobbin lace. The city belonged to Flanders until it was ceded to Louis XIV, in 1678. From then on, the fine Flemish bobbin laces, woven so extravagantly, were considered French. French men and women literally dripped in lace!

So fine was this lace that one pair of women's sleeve ruffles would take one Valenciennes lace worker 10 months of 15-hour days to complete. Lace was strongly associated with weddings and other joyous occasions. At the French court, etiquette prescribed that it was never worn by those in mourning. In 1739, when Louise Elisabeth, eldest daughter of Louis XV, wed the Prince of Spain, the bill for her lace trimmings, underwear, and nightgown cost the equivalent of 25,000 pounds; when Cardinal Fleury saw the trousseau, he said that he supposed it was to marry all seven sisters.[16]

By 1810, the Englishman John Leaver had invented and improved a machine that could twist threads and make a wide, strong lace mesh quickly. An attachment called the Jacquard advanced the technology by requiring a movement from only one side in a constant, fixed motion that resulted in lace that so closely resembled handmade lace that only a textile expert could discern the difference.

Americans of means ordered their lace from Europe, especially for elegant lace curtains and in the form of handkerchiefs, racy *bustiers*, fancy boudoir attire, and lace gloves. The lace industry was slow to develop in the United States because of tariffs imposed by England. However, during the brief Spanish-American War, when soldiers in Cuba and the Philippines died of malaria, which could have been prevented by mosquito netting, which the Leavers machinery also made, the laws were changed. The Tariff Act of 1909 provided free entry of Leavers lace machines for 17 months, and lace making came on a small scale to New England and the Midwest.

WHEN LINGERIE ENTERS THE WEDDING ALBUM

"Here, I'm Cutting the Cake . . . Here, I'm in a Nightie" read a headline in the Style section of the *New York Times* on May 17, 2009. Wedding photographers were shooting "boudoir" sessions to provide "sexy, play-ful shots of a bride, wearing, say, nothing but her fiancé's favorite sports jersey, or lingerie." One wedding photographer said these photos added "a bit of raciness to the wedding album," helping her business through lean times. "Much of the appeal of the boudoir sessions is that the brides want pictures of themselves in the best shape of their lives after the pre-wedding regimens of dieting and exercise. . . . It's empowering for these women."[17] And yet, surely, we want to resist our inclination, to prove we exist by taking pictures of ourselves, as these kittenish images do. Follow-ing this inclination to the end leads to the futile quest to show oneself in many guises—see me being athletic on water skis, soulful at a coun-try music concert, and frisky in the bedroom, before I am no more. As Susan Sontag said, photographs help people to "take possession of space in which they are insecure." At the opposite end of the spectrum, many couples are too busy, don't have the extra time or money or even space to make a wedding album from the photos taken by a professional or a friend. The couple's "wedding album" remains virtual, as invisible to the naked eye as their wedding night.

BEAUTIFUL TO TOUCH

Women do not purchase their wedding lingerie to be put in a garment bag or resold. The nightgown in the trousseau is an item that is used . . . and used up! Like the vicar in *The Vicar of Wakefield* (1766): "I . . . chose my wife, as she did her wedding-gown, not for a fine glossy surface, but such qualities as would wear well."[18] This is what makes bridal lingerie so de-lightful. While of luxurious fabrics and with special details, it is lovely and soft and also practical.

According to Marilynn Lipton, owner of Etoile Soleil in Westport, Connecticut, young brides do not select their own wedding-night linge-rie. Rather,

> Every woman wants to have her children live happily ever after, and she thinks this gives her daughter a good start. The mother or mother-in-law purchases wedding night lingerie. Friends may too but they'll get a cute and sexy nightgown without a robe. The moth-ers come in for something really special. Except for the older bride who selects for herself, it is very rare that the bride buys for herself for the wedding night. The first thing the shoppers care about is touch—does it have a soft hand? It's not a matter of how beautiful it is but how beautiful it feels.
>
> If the purchaser is a mother-in-law, she will ask us, "Is this ap-propriate?" In general we do a lot of handholding, for instance if the

bride is tailored and they're contemplating a frothy gown. She may sleep in a t-shirt and boxers, but they still want to get her a special gift. The bride will choose a pastel or even brown for items in her trousseau, where for the wedding night the thinking is classic, white or cream.

In our mobile society it seems, at first blink, irrational for a mother-in-law to provide the bridal lingerie. Yet, the gesture is confirmed by several young women we spoke with, and they appreciated it and did not find it overbearing.

The 20 years Ms. Lipton has been stocking her shop with exquisite underwear and gowns have seen a change in what sells:

Bridal lingerie now has softer lace—sometimes full-bodice; less silk (because it shows folds from being in luggage); more often shorter gowns, still with covers or robes (we call them jackets); more practicality—easily washable; more attention to fit, with a trend toward a shelf in the bodice for support; gowns that can go from sleep to casual; and pajama or boxer sets of a new elegance.[19]

NOTES

1.   Bertrice Small, *The Duchess* (New York: Random House, 2001), 213.

2.   Norbert Elias, *The History of Manners* (New York: Pantheon Books, 1978), 1:164.

3.   C. Willett Cunnington and Phillis Cunnington, *The History of Underclothes* (1951; Mineola, NY: Dover, 1992), 16.

4.   W. Carew Hazlitt, *Faiths and Folklore: A Dictionary of National Beliefs, Superstitions and Popular Customs, Past and Current, with Their Classical and Foreign Analogues, Described and Illustrated* (London: Reeves and Turner, 1905), 266.

5.   Laura Esquivel, *Like Water for Chocolate* (New York: Doubleday, 1992), 32–33.

6.   Gustave Flaubert, *Madame Bovary: Provincial Manners* (New York: Oxford University Press, 2008), 24.

7.   Cunnington and Cunnington, *History of Underclothes*, 218.

8.   George Marek, *The Eagles Die: Franz Joseph, Elisabeth, and Their Austria* (New York: Harper and Row, 1974), 105.

9.   Quoted in Brigitte Hamann, *The Reluctant Empress* (New York: Knopf, 1986), 46.

10.   Marek, *The Eagles Die*, 105–6.

11.   Marguerite d'Aincourt, *Études sur le Costume Feminin* (Paris: Rouveyre et G. Blond, 1883), 14–15, trans. Jane Merrill.

12.   Valerie Steele, *Paris Fashion: A Cultural History* (New York: Oxford University Press, 1988), 119.

13.   Comtesse de Tramar, *Le Bréviaire de la Femme* (Paris: Victor Havard, 1903), 10.

14.   Ibid., 171.

15.   Mary Eden and Richard Carrington, *The Philosophy of the Bed* (London: Spring Books, 1961), 38.

16.   Bury Palliser, *A History of Lace* (London: Samson Low, 1875), 146–47.

17.   Douglas Quenqua, "Here, I'm Cutting the Cake . . . Here, I'm in a Nightie." *New York Times*, Style section, May 17, 2009, 1.

18.   Oliver Goldsmith, *The Vicar of Wakefield* (New York: Heritage Club, 1939), 1.

19.   Interview with Marilynn Lipton, May 14, 2010.

CHAPTER 15

The Food of Love

Le flambeau de l'amour s'allume à la cuisine. (The torch of love is lit in the kitchen.)

—French proverb

TO EAT OR NOT TO EAT

In my [Jane's] imagination, the morning after holds all the sensual imagery, but for someone else, it's that impromptu midnight repast. When I interviewed people about the wedding night, they told me about many meals and the lovemaking that took place on this once-in-a-lifetime occasion. He made her grilled salmon and corn outdoors at their getaway lodge; they shared a glass of wine on the beach and watched the sun go down; the carrot cake they ordered for a wedding cake showed up only after the wedding, so they fed it to each other. So, food and romance? Absolutely.

Certain foods never cross your mind except when you are with the person you love, and then the most basic food may have more taste and texture, both of which leave an imprint on mind and memory: how on the wedding night you had this room service meal in a grand hotel in the city where you work and live, or how you dashed out for savory Tunisian *brika* when you married in Gibraltar; these are symbolic of place and emotion. Where else to eat foods in the "wrong" order, or make a meal of shared orders, all as if the two of you are one big person? The little in-

This 17th-century posset pot served a warm drink of eggs, sugar, milk, and bread-crumbs to newlyweds, as well as to the infirm. (© V&A Images/Victoria and Albert Museum, London.)

timacies commence that continue to grow in married life. There is such pleasure in simply standing next to the person you now belong with at the shop as you buy this or that item or in looking into each other's eyes across the table—all this because the two people know what the rest of wedding night/honeymoon will be like: an afternoon on the beach, the sharing of an outdoor shower, love-making on the balcony or in the cottage loft, back to the beach to watch the sunset, and then, after dark, ordering in or having provisions and a rental movie.

Leigh Cousins, relationship counselor and author, puts it succinctly:

The metaphorical connections between food and intimacy are many. Food is a way of entering the loved one's body. Food (the stuff of physical sustenance) is a motif for emotional sustenance. Feeding one another symbolizes the promise to care for each other, to hear and accept and answer and embrace and celebrate one another's earthbound needs and immerse in each other's mortality.[1]

NOW I CAN EAT

Since time immemorial, the wedding night has been associated with food. A vintage cartoon shows a couple leaving the church after their wedding, the bride svelte in her clingy gown and veil. In the thought balloon over her head—"Now I can eat!" Bridegrooms often get tipsy at their weddings because they imbibe with little food. Very possibly, the bride is famished, not from trying to fit into "the dress" but from the wedding's being an out-of-body experience.

At the wedding party, food speaks of the generosity of the hosts, and the toasts wish upon the couple a long and fruitful marriage. Thus, a New England wedding in Puritan times ended with kissing the bride, firing guns, and drinking rum. In contrast, the après-wedding eating and drinking of the couple alone or with a few boon companions are saturated with sexual connotation. Writing in the first century C.E., Plutarch said that the founder of Athenian democracy, Solon, bade brides eat a quince the first night of marriage, "intimating thereby it seems, that the bridegroom was to expect his first pleasure from the bride's mouth and conversation."[2]

A classic cultural collision in wedding planning occurs over whether guests will be served a complete meal. Elizabeth, a clothing store buyer in Boston, was a prime example of someone caught in the middle. Her older sister's wedding was the "cardboard" canapé variety. Elizabeth's parents were Episcopalian. Some families omit a dinner for the sensible reason that they wish to cut costs, but her parents insisted on a string quartet at her father's club, not a band, and no meal for Elizabeth's sister's reception. Elizabeth said, "My parents told my sister it was the height of vulgarity to serve real food. When my time to plan the wedding came, I remembered guests leaving hungry and looking for a restaurant in downtown Boston at nine P.M., and so we ate. When my father objected I convinced him with, 'Dad, we can borrow from other cultures.'" So, whether the guests will be hungry or well fed after the wedding depends partly on the traditions of the family or families planning the nuptials.

UNDER THE PILLOW

My navy parents attended many weddings. At home, I awaited the little box of wedding cake. I believed that if the box were put under my pillow, I would dream that very night about my future bridegroom. If my parents returned late at night, my mother knew to put the box under my pillow, even though she said it hadn't worked for her—no dream of my dad. However, she had gone to a gypsy fortuneteller, who said that she'd marry a man whose name began with "R," and that came true.

Gypsies were not on the scene in my day as in her youth, so I counted on the wedding cake.

My brother teased me that I had to eat the cake the next morning for the imagined bridegroom to reappear. From the moment I saw the box in the light of day, it was as if lit with white light, and, seduced by the story, I felt "something," if not a beloved's face. For a girl to have the token of the bride's cake was like lying in a field of poppies. It had little to do with a specific "him" but rather floated me to an unseen place and joyous state.

This state of expectation is captured in an 18th-century poem:

But, madam, as present take
This little paper of bride-cake;
Fast any Friday in the year,
When Venus mounts the starry sphere,
Thrust this at night in pillowbeer;
In morning slumber you will seem
T'enjoy your lover in a dream.[3]

Bride-cakes were given as favors to unmarried girls in early New England. Eliza Wolcott was the daughter of Oliver Wolcott Jr., the U.S. secretary of the Treasury after Alexander Hamilton, from 1795 to 1800, and later, like his father and grandfather, governor of Connecticut, from 1817 to 1827. While living in New York City, Eliza attended the wedding of her sister Laura, one year her senior, to Colonel Gibbs. Eliza sent back to Litchfield, Connecticut bits of wedding cake, which her cousins never received. In a letter to an uncle in Litchfield and dated February 24, 1811, Eliza wrote:

Instead of delivering the Trunk to Mrs Reeve as requested, I understand it was opened by Mr. Gibbs Mr Hing and Mr Aspinnall,—I have to request you, to order the Sheriff to take up these three young men, who were all concerned in taking the Cake. If they are penitent and make suitable apologies, I am willing they should be pardoned, this being as I wish to believe, their first offence, but if they deny the charge, I request you to detain them in jail, till I can send you Miss Sally Gracie's deposition, who heard Mr Aspennall [sic] make a full confession. I can prove them guilty, and if they are stubborn I suppose you will sentence them to be punished according to Law.[4]

Eliza would marry and have children, too, but Laura outlived Eliza by 15 years, surviving until 1870.

DRINK

Festive and at least symbolically Dionysian, drinking belongs to the wedding celebration. In Tudor England, drinking at wedding celebrations was so excessive that Queen Elizabeth tried to limit the amount of malt that could be brewed for a "bride-ale," the source of our term "bridal."[5] In 17th- and 18th-century England, it was standard to have a "bidden wedding," where guests left money for the newlyweds to offset their expenditure on the wedding party. The bride herself prepared a strong brew of "bride-ale" for sale to the guests. The bidders were young men sent out to recruit the wedding guests, all of whom were expected to contribute. While many today toast at the reception with champagne, other wedding drinks were more associated with the après-wedding.

As part of the charivari in France, young men brought a cauldron of caudle, wine mixed with spices, eggs, and bread, on a stick resting on their shoulders. The drink was to revive the couple after the wedding night.

POSSET

With more propriety, following a custom widespread in Europe, a priest used to appear in the bedroom with a benediction posset, boiled milk curdled with wine or ale. The couple drank it, and then the priest blessed the bed, sprinkled the couple with holy water, and filled the room with incense. In the eggnog family of drinks, the warm milk of posset soothed nerves and ensured a restful sleep. Posset sets of the bowl, pitcher, various containers for the ingredients, and spoons were a popular gift to newlyweds. The set at the Victoria and Albert Museum, in London, is made of porcelain, and many costly sets were made of silver.

A 17th-century poem by John Suckling, A *Ballad upon a Wedding*,[6] describes how bridesmaids delayed consummation of the marriage by coming into the bedroom with the posset:

> But, just as Heav'ns would have, to cross it,
> In came the bridesmaids with the posset:
> The bridegroom eat in spite;
> For, had he left the women to 'it,
> It would hae cost two hours to do't,
> Which were too much that night.

This poem, often quoted at English weddings, has the lively tempo and simple rhyming of a ballad.

MEAD

Mead, or honey wine, is one of mankind's oldest fermented drinks. In ancient times, honey was plentiful and easily fermented. In the *Symposium*, Plato states that the Greeks brewed mead before they learned how to make wine. In the *Odyssey*, the great adventurer drinks honey wine on several occasions. In southern Europe, wine pretty much replaced mead, but in the north, where wine was less plentiful, mead persisted. A great feast in *Beowulf* takes place in Mead Hall. A Northern European custom was to give the bride and groom a month's supply of mead, a practice that may have given us our word "honeymoon."

Mead brings to mind a picture of lords and ladies quaffing from silver goblets and a knight offering a mead cup to a pretty maid. The Celts made potent mead by adding the sap of the hazel tree, and it is in Ireland and Scandinavia that mead is mostly associated with the wedding night. It was said to ensure a man's virility and boost his strength. If the couple drank it during the honeymoon period, they were more likely to have a son.

The American godfather of mead, Robert A. Morse, started out making mead in a vat in his backyard, just as the reader of this book can.[7]

Basically, you water down honey, put it in a narrow-necked glass jug in the sun, sprinkle in some cloves, and, presto, home-brewed mead. There are also recipes for home-brewed sparkling mead, which requires two fermentations; the process resembles that for making champagne. In the United States, the mead makers who make an organic honey wine flavor it with currants, blackberries, raspberries, blueberries, or cranberries.

Morse said that goldenrod honey was too strong to eat but made his favorite mead. He offered a centuries-old recipe that goes like this: take one part honey to two parts water; boil till one part is evaporated, and skim; add cloves and ginger; then let it sit in the sun. When it is lukewarm, put it into the container, and add the flowers.

Now mead is enjoying a resurgence in North America, with dozens of "meaderies" dotting the United States and Canada. For example, the Lunenburg County Winery has been making honeymoon wine since the mid-1990s.[8] The mead Chris (my first husband) quaffed in northern Michigan tasted very distinct and resembled liquor, rather than wine or beer.

APHRODISIACS

In his *Libro de Buen Amor* (Book of Good Love), the 14th-century poet Juan Ruiz expounds on sex stimulants, many of them drawn from pharmacopeia introduced into Europe by the Arabs. He recommends for their particular aphrodisiacal property ginger, sandalwood, cumin seed, citrus fruits, marigolds, cloves, and "large quantities of vile carrots."[9]

Foods that are rarer, spicier, more expensive, and prettier than most, as well as sugary delicacies that tickle the throat or dainty finger foods take on aphrodisiac properties over time. The aphrodisiac is generally rare, like saffron, cardamom, or truffles.

One of my friends told me of the delicious sensuality of her first raw oysters—when her friend in Paris said to her, "Add nothing to it, put nothing on it, just taste the sea."

So, maybe, food and drink are transformed into aphrodisiacs by magical words—an attractive stranger's voice, a lover's look as he feeds you. Lists of aphrodisiacs are many but, alas, the essential element seems to be context, not chemistry. You, or a chef, can name a whole lot of things—some Indian foods, oysters in a seaport where they are a specialty, delicious raspberries from the garden, sherbet flavored with rose petals, or butterscotch sauce on ice cream—a host of foods that can somehow sound sinfully, sensually delicious, with aphrodisiac qualities, if you close your eyes and feel the smell and taste—and then look into the eyes of the person who is sharing these delicacies with you.

CONCOCTIONS

In the French Pyrenees, the bride and groom disappeared after the wedding feast. As the accordion (or, during the Renaissance, the lutes and fiddles) played music faster and faster, someone would shout, "They've gone, they've gone! It's time to prepare the *aillade*!"[10] At this, the guests shrieked with delight and dashed into the kitchen to boil up a god-awful brew with handfuls of garlic (French *aille*), salt and pepper, topped off with creative pinches from each person of ingredients such as a cinder or a spider's web.

Then the guests searched for the bridal pair, who had "hidden" in the bedroom. When found, the man and wife had to drink at least a mouthful of the *aillade* and declare it delicious. We can only conjecture why the guests did this—whether to divert a virgin's fear or scold the bridal pair, who might otherwise be walking on air, or because bibulous people become foolish, or all of these.

CHOCOLATE

What is it about chocolate? Even if you scan the dessert menu looking for an item other than chocolate, you may associate eating chocolate with your wedding night. When the Spanish princess Maria Theresa married the future Sun King, Louis XIV, she gave him a present of chocolate. This was a rare as well as a sweet gift, for the Spanish, who discovered chocolate when they conquered the Aztecs, kept secret its source and cultivation. However, as the Spanish empire dwindled, chocolate began to spread to the rest of Europe. This is when Maria Theresa gave it to Louis XIV as a precious gift. At the time, and well into the 19th century, chocolate was a food only for the elite—people rich enough to afford it. France actually made it illegal for anyone not of noble birth or of the clergy to drink it.

Interestingly enough, chocolate was originally used as an aphrodisiac among the Aztecs. The emperor Montezuma was a great drinker of chocolate, and legend has it that he drank numerous goblets of it daily in order to enhance his sex drive. This Aztec tradition lives on when hotels place chocolates on the pillows in the honeymoon suite.

Over centuries, Parisians have mocked their compatriots in the provinces as coarse dolts, while the rural population has looked on Parisians as hoity-toity snobs. According to folklorists, this explains the custom of *la rôtie*, or roast. The custom is very old, and over time it has changed from savory to sweet. The earliest custom involved a roast chicken placed in a chamber pot. In other recipes, the concoction may be eggs and cream, a milk soup with a string of garlic heads, or a spicy onion soup with a phallic-shaped carrot joined to garlic heads. All the variations were edible, if outlandish.

In the Auvergne region of France, two of the bourgeoisie's favorite luxuries for celebrating, chocolate and champagne, are combined and served in a chamber pot. This peculiar-looking, delicious-tasting food, called the *rôtie*, is fed to the bride and groom in the nuptial bed. The couple may keep this pot, sometimes painted with an eye, in their bedroom or use it as a vase for flowers in the entry of the house, as a souvenir of an important rite of passage into married life.[11]

After the wedding party, the bride and groom go to a house in a nearby village. Young men and women go from house to house looking for the couple. When they arrive, noisy and drunken, at the right house, they are told, "Sorry, the couple isn't here," whereupon they barge in and up the stairs and burst into the bedroom with the *rôtie*. The implication is that that the couple has not yet consummated their marriage, and the gang may perform the practice called "*vider le lit*" (empty the bed), tipping the bed so that the bride and bridegroom fall to the floor in a heap of bedclothes. The party stays until dawn, and, before they leave, they serve the newlyweds a hearty onion soup.

La rôtie seems to say that you can take the wedding out of the past but you can't take the past out of the wedding. Of this custom, Georges Sand wrote, in her story "A Country Wedding":

We won't discuss the toast that is brought to the marriage bed; that's a very silly custom, which upsets the modesty of the bride and tends to corrupt that of the other young girls present.[12]

This does not sound like a tradition a couple would willingly revive.

SOUPS

A French soup served late at night with the intention not to ridicule but to stimulate the passions is called *le resveil* (the arousing or awakening), referring to its property of increasing the couple's ardor. *Le resveil* was served to Martin Guerre, the interloper who pretended to be a woman's husband returned from an absence of many years, whose tale was told in a classic movie starring Gérard Depardieu as Martin.[13] In Brittany, *le resveil* was served to the newlyweds in their marriage bed three days after the wedding.

The idea of waking up famished and having breakfast in bed seems sensual and luxurious. Such morning-after customs reflect a sense that couples that like to see each other in the morning have a good chance of happy marriage. As English humorist A. P. Herbert quipped, "The critical period in matrimony is breakfast-time."[14]

Food and ritual (which wedding nights involve) go hand in hand and are as powerful as anything we humans do. Think about taking communion and the symbols of breaking bread. Wedding nights are champagne (effervescent and special) and strawberries (heart shaped, red, sweet, and delicate). Chocolate and caviar (not together, of course), a night of lovemaking and symbolic foods; if you do the irreverent thing and put chocolate and caviar together, you get, naturally, a lot of laughs.

NOTES

1.   Correspondence with Leigh Cousins, June 30 and July 6, 2010.

2.   Plutarch, *Plutarch's Morals: Ethical Essays* (London: George Bell and Sons, 1888), 70.

3.   Kris Bulcroft, *Romancing the Honeymoon: Consummating Marriage in Modern Society* (Thousand Oaks, CA: Sage, 1999), 23.

4.   Letter to Frederick Wolcott, Esq., Wolcott Family Collection, Litchfield (CT) Historical Society.

5.   Bulcroft, *Romancing the Honeymoon,* 23. See also Nina Epton, *Love and the English* (Cleveland, OH: World, 1961), 95.

6.   John Suckling, "A Ballad upon a Wedding," www.luminarium.org/sevenlit/suckling/wedding.htm.

7.   Robert Morse, *Making Mead (Honey Wine)* (Ithaca, NY: Wicwas Press, 1980).

8.   Megan Venner, "The Original Honeymoon Wine," *Good Taste,* Spring 2010, 30.

9.   Nina Epton, *Love and the Spanish* (London: Cassell, 1961), 26.

10.   Nina Epton, *Love and the French* (Cleveland: World, 1960), 112.

11.   Deborah Reed-Danahay, "Champagne and Chocolate: 'Taste' and Inversion in a French Wedding Ritual," *American Anthropologist* 98 (December 1996): 750–51.

12.   George Sand, *The Devil's Pool and Other Stories,* trans. E. H. Blackmore and A. M. Blackmore (Albany: State University of New York Press, 2004), 173.

13.   For an English version of this French tale, see Natalie Zemon Davis, *The Return of Martin Guerre* (Cambridge, MA: Harvard University Press, 1983), 20–21.

14.   Robert Andrews, ed., *Columbia Book of Quotations* (New York: Columbia University Press, 1993), 108.

CHAPTER 16

Arabian and Other Nights

A wedding night is a perfect frame for a short novel, an irresistible microcosm with sensual, comic, tragic possibilities.

—Ian McEwan[1]

According to Freudian psychiatrist Bruno Bettelheim, if we go to fiction to resolve complicated problems, no single story can give us a solution.[2] This chapter discusses a wide variety of fictional wedding nights, which, from a certain angle, provide the impetus for personal growth and integration throughout our lives.

900 C.E.: *THE THOUSAND AND ONE NIGHTS*

Though known in the English-speaking world as *The Arabian Nights*, the literal translation of the Arabic is *The Thousand Nights and a Night*. The latter part of the title, *and a Night*, captures the essential plot and its hold on the imagination. For 1,000 nights, there is one more night for Scheherazade (from the Arabic *Shahrazad*), the vizier's daughter, to tell a tale and avert her death. For 1,000 nights, there is one more wedding night of storytelling.

A vast store of tales from India, Persia, and the Arab world were compiled in the ninth century C.E. in the frame of stories told by Scheherazade over 1,001 nights. They include tales of historical figures such as Harun al-Rashid and fanciful creatures such as Sinbad the Sailor. The collection of stories includes romances such as the story "Aladdin and the Magic Lamp," comedies such as "The Ass, the Ox and the Laborer," tragedies such as "The Three Apples," and abundant erotica such as the story of Nur al-Din and the Damsel Anis al-Jalis.[3] These tales feature magic lamps, flying carpets, and seductive marionettes, as well as saints, thieves, and adulterers. Many of the tales recount the multiple faces of love—faithful and unfaithful, requited and unrequited, jealous and unwavering.

When first imported from Egypt by the French scholar Antoine Galland in 1704, *The Arabian Nights* immediately caught the fancy of French readers. Galland translated the massive collection tale by tale for the newspaper *Mercure*. The task kept the Frenchman working in his bedroom until late at night. Since many of the tales end in suspense, crowds of avid readers would gather below his room, pitching pebbles at his window and clamoring for the next installment.

Many tales are interlaced in *The Arabian Nights*, but the one that frames them all belongs to King Shahryar and the lovely Scheherazade. It all starts when Shahzaman, Shahryar's younger brother, discovers that his bride is cuckolding him. Shahzaman executes her, abandons his kingdom, and joins his brother, Shahryar. When the brothers discover that Shahryar's wife is equally unfaithful—sleeping with eunuchs who are in fact not eunuchs—they conclude that all women are deceivers. Each brother returns to his own kingdom, vowing to deflower a virgin every night and kill her in the morning. Women are for men's sexual delectation and nothing else.

Onto this grim scene comes the sparkle of female intelligence in the person of the vizier's elder daughter, the clever and assertive Scheherazade. To end the terror, Scheherazade volunteers to wed the king and restore his better sense. How to do this? Clearly, uncommitted sex won't do it—he has been having plenty of that. Instead, Scheherazade offers him romance in the form of stories about the full range of human needs and desires. Each night ends before Scheherazade completes a tale, leaving the king with the choice of executing the bride the next morning or letting her live to finish the tale.

In fact, it takes two women to pull Shahryar out of his murderous funk. Scheherazade receives help from her sister, Dunyazade. At the crucial moment between intercourse and sleep, Scheherazade asks the king if she may bid goodnight to her sister. When Dunyazade enters the bedchamber, she asks Scheherazade for a story. Then, at daybreak, Dunyazade increases the king's suspense by interrupting the tale before its climax. This trick stays Shahryar's hand long enough—almost three years—for Scheherazade to heal his heart, restore his reason and sense of justice, and save the kingdom from ruin. After the last night, Scheherazade brings to the king the three children she has conceived and born during this extended stretch of storytelling and lovemaking. She requests that the king release her from his vow of death. Hearing this request, Shahryar weeps and tells her that he had pardoned her long before this night. To the court, he declares, "As for this Shahrazad, her like is not found in the lands; so praise be to Him who appointed her a means for delivering His creatures from oppression and slaughter!"[4]

Within the frame story, several tales touch on the wedding night. On the 384th night, Scheherazade tells the tale of Mutalammis and his wife, Umaymah. Like Odysseus, Mutalammis has been away from home so long that his tribe thinks him dead. Suitors call on Umaymah, and she at first refuses them. However, the suitors are numerous, and Umaymah's family and friends entreat her to not waste her life as a childless widow. Umaymah relents and is betrothed to a man of her tribe. On the night of the wedding, her long-absent husband, Mutalammis, returns home and learns that Umaymah is about to marry another man. As is still the custom in Arab countries, the men and women celebrate separately, and then the groom enters the women's tent for his first direct look at the bride. In the tale, as the prospective bride and groom sit side by side on the bridal couch, Mutalammis enters the women's quarters and hears his wife sigh:

Would Heaven I knew (but many are the shifts of joy and woe)
In what far distant land thou art, my Mutalammis, oh!

From the crowd, Mutalammis responds:

Right near at hand, Umaymah mine! whene'er the caravan
Halted, I never ceased for thee to pine, I would thou know.

The bridegroom understands what's happening and leaves the two to their reunion. The tale concludes by stating that Mutalammis and Umaymah "bode together in all comfort and solace of life and in all its joys and jollities till death parted them."[5]

The Thousand and One Nights propagated stories ranging from Boccaccio's *Decameron* to familiar Western fairy tales like "The Three Feathers" and "Rapunzel." Novelist John Barth wrote a dazzling modern version, told from the point of view of Dunyazade, that includes this passage: "'Did you really imagine your sister fooled Shahryar for a thousand nights with her mamelukes and dildoes?' Shah Zaman laughed. 'A man couldn't stay king very long if he didn't even know what was going on in the harem! And why do you suppose he permitted it, if not that he loved her too much, and was too sick of his other policy?'"[6]

400–100 B.C.E.: GREEK AND ROMAN
WEDDING POEMS

As described in chapter 2, the Greeks established the formal procession of the bride to the groom's house. As family and friends led the bride to her new home, boys and girls would meet them at the door with a song called an *epithalamion,* combining the Greek words for "of " and "nuptial chamber." In his ode to Hieron of Syracuse, Pindar (fifth century B.C.E.) describes the wedding feast that an impatient woman never celebrated and the wedding song that she never heard:

> She waited not to see the marriage feast,
> Nor stayed to hear
> The sound of swelling bridal hymns,
> Such notes as maiden friends of a like age are wont
> To spread in soothing songs upon the evening air.[7]

In the third century B.C.E., Theocritus addressed a wedding song to Helen. He praised "maidens with hyacinth blossoms wreathed in their hair . . . [singing] to one strain, and with feet interweaving / [Beating] out the measure, and the house rang to their hymns." In this poem, Theocritus teases the bridegroom, Menelaos, for being sleepy with drink and going to bed alone while Helen plays with her friends. The poet praises "roselike" Helen for her weaving and mastery of the lyre and wishes the couple's children to be like Helen's mother. The poem ends,

> Sleep, breathing love and desire to each other's breast,
> Nor forget to awake at the first light of dawn.
> At daybreak we will return, when the first minstrel
> Lifts up his bright-plumed neck and crows from his nest.
> Hymen, O Hymenaios, rejoice in this wedding![8]

The Romans adopted the poetic tradition of wedding songs along with the basic three-step Greek wedding. Supreme among these poems is an epithalamium by Catullus (first century B.C.E.). Catullus hailed from the northern Italian city of Verona, which 1,500 years later, was the setting for Shakespeare's *Romeo and Juliet.* Catullus fell madly in love with Verona's most dazzling lady, who, alas, did not return his passionate affection as the young poet desired. Subsequently, Catullus enjoyed a series of more casual loves until he again fell hard, this time for Clodia, "a lover of luxurious living, and never happy unless she had a string of young men in attendance."[9] In his poems to Clodia, he nicknames her "Lesbia" after the reputation of Lesbos for its beautiful women. (In Catullus's time,

Lesbos did not connote lesbianism; that came much later.) Coleridge, one of many English poets who translated Catullus, rendered Catullus's famous lines about kissing Clodia as follows:

My Lesbia, let us love and live,
And to the winds, my Lesbia, give
Each cold restraint, each boding fear
Of age and all her saws severe . . .
A thousand kisses take and give!
Another thousand!—to the store
Add hundreds—then a thousand more!
And when they to a million mount,
Let confusion take the account,—
That you, the number never knowing,
May continue still bestowing—
That I for joys may never pine,
Which never can again be mine!

After a couple of years, the kisses wore thin on Clodia's lips, and she left the poet for a much younger man. Catullus left town for the provinces in Asia Minor and late in life published his poems, many to Clodia, but also a lively *epithalamion,* or wedding song. The poem contains addresses to Hymen, the god of marriage, and celebrates the wedding of Junia, "lovely as Venus." The poet asks Hymen to bind Junia's heart to her new husband "as clings / ivy this way and that, as twine tendrils around the tree trunk." This poem describes the processing bride, dressed in a "flame-tinted veil" and yellow slippers. In her hair are "blossoms of sweet-scented marjoram." In praise of Hymen, Catullus writes:

There's no god to be sought after
more by lovers and loved ones . . .
you all tremulous parents beg
on their children's behalf; for you
intact virgins ungirdle; you
capture each novice husband's keen
(and uneasy) attention.

During the procession, led by "bright torches" with "golden manes," the groom scatters nuts to boys lining the street. The poet ribs the groom that he must give up playing with nuts—and boys—and turn his loyalty to Hymen and his bride. What was licit before marriage—sex with boys—is no longer available:

Scented bridegroom, it's rumored you're
finding it hard to abstain from your
nice smooth boys, but abstain you must . . .

The bride and groom approach her new home toward the end of the day. As the day turns to night, festivities come to an end. It is time to consummate the marriage. The bride lifts her feet

. . . with all best
Omens over the threshold and
[passes] through the polished entrance-way.

Inside the *thalamion*, the marriage bedchamber, her husband reclines on a "purple-draped couch," and married women prepare the bride for her wedding night, a night that combines pleasure and new responsibilities.

Play as pleasure dictates, and soon
give us children . . .
Close the doors, you unmarried girls
playtime's over for us. You good
married couple, live happy and
exercise your youth's vigor in
constant bouts of its duty.[10]

1400 C.E.: GEOFFREY CHAUCER, *THE CANTERBURY TALES*

Chaucer created a proto-feminist in the Wife of Bath, one of his most popular characters, an entrepreneur and earthy storyteller of her own marriages to five successive husbands. In her Tale, she recounts the story of a knight who rapes a maiden. Condemned by King Arthur, the knight is saved by the intervention of the queen, who metes out another punishment: to travel the countryside for a year to find out "What thing it is that women most desire."[11] For a year, the knight wanders and hears many answers from many women, leaving him perplexed. On his return to the queen and certain death, he meets a hag, who tells him that she has the answer if he will grant her any wish. The knight agrees, and they proceed to the queen's court. There the hag tells the knight that, above all, women desire sovereignty over their husbands. The queen likes the answer and pardons the knight for his crime. To the knight's dismay, the old woman's wish is for the knight to marry her. On their wedding night, the knight is distraught about having to marry such an ugly woman. The hag lectures him on the true definition of nobility (what Chaucer calls gentilesse) as a Christian virtue in which high lineage, youth, and beauty are irrelevant. He can have a wife who is ugly and faithful or a wife who beautiful and unfaithful.

> This knight considered, and did sorely sigh
> But at the last replied as you shall hear:
> "My lady and my love, and wife so dear,
> I put myself in your wise governing;"

The crone replies:

> "Then I have got of you the mastery,
> Since I may choose and govern, in earnest?"
> "Yes, truly, wife," said he, "I hold that best."

Having achieved mastery over the man, the woman becomes fair and faithful. Dominion frees her sexual desire, and they get on with their sexual union.

> For joy he clasped her in his strong arms two,
> His heart bathed in a bath of utter bliss;
> A thousand times, all in a row, he'd kiss.
> And she obeyed his wish in everything
> That might give pleasure to his love-making.[12]

1595: EDMUND SPENSER, *EPITHALAMION*

Foremost among the English masters of wedding poems was Edmund Spenser.[13] He was recognized as a great poet when Shakespeare and Marlowe were young up-and-comers. Shakespeare read Spenser and affectionately mingled respect and disrespect in teasing him.

Spenser married young, and his first wife died soon after. He was in his forties by the time he wooed Elizabeth Boyle, who was younger and of higher social status. The marriage took place on the summer solstice in 1594, leading the poet to make a joke about "why I picked the longest day and shortest night to get married." The next year, Spenser wrote *Amoretti and Epithalamion*, a sequence of poems, as a wedding gift to his new wife. The *Amoretti* are love sonnets that lead up to the *Epithalamion*, or wedding poem.

Spenser changed the traditional love sonnet from laments about a lost love to an account of courtship leading to marriage. Earlier poets such as the Italian Petrarch and the English Philip Sidney had written about unattainable mistresses who either reject the poet (Sidney's "Stella") or die and ascend into heaven (Petrarch's "Laura"). In Spenser's sonnets, the woman says yes. Though initially proud and disdainful, she is won over and yields to love and married bliss.

When his chosen bride accepts him in the 67th sonnet of the *Amoretti*, Spenser describes it as a mystery, and the poem at this juncture has a tone of awe. He employs the traditional metaphor of hunting a deer, which in earlier poems typically has fled from the hunter. But here, instead of escaping, the deer comes back: "there she beholding me sought not to fly . . . strange to see a beast so goodly won." In these lines, the Protestant ideal of companionate marriage enters into and transforms the European love lyric.

Spenser's ideal of love was deeply religious and sacramental but also complex, because the sonnets have a darker side. All through the poem are hints that life is brief: "for short time and endless moment." The marriage of Spenser and Boyle would last five years, and after his death Elizabeth would remarry and be widowed again and then marry a third time.

Spenser constructed the *Epithalamion* with the precision of watchworks. Its numerological structure begins before dawn and continues through the hours, stanza by stanza, ending in the middle of the wedding night with consummation. Spenser abides by the Renaissance belief that mathematical harmonies structure the universe. Spenser sees his courtship of Boyle as harmoniously embedded within the larger universe.[14]

It's clear in the sonnet sequence that his bride was a very strong-willed young woman.

> See how the Tyrannesse doeth joy to see
> The huge massacres which her eyes do make;
> And humbled harts brings captive unto thee,
> That thou of them mayst mightie vengeance take.[15]

Spenser casts her in the role of someone proud and serious: persuading her to consent takes a long while. The woman is the dominant partner. His struggle is how to be a partner, how to submit without being a prisoner of her pride, and how she can submit without submitting. The poet goes round and round on this in the sonnet sequence: why am I suffering, and will our story ever have a happy ending?

In the *Epithalamion*, Spenser calls on the Muses:

> Go to the bowre of my beloved love,
> My truest turtle dove,
> Bid her awake, for Hymen is awake . . .

Doe ye to her of joy and solace sing,
That all the woods may answer and your eccho ring.[16]

Calling on the young women and men who accompany the bride and
groom, Spenser sets the day of summer solstice—"The joyfulst day that
ever sunne did see"—and says, later in the poem,

But for this time it ill ordained was,
To chose the longest day in all the yeare,
And shortest night, when longest fitter weare;

The bride wears "perling flowers," giving a "golden mantle her attire."
Advertising her to the daughters of local merchants, the poet/husband
describes his catch:

Her goodly eyes lyke Saphyres shining bright,
Her forehead yvory white,
Her cheekes lyke apples which the sun hath rudded,
Her lips lyke cherryes charming men to byte,
Her brest like to a bowle of creame uncrudded,
Her paps lyke lyllies budded.

Once we understand that the initially off-putting "uncrudded" means
"uncurdled," we have breasts like lily buds floating in heavy cream. As the
day's festivities wind down, Spenser calls on the bridesmaids:

Now bring the Bryde into the brydall boures.
Now night is come, now soone her disarays,
And in her bed her lay;
Lay her in lilies and in violets,
And silken courteins over her display,
And odourd sheetes, and Arras coverlets.
Behold how goodly my faire love does ly . . .
Now it is night, ye damsels may be gon,
And leave my love alone,
And leave likewise your former lay to sing:
The woods no more shal answere, nor your eccho ring . . .

The last lines of the previous stanzas describe the surrounding wood-
lands, which respond to the wedding celebrations. Then, in this stanza, as
the couple draw the curtains of their bed, the public celebration ceases,
and the woods return to silence.

1633: JOHN DONNE, *EPITHALAMION*

In John Donne's wedding poem, written a generation after Spenser's, the bride brings her feather bed, and the poem progresses from the après-wedding to the next morning, when the poet asks who will be the first to draw the curtain and let in the light, he or she. Donne, who in another poem, *To His Mistress Going to Bed,* compares caressing a woman's body to the recent discovery of America—"License my roving hands, and let them go / Before, behind, between, above, below. / Oh, my America, my Newfoundland"—in this poem conveys foreplay in transcendental terms:

> A Bride, before a good night could be said,
> Should vanish from her cloathes, into her bed,
> As Soules from bodies steale, and are spy'd.
> But now she is laid; What though shee bee?
> Yet there are more delayes, For, where is he?
> He comes, and passes through Spheare after Spheare,
> First her sheetes, then her Armes, then any where.
> Let not this day, then, but this night be thine,
> Thy day was but the eve to this, O Valentine.[17]

NOVELS

The novel emerged in England in the mid-1700s. They were romances, and women wrote many of them. The new middle class read them, and, more than two centuries later, English-reading peoples are blessed with a steady flow of romances, detective stories, science fiction, and many other genres of the novel. This section highlights wedding nights in novels from the early 1800s up to current times.

1748: *FANNY HILL; OR, MEMOIRS OF A WOMAN OF PLEASURE*

The rust of irrelevancy does not occur on the great love stories of literature. *War and Peace* is a masterpiece, but *Anna Karenina* has the heartbeat of private author-to-reader truth. John Cleland's novel *Fanny Hill*, while not appropriate reading for the young, remains a "fresh classic." Fanny is by turns brazen, plucky, crafty, decadent, purely sensual, materialistic, and always in control and superior to the erotic episodes of her story. Just as we feel all is well when Odysseus returns from his adventures to remain with Penelope, so, too, when Fanny reunites with her first love, Charles, she and the reader forget the erotic episodes that have gone before.

At the story's end, Charles returns from India, reduced to his essential self, with no financial assets. Charles and Fanny meet by accident at an inn, and, after they eat and catch up, the innkeeper shows them to the room with the best bed he has. After matter-of-factly narrating her many erotic adventures with both sexes, Fanny shows shyness about sex.

> And here, decency forgive me! if, once more I violate thy laws and, keeping the curtains undrawn, sacrifice thee for the last time to that confidence without reserve, with which I engaged to recount to you the most striking circumstances of my youthful disorders.[18]

The very modern Fanny observes that being with Charles makes her feel lovesick and yearn for him, tempered by sudden diffidence and modesty: "all held me in a subjection of soul incomparably dearer to me than the liberty of heart which I had been long, too long! the mistress of, in the course of those grosser gallantries." Only Charles has the "secret to excite" the emotions that "constitute the very life the essence of pleasure." In her narration, Fanny goes on to detail the ecstasy her lover's "scepter-member" brings her by the "sentiment of consciousness of its belonging to my supremely beloved youth." The thought of love and sensation are streams that "poured such an ocean of intoxicating bliss on a weak vessel, all too narrow to contain it, that I lay overwhelmed, absorbed, lost in an abyss of joy, and dying of nothing but immoderate delight."

After Fanny confesses her vices, Charles forgives her and asks her to marry him. Their night in the inn is therefore their real wedding night. This was not, however, enough to redeem the story in the eyes of the law, and, for more than two centuries after John Cleland wrote the novel, in debtors' prison, it was banned for obscenity. Putnam published *Fanny Hill* in 1963, and, in 1966, the Supreme Court ruled the novel did not meet the current standard for obscenity.

1818: FRANKENSTEIN; OR, THE
MODERN PROMETHEUS

Mary Shelley was only 18 when she wrote *Frankenstein; or, the Modern Prometheus*, first published in London in 1818. In the novel, set a century earlier, Victor Frankenstein, who narrates, has discovered a talent to "give life." With a firm faith in science, he creates a living being from body parts scavenged in graveyards. This creation ought to have been an Adonis, but somehow the scrap-method results in a ghoul, who is oversensitive, along the lines of Goethe's *Young Werther*, thirsting for revenge against anyone who shows or might show repulsion for his person.

The monster creature reasons that the only way to relieve his unbearable loneliness is for Victor to create a woman for him. Victor begins, but he eventually shrinks from the task and stops. Meanwhile, the monster is following his creator's every move, one terrifying step behind. The monster threatens Victor:

> "I will be with you on your wedding-night!" Such was my sentence, and on that night would the daemon employ every art to destroy me, and tear me from the glimpse of happiness which promised partly to console my sufferings.[19]

Through the dark days of guilty wandering and even prison, when Victor is accused of one of the monster's murders, Victor's childhood love, Elizabeth, stays true. At last, Victor tries to put the horrors behind him, but when Elizabeth meets him in Geneva, he doesn't find hoped-for tranquility. Contrarily, he has fits of madness as their marriage day approaches. Elizabeth is innocent of Victor's monster creation.

On the night of his wedding to his childhood love, Victor's fears only mount. After the ceremony, they take a boat to Evian as the start of a nuptial journey.

> The day was fair, the wind favourable; all smiled on our nuptial embarkation. . . . These were the last moments of my life during which I enjoyed the feeling of happiness.[20]

They land at eight, and the moon shines high in the sky until clouds obscure it, and heavy rains descend. Victor tells Elizabeth that his agitation will end as soon as this "dreadful" night is done. Victor tells her to retire for the night. As he begins to search for the monster, he hears Elizabeth scream and realizes it was never his death the monster intended but his bride's. Now the monster, from self-loathing, has killed not only Victor's best friend but also his bride, as well as sundry others. Victor's father dies of grief, and Victor commits to seeking revenge, no matter what it takes.

Mary Shelley's own marriage would begin with romance, but three of her four children would die early. The sexual freedom that Shelley espoused was better for the gander and not the goose. While both Mary and Percy believed that emotional ties were more important than legal ones, she suffered during their marriage when his romantic attention strayed to other women. Frankenstein is the man longing for completion in a mate, but the wedding night looms in every moment of the story as the supreme disappointment and danger.

1874: *DANIEL DERONDA*

Whereas male authors often overstress the wedding night with drama or skip over it, female authors are more likely to write about their expectations and feelings regarding this significant rite of passage. George Eliot portrays two contrasting wedding nights in *Daniel Deronda,* whose moral hero breaks away from conventions and discovers he was born a Jew. The wedding night that concludes the book is satisfying because the girl, Mirah, is intelligent, patient, good, and deserving, and she and Daniel have a deep bond. However, it is the novel's first wedding night, involving a woman with whom Daniel was briefly smitten, that offers the deeper psychological insights.

Wrongheadedly, the impoverished Gwendolen marries Grandcourt, the richest man she can find, to secure a fortune. After the ceremony, they drive back to his estate. She becomes increasingly excited—her heart is aflutter not only at the prospect of being the lady of the manor but also with "some dim forecast, the insistent penetration of suppressed experience, mixing the expectation of a triumph with the dread of a crisis." She is so worked up that she doesn't quite realize he kisses her as they ride in the carriage, but on some level the kiss keys her up even more: "She turned his gentle seizure of her hand into a grasp of his hand by both hers, with an increased vivacity as of a kitten that will not sit quiet to be petted."[21]

Left alone to change for dinner, nearing the hour of consummation, Gwendolen receives a letter, delivered to her bedchamber by her new husband's mistress and the mother of his children. The bridegroom has a prior attachment! The letter dashes Gwendolen's dream of a secure, predictable marriage. The diamond necklace her new husband has given her as a wedding-night token was the property of a jilted lover before her. The necklace is now toxic to the bride, and her husband finds her shrieking, with the diamonds scattered around on the floor. "Was it a fit of madness?" he asks himself, but he doesn't come clean or try to deal with the situation.[22] Upon receiving the necklace, Gwendolen feels overwhelmed with guilt for disinheriting his children. Gwendolen recognizes that the marriage, undertaken for security, which seemed so sensible, is really a snake pit. When Gwendolen and Grandcourt go on their honeymoon in the Mediterranean, he falls off the boat. Gwendolen futilely tries to save him. Alone, Gwendolen realizes that her true love is Daniel, who is now happily married and leading a meaningful life.

1936: *GONE WITH THE WIND*

What is it about Scarlett O'Hara that captivates young women? We perused a 1973 edition of Margaret Mitchell's classic novel. It was the 82nd printing. That works out to more than two press runs a year since the novel's birth. *Gone with the Wind* has been an American coming-of-age book for a vast number of teenage girls. Scarlett's first wedding night, with Charles Hamilton, takes place after a short two-week engagement, Scarlett on the rebound after her beloved Ashley Wilkes asks for the hand of Charles's sister, Melanie. As Charles courts Scarlett, she thinks, "Why not take this pretty, flushed boy? He was as good as anyone else and she didn't care."[23] After the wedding, Scarlett is unprepared for the wedding night. "Of course, she knew married people occupied the same bed but she had never given the matter a thought before. . . . Now for the first time since the barbecue she realized just what she had brought on herself."[24]

Scarlett refuses to let Charles into her bed, but, the next night, the night that follows Ashley and Melanie's wedding, the sobbing Scarlett accepts Charles and consummates the marriage. Charles goes off to fight in the Civil War and dies. Scarlett is pregnant and gives birth to a son she does not want. Unlike more conventional Southern women who endured sex to have a child, Scarlett loses the man to war and has to endure his offspring. She is left with her longing for Ashley, the man who got away, the beloved she will never marry.

Scarlett does marry other men, first her sister Suellen's beau, Frank Kennedy, and then the notorious Rhett Butler. The Butlers go on a bridal tour to New Orleans, but the novelist discloses nothing about their wedding night. Scarlett, who has flouted social convention her whole adult life, now has the financial security she needs to be her own woman. Yet, during the honeymoon, she frets about society's tut-tutting over her marriage to a man she once despised. That is, she wants to make her own rules, but not so much that her peers reject her. Rhett sets her straight: "If I were a low-bred, poverty-stricken villain, people wouldn't be so mad. But a rich, flourishing villain—of course, that's unforgiveable."[25]

Nights of true passion with Rhett ensue, but, unfortunately for Scarlett, these lead to further misunderstandings and ruptures. When Melanie

Wilkes dies, Scarlett is astonished to realize that her longstanding yearning for Ashley is over. As she tries to express her new insight to Rhett, he
walks out on her, uttering that famous line: "Frankly my dear. . . ." The
book ends with Scarlett promising herself to think about this "tomorrow
at Tara [her family plantation]."

1937: *BUSMAN'S HONEYMOON:* A LOVE STORY WITH DETECTIVE INTERRUPTIONS

In Dorothy Sayers's *Busman's Honeymoon*, the appearance of a body com-
plicates the honeymoon of Peter Wimsey and Harriet Vane. Peter and
Harriet's courtship has unfolded in three previous novels. In *Strong Poison*, Lord Peter Wimsey and the reader meet Harriet Vane when she is in
the dock. The mystery writer is accused of murdering her former lover,
and Peter is the amateur detective who finds the actual culprit. This novel
ends with Peter proposing to Harriet; she rejects him. In *Have His Car-
case*, Harriet discovers a body on a deserted beach. She is on a solo walking tour trying to forget the public humiliation of the *Strong Poison* trial.
Harriet welcomes Peter's help in solving this seemingly impossible suicide (or is it murder?). He proposes again; again she rejects him. In their
third shared case, in *Gaudy Night*, Harriet tries to solve the mystery of a
poisoned-pen prankster at the woman's college in Oxford University. She
needs Peter's help to unmask the culprit; Peter proposes in Latin, and Harriet accepts, also in Latin.

Dorothy Sayers set her detective novels in England of the 1920s and
1930s. Her characters are so appealing that generations of readers have
recommended her books to younger readers, especially the four books
and several short stories that follow the complicated relationship and
growing love of Lord Peter Wimsey and Harriet Vane. If you go to an on-
line bookstore and search for "Harriet Vane," you will find the original
novels by Sayers and contemporary novels by Jill Paton Walsh that are
based on story outlines left by Sayers. Try to set up a new e-mail account
as Harriet Vane and you will discover that dozens have been there before
you. The Dorothy L. Sayers Society is the official fan club (www.sayers
.org.uk/).

Busman's Honeymoon is divided into "Prothalamion" and "Epithalamion"—that is, before and after the wedding—and the sleuthing begins when Peter and Harriet pass up "Hotel Gigantic" on the Continent
to spend their honeymoon at their newly acquired country cottage, accompanied by Bunter, Peter's invaluable valet. The former owner, despite having promised to meet them at the house to turn over the keys, is

absent. The house is unprepared for the new owners, and the house shows many signs of neglect. Chimneys smoke, the lamps burn out, the bed is unmade, and a sign at the front gate says "No bread and milk till further notice." Bunter saves the day with a prepacked basket dinner of soup, foie gras, quail, and wine.

As Bunter takes a hot kettle of water upstairs for Harriet's bath (the cottage has no bathroom), Harriet asks Peter, "Are you sorry we didn't go to Paris or Menton after all?" In response to his emphatically negative response, she says, "Such a series of domestic accidents could only happen to married people. There's none of that artificial honeymoon glitter that prevents people from discovering each other's real characters. You stand the test of tribulation remarkably well." He thanks her and says, "I really don't know that there's a great deal to complain of. I've got you, that's the chief thing, and food and fire of sorts, and a roof over my head. What more could any man want?"[26]

Despite the domestic accidents, Peter and Harriet's wedding night ends in the goose-feather four-poster bed with clean (but threadbare) linen sheets. Referring to the old ballad "Raggle Taggle Gypsy," in which the bride deserts her nuptial goose-feather bed for "a cold open field, / Along with the wraggle taggle gypsies," Harriet gushes, "Oh, Peter! The ballad was right. It is a goose feather bed!"[27]

Sayers declines to give us all the wedding-night details:

> It is no part of the historian's duty to indulge in what a critic has called "interesting revelations of the marriage-bed." It is enough that the dutiful Mervyn Bunter at length set aside his writing materials, blew out the candle and composed his limbs to rest; and that, of the sleepers beneath that ancient roof, he that had the hardest and coldest couch enjoyed the quietest slumbers."[28]

In the morning, Harriet awakes first, contemplates her new husband, who is still asleep, and reflects on the wedding night's passion:

> If his first words were French one would at least feel certain that he retained an agreeable impression of the night's proceedings; on the whole, however, English would be preferable, as showing that he remembered quite distinctly who one was.

No, this is not the first sexual encounter for either Peter or Harriet. Peter awakes and utters only "M'mmm." Harriet impatiently asks whether he knows who she is. Peter responds:

Yes, my Shulamite, I do, so you needn't lay traps for my tongue. In
the course of a mis-spent life I have learnt that it is a gentleman's
first duty to remember in the morning who it was he took to bed
with him. You are Harriet.[29]

Later that morning, Harriet is picking flowers in the garden when she
hears a commotion in the house. It is the chimney sweeper, Mr. Puffett,
hard at work. Upon greeting him, Harriet extends her hand. It is an awkward moment of class difference and dirt.

Mr. Puffett looked at it, looked at his own, pulled up his sweaters to
get at his trousers pocket, extracted a newly laundered red-cotton
handkerchief, shook it slowly from its fold, draped it across his palm
and so grasped Harriet's fingers, rather in the manner of a royal proxy
bedding his master's bride with the sheet between them.[30]

1962: OLD MORALITY

Master short-story writer and author of the novel *Ship of Fools*, Katherine
Anne Porter was married in 1906, three weeks after her 16th birthday, in
a double ceremony with her sister, who was five years older. Her infatu-
ation with John Henry Koontz, son of a wealthy Texas rancher, barely
outlasted the ceremony. Porter told a close friend many years later that
she had "held out" for 47 days before the marriage was consummated,
implying that the experience had been tantamount to rape.[31] Decades
later, when she was writing *Ship of Fools*, she created a fictional portrait
of Koontz in the character of William Denny, a crude, insecure, bigoted
young man who carries aboard ship the fully illustrated book *Recreational
Aspects of Sex as Mental Prophylaxis: A Guide to True Happiness in Life*.

Raised by her prim Victorian grandmother, Katherine was kept ignorant about sex, while her father idealized his deceased wife and made his
daughters wary of boys. Only an aunt was less reticent and passed on some
tips, which, according to Porter's biographer, included advising Katherine, before her wedding, to get into the habit of sitting in a cold bath before going to bed with her husband. "'That makes you tight, harder to get
into,' she explained. 'Men like that.'"[32]

In "Old Morality," Amy is the glamorous aunt who died young. Her
niece wants to hear the story of her elopement and is told, "She ran into
the gray cold and stepped into the carriage and turned and smiled with
her face as pale as death, and called out 'Good-by, good-by,' and refused
her cloak, and said, 'Give me a glass of wine.' And none of us saw her
alive again!"[33] Amy has threatened her family, saying that she will be an

old maid because she wants thrills and romance nonstop, but a man woos
her long and wins her. At the wedding, Amy flouts convention and wears
a jet-black gown: "I shall wear mourning if I like . . . it *is* my funeral, you
know."[34]

2008: ON CHESIL BEACH

Ian McEwan's novel *On Chesil Beach* opens with the wedding night of Edward Mayhew and Florence Ponting. They are eating a hotel dinner that
neither wants. The year is 1962; Edward and Florence enjoy a love that
bridges a class and educational divide that separates the marginal May-
hews and the well-established Pontings. The wedding night takes place at
a time when good girls saved themselves for marriage. Edward and Florence are virgins, and, as they nibble at the roast beef and boiled veg-
etables, each internally plots the next move from the table to the bed,
"where their new maturity would be tested, when they would lie down together on the four-poster bed and reveal themselves fully to each other."

Florence is more than nervous about her first sexual intercourse. She
dreads penetration and has kept Edward's physical attentions well north
of her private parts. Yet, she knows consummation is her duty. Edward is
a normally sexed young man and during their year-long courtship managed to kiss a bare breast, but Florence has rebuffed his attempt to ease her
hand onto his crotch. As a result of Florence's restraint, their courtship
has resembled a musical *pavane*, "a stately unfolding, bound by protocols
never agreed or voiced but generally observed."

As they finish their dessert of trifle and the waiters leave the room,
silence descends on the normally talkative couple. Neither understands
that the first time in bed lacks the verbal familiarity they enjoy when
talking about Florence's music or Edward's books. To mask her fear of
sex, Florence leads them to the bed, which squeaks as they move, "a reminder of other honeymoon couples who had passed through all surely
more adept than they were . . . a solemn queue stretching out into the cor-
ridor, downstairs to the reception, back through time." They awkwardly
undress—the zipper on her dress sticks, Edward fails to finish the job—
and Florence, lying on her back like a fish out of water, for the first time
touches the male organ. Edward, pent up after a week's abstinence from
"self-pleasuring," explodes semen, wetting Florence with its stickiness
from stomach to chin. Though ashamed of her "primal disgust," Florence
impulsively wipes herself with a pillow, throws on her dress, and runs from
the room and the hotel to the pebble beach.

She needs time to collect herself, but time is not on her side, or Edward's. Edward finds her, and their first conversation about sex is

acrimonious and stirs up their many differences, of the sort that married couples work out over the years. Desperate to salvage the night, Florence proposes an open marriage in which Edward would be free to sleep with other women. This proposal stuns Edward, who reminds Florence of her vow, "With my body I thee worship." Florence needs Edward's patience; Edward needs Florence's body. Just as she led the way to the bed, Florence returns to the hotel. Edward, feeling deceived and hurt, does not follow. Florence checks out. The wedding night and the marriage are over.

But not the poignant longing for each other. This they carry for the rest of their lives.

2010: A MATTER OF CLASS

Mary Balogh is a best-selling author of historical romances. She uses wedding-night expectations and yearning and wedding-night potentiality and dreams in her funny and wise narratives. What does the concept of a wedding night evoke in her as a writer? We interviewed her and listened.

Why do you write so many versions of the wedding night into your characters' lives?

Because my books are set in the early 19th century, and divorce was virtually out of the question, a wedding night is the beginning of something lifelong. The actual events of the night may or may not be sensational (a lot depends upon whether the marriage occurs early in the book or toward the end). But always they lead to a lasting relationship that will be firmly based upon friendship, affection, love, passion and—yes, it is basic to the whole thing—a firm sense of self-worth.

I suppose many people feel that what happens behind the closed bedroom door should remain private. I feel that sex is such an important (though not the only) part of the love relationship that it must be shown. Sex scenes in my books always show what is right or what is wrong or what is slowly developing in the love relationship. My sex scenes are not gratuitous, and they are never tacked on because this is page such-and-such and it is time for a sex scene. They are integral to the whole story.

I hope that all readers, married or otherwise, will see every part of my story, including the sex scenes, as real and believable. I hope to show readers that love is the key element in a relationship but that sex is a wonderful physical expression of that love. I always try to show that sex in itself, even if marvelously enjoyable, is not enough to make for a satisfying ever-after kind of love.

What does the male protagonist feel on the wedding night?

Mostly lust. But a lot else, too, if this is the end of the story and he has learned to love. What he feels depends entirely upon the story.

What does the female protagonist feel on the wedding night?

Again, it depends greatly upon where in the story the scene comes. In historical romance, the heroine will most often be a virgin on her wedding night, and this fact will have all a definite impact on her feelings. But the feelings will vary depending upon her character and feelings for the hero.

Is a wedding night passionate and special even if the couple has already "known" each other?

Probably, especially if they have already had one or more sexual encounter. But a wedding night is not necessarily either passionate or "special." It may be only the beginning of a long and difficult love relationship.

Often, true love occurs well after the first coupling, on either side of the wedding night, which has a unique importance for the couple all the same. In *A Matter of Class*, Reginald Marsh Sr. has enormous wealth but no pedigree. To gain social status, he orders his son, Reginald Jr., "Reggie," to marry Lady Annabelle Ashton, the daughter of the neighboring earl; if he does not, he will lose his inheritance. Annabelle is available because she has become damaged goods by trying to run off with a coachman. Her father, the earl, sees marriage to Reggie as her only chance to avoid spinsterhood. So, the two enter into an engagement neither desires, but, over the course of their courtship, resentment turns to attraction. On their wedding night, the last vestiges of antagonism melt into sexual passion.

"Oh, Reggie," she sighed and melted against him. "I think you are . . . I do love you."
"Anna." He found her mouth with his and kissed her deeply. "My love, I hope you had plenty of sleep last night. You will not get much tonight. I am going to make love to you over and over until you get as much pleasure from it as I do—and you did not quite get last autumn. And then, when you do share the pleasure, I am going to keep on making love just to prove that it was no freakish accident."
"Words, words, words," she said against his mouth. "When are you going to show me action, boaster?"

She laughed softly and then half shrieked as he growled and swung her up into his arms. He strode to the bed with her and tossed her onto it.

"Right, if it is action you want, it is action you will get," he said, divesting himself of the cumbersome dressing gown and nightshirt before joining her there. "My love," he added.[35]

The wedding night is the summa, even though reference is made to previous embraces. That typifies many of the romances today, when it is unrealistic to wait until the wedding night (which heroines did in the Harlequin romances of the 1970s). In this scene, both Annabelle and Reggie utter the magic words "I do," echoing the wedding vows. Most men are unlikely to read the romances or understand their appeal, but they transport many of us, and me in a certain mood, to a dulcet world.

NOTES

1.   Email from Ian McEwan, May 1, 2010.

2.   Bruno Bettelheim, *The Meaning and Importance of Fairy Tales* (New York: Random House, 1976), 87–88.

3.   "Alf Laila wa-Laila," *E. J. Brill's First Encyclopedia of Islam* (Leiden: Brill, 1960), 1:252–56.

4.   Richard Burton, trans., *A Plain and Literal Translation of the Arabian Nights Entertainments Now Entitled The Book of the Thousand Nights and a Night* (Denver: The Burton Club, 1905), 10:55.

5.   Ibid., 5:75.

6.   John Barth, *Chimera* (New York: Houghton Mifflin, 1972), 54.

7.   Pindar, *The Odes of Pindar Translated into English Verse by Geoffrey S. Conway* (London: J. M. Dent & Sons, 1972), 98.

8.   Theocritus, *The Idylls of Theocritus; a Verse Translation by Thelma Sargent* (New York: Norton, 1982), 74.

9.   E. Roylston Pike, *Love in Ancient Rome* (London: Frederick Muller, 1965), 77.

10.   Catullus, *The Poems of Catullus; a Bilingual Edition*, trans. Peter Green (Berkeley: University of California Press, 2005), 107ff.

11.   Geoffrey Chaucer, *Canterbury Tales*, rendered into modern English by J. U. Nicholson (Garden City, NY: International Collectors Library, 1934), 335.

12.   Ibid., 344.

13.   This section on Spenser comes largely from personal communications with David Lee Miller, Professor of English at the University of South Carolina.

14.   Based on conversations with David Lee Miller, Carolina Distinguished Professor of English and Comparative Literature, University of South Carolina.

15.   Edmund Spenser, *Epithalium*, Sonnet 10, *The Norton Anthology of Poetry*, trans. Arthur Eastman (New York: Norton, 1970), 147.

16.   Ibid., 150 ff.

17.   John Donne, *The Epithalamiums Anniversaries and Epicedes* (Oxford: Clarendon Press, 1978), 9.

18.   John Cleland, *John Cleland's Memoirs of a Woman of Pleasure* (New York: Putnam, 1963), 288.

19.   Mary Shelley, *Frankenstein; or the Modern Prometheus* (New York: Dutton, 1960), 203.

20.   Ibid., 208.

21.   George Eliot, *Daniel Deronda* (Boston: Riverside Press, 1909), 116.

22.   Ibid., 120.

23.   Margaret Mitchell, *Gone with the Wind* (New York: Macmillan, 1973), 125.

24.   Ibid., 130.

25.   Ibid., 846.

26.   Dorothy Sayers, *Busman's Honeymoon: A Love Story with Detective Interruptions* (New York: Avon, 1968), 55.

27.   Ibid., 51.

28.   Ibid., 57.

29.   Ibid., 59.

30.   Ibid., 67.

31.   Darlene Harbour Unrue, *Katherine Anne Porter: The Life of an Artist* (Jackson: University Press of Mississippi, 2005), 41.

32.   Ibid.

33.   *The Collected Stories of Katherine Anne Porter* (New York: Harcourt Brace Jovanovich, 1979), 176.

34.   Ibid., 182.

35.   Mary Balogh, *A Matter of Class* (New York: Vanguard, 2010), 190.

CHAPTER 17

An Occasion for Mirth

Joking is a priest in disguise who weds every couple.

—Jean Paul Richter[1]

Jokes come in all shapes and sizes, from loopy shaggy-dog stories to crisp one-liners. Most jokes, though, are short and snappy and have a twist at the end. In *Hamlet*, the talkative Polonius pronounces, "Therefore since brevity is the soul of wit / And tediousness the limbs and outward flourishes / I will be brief."[2] Of course, Polonius is never brief! Sigmund Freud punctuates the brevity of most jokes by declaring that they have "too few words."[3] That is, the brevity of a joke excites the imagination—in the case of wedding-night jokes, sexual imagination—and pulls us into a scenario of the mind where our sense of humor dwells.

If successful, jokes make us laugh or chortle out loud. Typically, a joke has one chance to rouse us; if someone has to explain it, the joke falls flat as a pancake. To be funny, the sexual joke needs to appeal to sexual desire. For this reason, certain jokes designed to appeal to male lust may strike women as stupid, juvenile, or unfinished.

Some blessed souls have a huge repertory of jokes, but most of us find jokes hard to remember, especially if heard or read in a cluster. For example, a collection of knock-knock, doctor, or lawyer jokes seems way too much. And we quickly forget most jokes, even the funniest ones. In this regard, Freud likens jokes to dreams: in the moment, they tickle us until we squeal, but they naturally inhabit the realm of dreams and arouse a wide, usually dark, range of emotions.

Jokes with the "hook" of the wedding night have an old-fashioned feeling to them because of our changing mores. In a sense, we look back at them, and their hilarity often seems quaint or like something that belongs to a previous era. Also, with the advantage of retrospect, we see they fall into one of four distinct types: (1) jokes about the sexual excess of the first night; (2) jokes about the bride as questionable virgin; (3) jokes about the naïve bride or groom; and (4) jokes about the mismatch of male and female sexual desire and capacity. All four genres satisfy one requirement of jokes—that the punch lines relieve tension or expectation created by the set-up. For example, a woman writes to the comedian George Burns:

> Dear George—I just read a survey that says 85% of American women have sex before they're married. Do you believe this?—Pre-Nuptial

George answers:

> Dear Pre—No. But I don't believe that 85% of them have it after they're married either.[4]

"I wanted to do that."

(Reproduced with permission of The Cartoon Bank/ Conde Nast Publications.)

Although we acknowledge that jokes tend to lose their humor when analyzed, let's parse this joke. It moves to the gag as follows: Pre-Nuptial's question establishes a familiar framework of premarital sex—how many of us are doing it before we tie the knot? The answer starts in that framework and then jumps to a slightly new one—marital sex. That small jump is enough to elicit a laugh. Then we feel a commonality, as well, with others who "get" the joke with us. That sense of sharing human foibles is what Henri Bergson famously defined as the source of comedy.[5]

SEXUAL EXCESS

The first category of wedding-night jokes, sexual excess, imagines a world of abandon, what Orwell called "enthusiastic indecency."[6] Orwell gives this example:

> The bridegroom is getting out of bed the morning after his wedding night; he says "The first morning in our own little home, darling!" and tells his bride he'll go get the milk and paper and bring his bride a cup of tea. The inset is of the front doorstep, on which are four newspapers and four milk bottles.

Comedian Milton Berle places this joke in a hotel, with the woman ravenous:

> After the fourth day of a nonstop honeymoon, the newlyweds walked into the hotel restaurant. The waiter came over and asked for their orders. The bride purred to her husband, "You know what I like, sweetheart." The groom said, "Sure, but we have to eat something one of these days."[7]

Sexual excess lies at the funny bone of many wedding-night jokes. In these jokes, the daily routine goes out the window in the midst of uninterrupted sex. Neither person thinks about the outside world; both are interested only in their carnal delight. Time stops; sleeping and eating cease. Here is a mirror version (where the man is insatiable), using a pun:

> After a week in the hotel room without going out the groom decides to take his bride to a movie. He calls to her in the bathroom, "Honey, would you like to see Oliver Twist?" "No thanks, I've seen it do everything else."[8]

Milton Berle, an avid and avowed collector of jokes—among comedians, this is known as "borrowing," and it's legitimate so long as the borrower enhances the joke—uses puns in another riff on sexual excess:

The Cabots and Lodges, two old and respected families, finally joined hands in the marriage of Hortense Cabot and Carter Lodge. Because the families were important in the area, the fathers arranged for security at the honeymoon hotel. The private detective hired for the evening stood guard all night in front of the door to the suite. The next day the detective reported back to the fathers, who asked, "What happened last night?" The detective said, "Well, when the groom carried the bride into the room, she told him, 'I offer you my honor.' He answered, 'I honor your offer.' And that's how it went all night—honor, offer, honor, offer."[9]

In each of these jokes, the opening statement sets the audience in a familiar environment and shifts the logic to another frame. In the first two jokes, the shift takes place from the fantasy of uninterrupted sex to picking up the daily newspaper or eating a meal. In the Cabots-and-Lodges joke—one of an entire corpus based on these staunch patrician families—we begin with the exclusive world of prominent Bostonians, the fancy honeymoon suite, a private guard, and the formal language of "honor." The punch line shifts the frame to a crude pun and the physical motions of sexual intercourse.

Men, of course, are competitive and like to compare their scores.

Two friends arrange a double wedding night and get rooms next to each other. They undertake to compete in intercourse and to chalk up their scores on the wall. The first man chalks up a 1 and then another and another, but can do no more. In the morning the other groom and his bride come to look at their competitors' score and read 111 as one hundred and eleven. "You win," says the friend. "That's a dozen more than we could manage."[10]

And in a similar vein: "Two brides meet in a honeymoon hotel. One says, 'Does your husband snore in his sleep?' The other replies, 'I don't know. We've only been married three days.'"

Jokes are as old as settled life, as old as the historical record. Collections of clay tablets that preserve the wedding-night songs we enjoyed in chapter 2 also include jokes. A tablet written around 1900 B.C.E. includes a scatological joke (from the Greek word for excrement); the Sumerian quip reveals another characteristic of jokes—they surprise us by bringing the unmentionable into view.[11] The Greeks and Romans loved jokes and compiled numerous anthologies. In classical Athens, the Group of 60 gathered regularly to share jokes, and Philip of Macedon, both ruler of Greece and student of Aristotle, paid to have the proceedings recorded for his pleasurable reading.[12] In ancient Rome, Melissus collected 150 anthologies of jokes, and a third- or fourth-century C.E. Greek anthology, *Philogelos* (Laughter Lover), lists 260 jokes; alas, no wedding-night jokes survive in these Greek and Latin compilations.

Serious thinkers have made attempts to explain why jokes are funny. Plato (427–348 B.C.E.) thought of them as ridicule aimed at the helpless. To this philosopher, jokes were close to ridicule. The following analysis from George Carlin essentially falls into this type:

> Down the aisle. Now, generally, all this obsession with appearance has one purpose. It's supposed to lead to romance and—it is devoutly wished by some—a wedding. A wedding is another one of those good deals women get: The man "takes a wife," the woman is "given away," her family pays for the whole thing, and everyone stands around hoping she gets pregnant immediately.[13]

In this joke, Carlin sets up the familiar pattern—a romance leads to marriage leads to children—but he unsettles the conventional pattern by highlighting certain wedding phrases—"takes a wife," who is "given away"—as a series of economic transactions that mock the bride and her family as ignorant, helpless victims. Many ethnic jokes also fit this category, as do jokes about blondes.

Funnier to our ears are jokes that mock the high, rather than the low. The following British joke assumes a wide class divide:

> The virgin daughter of a titled English family gets married. After intercourse she says to the groom, "Is this what the common people call 'fucking'?" Her husband admits it is. "Well, it's FAR too good for them!"[14]

Another version of this joke has Queen Victoria asking Prince Albert after a night of sexual pleasure, "Do the common people do this too?"[15] Both of these jokes play on the idea that people in the upper echelon of society are sexually naïve—more in love with their dogs than with each other—and that the common folk have superior and great sex. The humor is that sex does not cross the class divide, even though all couples do it, or could do it. Later in this chapter, we will see other jokes about naïve husbands and wives on their wedding nights, but this one reflects upper-class suspicion that the lower classes not only have better sex lives but might take over.

Plato's student Aristotle (384–322 B.C.E.) opined that jokes are about ugly things that do not disgust us. Aristotle also pointed out that jokes contain the unexpected. Unfortunately, he did not leave us any examples, but other joke analysts point out that caricatures perform this function: in visual form, the way in which cartoonists have portrayed the voluptuous bride; in verbal form, the range of gender or ethnic stereotypes. The following wedding-night joke brings to our attention an antagonism that might flare up between a bride and a groom—and takes it to the comic limit:

> Two newlyweds are on their honeymoon. As they undress for bed the husband tosses his pants to his bride, saying, "Here, put these on." She puts them on but the waist is twice the size of her body. "I can't wear your pants," she says. "That's right," says the husband. "And don't you ever forget it. I wear the pants in this family." With that the bride throws him her panties. "Try these on," she says. The husband tries them on but can only get them as far as his knees. "Hell," he says. "I can't get into your panties." His bride replies, "That's right, and that's the way it's going to be until you change your attitude."[16]

This joke fits the criterion of ugliness because it is bad form for the husband to issue his challenge on their wedding night. Having the couple toss their clothes at each other jars our expectations of undressing for a night of sexual pleasure. The traditional mood of wedding-night sweetness tilts and addresses our sense of needing correction by forcing the man to squeeze into his wife's underwear. The punch line establishes sexual parity, and, as we laugh, we inwardly cheer her for her bravado.

Immanuel Kant (1724–1803), who never married lest marital life detract him from philosophy, firmly established the two-frames theory mentioned earlier: "Laughter is an affectation arising from an expectation that is strained, and which suddenly reduces to nothing."[17] That is, jokes are a "play of thought" that starts with something and ends without it. They begin with a deception, a logical trick, which dissolves in the punch line. One of Kant's jokes: "A man grieved so much that his wig turned white." The white wig belies the grief. The listeners are tricked and enjoy it. The German philosopher saw humor as a rapid shift from understanding a situation one way to understanding it as something else. According to Kant, because they end in "nothing," jokes are good for our well-being; they bring us to a state of rest after an initial jolt. It's the change that causes laughter and nurtures good health.

Apprehension about sex underlies many wedding-night jokes. In 1905, Sigmund Freud wrote a major essay, "Jokes and Their Relation to the

Unconscious," in which he analyzed jokes as forms of aggression. According to Freud, the aggression bursts forth into consciousness—from id to ego—and the subsequent relief of tension drives the laughter. In simple Freudian terms, the controlling superego allows the individual ego to express the pleasure-seeking id in jokes. Freud argued that we repress unconscious drives because they are socially unacceptable—for example, much of our sex drive or competition between son and father for the mother or between daughter and mother for the father—and then condense and translate them into acceptable expressions—a joke or laughter at a joke. The illicit pleasure seeking (by the id), of which sex is a prime example, coils our nerves—a discomfort that laughing at a good joke releases. The joke is a more or less harmless expression of an aggressive drive. Though debatable, Freud's psychological interpretation of jokes informs most contemporary analysis of them, both their content and our motivation to tell and laugh at them.

BRIDE AS QUESTIONABLE VIRGIN

The second type of wedding-night jokes hinges on the age-old male vigilance over whether his wife's offspring are truly his own. Underlying this concern is the attitude that the bride is a sexual object to all men. Wedding receptions deal with this by allowing the other men to dance with and often kiss the bride. Both activities allow men to act on their sexual desire in a socially acceptable way. That wedding receptions spill over into unrestrained drinking and distasteful toasting is evidence of this strong but submerged desire. The bride can kiss and dance without sacrificing her sexual virginity, which is what matters to the groom as he contemplates the paternity of his children. In Polish weddings, this ritual is especially strong. The bride holds a plate, and the man desiring the first kiss breaks the plate with a coin. Who cracked open the plate? The man with money, but it is only a plate!

Questionable-bride jokes, then, reveal the husband's wary interest in the bride's previous sexual activity. Is she what she appears or claims to be?

> Best friend to groom: "You don't want to marry that girl—everybody in Centerville has screwed her!" Bridegroom, after a pause: "Well, uh, is Centerville such a big place?"[18]

In this joke, the new husband accepts his status as one of many—but not too many—sexual partners. In other jokes, the apparent virgin bride reveals her seamy past as a casual aside.

A young man tries very hard to seduce a girl on the promise of marriage, but she steadfastly refuses to give herself to him till their wedding night. After making love to her then, he admits ruefully: "You know, you were right not to let me before—I never would have married you if you had." "Don't I know it," says the bride, "that's the way the last five guys fooled me."[19]

Here's the same idea in a play of words:

Man to wife on their wedding night: "Are you sure that I'm the first man you have slept with?" Wife: "Of course, honey. I stayed awake with all the others."[20]

Another version plays on the status of a clergyman.

A minister, on his wedding night, comes back from brushing his teeth in the bathroom and finds his bride lying naked on her back on the bed. The minister is dismayed. "Why I expected to find you on your knees," he says reproachfully. "Well, all right," says the bride, "but it always gives me the hiccups."[21]

NAÏVE BRIDES AND GROOMS

Jokes about the sexual ignorance of the bride and groom, the third category of wedding-night jokes, reflect on more than lack of knowledge or experience. They invariably evoke some of the awe of a person's first sexual intercourse with a new man or woman. A sweet one goes:

A sheltered girl is afraid to go away on her honeymoon with her new husband, and tells this to her mother. "But honey, you gotta go with him. Didn't I go on my honeymoon with Daddy?" "Sure, but you went with Daddy. I got to go with this strange man!"[22]

In another, the bride lies on the bed in her wedding gown because her husband told her that they would be "going to town about 11 o'clock." The two jokes are similar in that the first reflects bridal jitters over first-time sex with a man, which she contrasts with her mother's being safe and cozy in her father's embrace—Freud's Electra complex. The second reflects bridal resistance to the new man, to going to his town rather than staying in her familiar town (and body). In some of these jokes, the wedding night takes place in the girl's home, with the mother nearby to help. Here's a popular Italian joke:

Sophie, a good virgin Catholic, got married and on her wedding night she stayed at her mother's house because she was nervous. But her mother reassured her, "Don't worry, Sophie. Luca's a good man; he'll take care of you." So Sophie went up the bedroom, and Luca took off his shirt, exposing his hairy chest. Sophie ran downstairs. "Mama, Luca's got a big hairy chest." "Don't worry, Sophie. All good men have hairy chests. Go upstairs; he'll take care of you." Sophie returned upstairs, and Luca took off his pants, exposing his hairy legs. Sophie again ran downstairs. "Mama, Luca's got hairy legs." "Sophie, don't worry. All good men have hairy legs. Luca's a good man, and he'll take care of you." So, Sophie went upstairs. Luca takes off his socks, and on his left foot he's missing three toes. Sophie runs downstairs. "Mama, Luca's got a foot and a half." "Stay here," says the mother. "This is a job for Mama!"[23]

Here, for an instant, a mother and daughter are competing for a young man. Via the joke, it's as though the trapdoor of the unconscious flies open before it slams shut. Freudians make much of sexual competition between children and parents, most famously reflected in the Oedipal complex, in which the son desires to overcome the father in order to sleep with his mother, his first, infantile sex object. In the topsyturvy world of the joke, the mother retains control over her daughter's sexuality, and the son gets to have sex with a combination mother and bride.

In a variation on this theme, the experienced mother-in-law is already "torn" and submits to the husband in place of the daughter:

The fellow is so stingy that he slept with his mother-in-law to save the "wear and tear" on his pretty new wife.

A cartoon in a World War II–era men's magazine shows the mother-in-law sitting on the lap of her son-in-law. The wife looks on angrily, and the husband says: "But I thought you said to make your mother at home."[24] In a 1950s men's magazine:

The groom and the bride's mother are shown sitting facing each other in a breakfast alcove in their pajamas and dressing-gowns, while the bride is coming in with the breakfast, saying enthusiastically, "I just knew that you'd get along with Mother." Under the table, unseen by the bride, the older woman has slipped off her bedroom slipper and has her bare foot thrust halfway up the groom's pajama-leg caressing him.[25]

The joke is that, while the bride holds the spotlight, her mother gets more satisfaction. Mothers are often depicted in these jokes as advice givers:

British mother to her bride: "Always remember, dear, that the marital act is the most unspeakable, reprehensible thing in the world." "But Mother, you had six children." "Yes, dear, I simply closed my eyes and thought of England!"[26]

A contemporary version:

A daughter about to be married says to her mother, "I need some advice." "Well, dear, tonight when your husband wants to get into bed with you, just remember that all men are beasts and do everything he asks." The daughter responds, "Oh, hell, Mother, I know all about making love. What I want to know is how do I scramble eggs for breakfast."[27]

Naïve grooms are also the butt of jokes, in this case fumbling even with the bed curtains.

The numskull groom on his wedding night does not know how to get into the bed because the curtains are drawn. He scales one of the posts, clambers to the canopy and falls upon his bride below.[28]

To the naïve groom, the female anatomy is mysterious. To cope with all that which is unknown, he often seeks advice.

A sexual neophyte is told by his doctor "to put the longest thing he has in the hairiest thing his wife has" in order to make her pregnant. Weeks later he complains, "Well, I put my nose in her armpit every night, but no luck yet."[29]

MISMATCHED SEXUAL DESIRE

The final category of jokes, involving mismatched sexual desire, often focuses on the groom's erection. The male feels potent, but will he actually satisfy his bride? Will the woman's evaluation match the man's self-evaluation? The issue of satisfying one's partner drives these jokes. In some, the woman flaunts her sexual superiority; in others, the man comes across as indefatigable, with unlimited sexual capacity.

A rapid-fire joke takes the point of view of the woman's superiority: "A bride's second disappointment—Niagara Falls." Another brief joke has the bride in the missionary position. "Bruce," she says, "the ceiling needs painting."

What the bride does *not* say to her groom can also provide humor:

It's cute.
Wow, and your feet are so big.
That's okay, we'll work around it.

From comedy-zone.net:

On their first night together, the newlyweds change clothes. The bride comes out of the bathroom, showered and wearing her robe. The proud husband says, "My dear, we are married now, you can open your robe." The bride does this, and the groom is astonished at her beautiful body. "May I take your picture?" The bride is puzzled. "My picture?" He answers, "Yes, my dear, so that I can carry your beauty next to my heart."

He takes her picture and then heads to the bathroom to change. When he comes out, showered and wearing his robe, the new wife asks, "Why are you wearing a robe? We are married now." The husband opens his robe, and the bride exclaims, "Oh my, let me get a picture of that." He beams and asks, "Why?" She answers, "So I can get it enlarged!"[30]

And from Milton Berle:

The newlyweds could hardly wait to get to their room. Both tore their clothes off. The groom puffed up his chest and said, "A hundred eighty pounds of dynamite." The bride said, "It's the three-inch fuse that worries me."[31]

In this joke, the groom's comparison of himself to dynamite backfires when the bride focuses on his sexual organ and, picking up on his own analogy, describes it as a short fuse—a double punch that calls into question both the groom's size and his ability to satisfy her sexually. The fuse image also captures both the excitement of the moment and the physiological differences between male and female arousal. In typical self-deprecation, Rodney Dangerfield of "I don't get no respect" fame confesses:

Hey, I gotta be honest with you. I'm not a fabulous lover. My wife and I were in bed on our wedding night and she said, "Well, honey, this is it." I said, "Honey, that was it."[32]

Henny Youngman of "Take my wife . . . please" fame also made fun of his sexual performance and turned a cliché upside down: "My wife and I went back to the hotel where we spent our wedding night. Only this time, I stayed in the bathroom and cried."[33]

Elephant jokes, all the rage in the 1960s, appeal to our childish delight in the illogical—elephants wearing sneakers, elephants occupying a shelf in the fridge, elephants sitting in trees—and usually stay clear of sexual humor. But not uniformly—they can veer off-color, too, as in this sequence:

What is the difference between an elephant and a plum? Their color. What did Tarzan say to Jane when he saw the elephants coming? Here come the elephants. What did Jane say when she saw the elephants coming? Here come the plums. She was colorblind.

Libraries shelve anthologies of elephant jokes in the juvenile section, and adults enjoy elephant jokes because they take us back to the innocence of childhood. However, the elephant-joke cycle generated at least one wedding-night cartoon.[34] We see a tent pitched next to a parked car with a Just Married sign. It is night. Looming behind the tent is an elephant with his trunk reaching into the tent door. From the tent comes the exclamation, "Great heavens, Paul!" In his book on joke cycles,[35] Alan Dundes, known on the University of California at Berkeley campus as the "joke professor," analyzes why various joke cycles, such as jokes about blonds, elephants, recent immigrants (e.g., the Irish, Poles, or "Jewish American princesses"), and light bulbs come into existence at specific times. He sees power struggles at work. Dundes also analyzes cucumber jokes, popular in the 1970s, in which the female in the joke flaunts her sexual self-sufficiency by substituting a cucumber for intercourse with a man. "With a cucumber, you don't have to be virgin more than once."[36]

On the other side of the battle-of-the-sexes are jokes favorable to men, where a man is so well endowed that a woman can barely handle him:

Two bridegrooms in a honeymoon hotel compare notes on their first night. "How did you leave your wife this morning?" asks one. "On the bed, smoking," replies the other. "Wow," says the first. "Mine is just a little sore."[37]

Milton Berle gives us a newlywed version of the "woman has a head-ache" joke:

Two people met in Laguna Niguel, a retirement community in California. Both were ninety years old. Since love knows no years, one
look was enough for them to know this was it. They were married a
week after they met. On the first night of the honeymoon, they got
into bed, held hands, and squeezed them. On the second night, they
squeezed hands again. On the third night, the husband pressed his
wife's hand. She said, "Not tonight. I have a headache."[38]

Another Berle joke asserts superior male sexual prowess even when the
bridegroom is old:

They made a rather strange couple. He was seventy-five if a day. She
was at most twenty-one. However, on the fourth day of the honeymoon, it was the bride who was begging for mercy. The new groom
hadn't left her alone for five minutes. While he was shaving and
getting ready to pounce on his new wife again, the bride managed
to get out of the suite and into the hotel coffee shop. The waitress
who'd seen them upon their arrival said, "What's going on? You're
young, and you look like hell." The bride said, "The old geezer
double-crossed me. When he told me he'd been saving up for fifty
years, I thought he meant money!"[39]

First we saw that philosophers analyzed jokes before anyone else. Then
we saw how Freud opened up the unconscious, with all its irreverent, id-
driven, and primitive motifs, as a mine of information. Today, neurologists
are putting their science to understanding jokes. Surprisingly, there seems
to be an "L-spot" in our brain that triggers laughter, and there is some evidence that the joke's change in frames drives a change in brain activity
from the left side, which processes the set-up, to the right side, which reg-
isters the punch line.[40] So, a joke's humor involves a lot of synapses carrying the illogic from one side of the brain to the other.

THE VALUE OF MIRTH

Some of us were thrilled as children by the circus act in which a prepos-
terous number of clowns exit from a small car. I didn't see it at the circus,
but my father, a naval officer, commuted to the Pentagon in a car that
held a similar fascination for my brother and me. Our father, who survived a ship that went down at Pearl Harbor, was driven and tense then,

but we saw him skip into his car pool in the morning, and, when he got out of it at night, he was laughing and sometimes lowering his head back in to hear the end of a joke. His nickname at Annapolis was Giggles. My brother and I did not know this side of him, except when he repeated in the kitchen funny stories to our mother, which the men in the car, all of whom had been badly wounded in the World War II or during the Korean War, had regaled him with that day. Sometimes I ran out to meet my father in order to feel that car shaking with laughter and to glimpse him so merry. Thus, we all see in the wedding night an occasion for mirth as well as jokes per se, because we need to laugh into some sense the ups and downs in our lives.

Janie Chang, born in Taiwan and a computer consultant and author in Vancouver, wrote down the oral corpus of stories that her family had preserved for many generations. For instance, Suefen was from a great family and was marrying the eldest and only son of a family whose fortunes she was going to repair. But, on the day of her arrival, Suefen was not thinking of her elevated position on the household. She was too terrified anticipating her wedding night. The only men she had known up to this time were her father, her brothers, and a few elderly family servants.

When she had become a mother and then a grandmother, she was finally able to joke about that night, saying that she went to her bedroom after the festivities and lay in her marriage bed waiting for her bridegroom to part the bed curtains, trembling with fear and sweating as though with fever. Whenever she told the tale, she would giggle and hide her face behind her fan, for she considered this a personal and rather risqué story.[41]

In old age, the woman who stepped out of the red sedan chair to become the bride of a perfect stranger giggled and remembered. Humor in this precinct of high emotion can transform the muted embarrassment and bring the recollection within our control. Tears of laughter at our foibles often make our wedding nights shimmer and sparkle in memory.

General giggling about the wedding night (beyond jokes per se) also places on a balance scale the respective sexual desire of bride and groom/ husband and wife, because, as we all know, the libidos of every couple are continually jockeying for equality. "Have you ever tried to guide a bride?" asks Ogden Nash in a poem, answering this in the next stanza:

Dear bride, remember, if you can
That thing you married is a man.
His thoughts are low, his mind is earthy,
Of you he is totally unworthy;
Wherein lies a lesson too few have larnt it—
That's the reason you married him aren't it?[42]

If we switch the genders and begin "Dear groom, remember, if you can . . . etc.," the humor works as well. The point is that male and female always need to adjust to each other sexually, which makes, in life, for considerable fun.

NOTES

1.   Quoted in Sigmund Freud, *Jokes and Their Relation to the Unconscious* (London: Hogarth Press, 1975), 11.

2.   *Hamlet*, Act II, scene 2.

3.   Freud, *Jokes and Their Relation to the Unconscious*, 13.

4.   George Burns, *Dear George: Advice and Answers from America's Leading Expert on Everything from A to B* (New York: G. P. Putnam's Sons, 1985), 172.

5.   Henri Bergson published his seminal essay on comedy, *Le Rire*, in 1900 and received the Nobel Prize in Literature in 1927.

6.   George Orwell, "The Art of Donald McGill," *Horizon*, September 1941; reprinted in Orwell, *My Country Right or Left, 1940–1943* (London: Secker and Warburg, 1968), 160.

7.   Milton Berle, *Milton Berle's Private Joke Files: Over 10,000 of His Best Gags, Anecdotes and One-liners* (New York: Three Rivers Press, 1989), 325.

8.   Gerson Legman, *Rationale of the Dirty Joke: An Analysis of Sexual Humor; First Series* (New York: Grove Press, 1982), 490. Many of the jokes used in this chapter are based on Legman and other anthologies, and with liberties.

9.   Berle, *Milton Berle's Private Joke Files*, 324.

10.   Legman, *Rationale of the Dirty Joke*, 497.

11.   "World's Oldest Joke Traced Back to 1900 BC," Reuter's News, July 1, 2008, http://www.reuters.com/article/idUSKUA1485120080731.

12.   For a delightful introduction to jokes, see Jim Holt, *Stop Me If You've Heard This Before: A History and Philosophy of Jokes* (New York: Norton, 2008).

13.   George Carlin, *When Will Jesus Bring the Porkchops?* (New York: Hyperion, 2004), 25. This mocking tendency is especially strong in Carlin's shticks about religion, in which he attempts the total demolition of his opponent.

14.   Legman, *Rationale of the Dirty Joke*, 494.

15.   Ibid., 494.

16.   Steven Arnott and Mike Haskins, *Man Walks into a Bar* (Berkeley, CA: Ulysses Press, 2007), 287.

17.   Immanuel Kant, *Critique of Judgment*, trans. James Creed Meredith (Oxford: Clarendon Press, 1989), 199.

18.   Legman, *Rationale of the Dirty Joke*, 457.

19.   Ibid., 458.

20.   Based on http://www.freejokesms.come/free-adults-jokes/man-2-wife-on-wedding-night.html.

21.   Legman, *Rationale of the Dirty Joke*, 551.

22.   Ibid., 493.

23.   See http//humorsphere.com/humor/Italian_jokes.htm.

24. Legman, *Rationale of the Dirty Joke*, 471.

25. Ibid., 452.

26. Ibid., 445.

27. Ibid., 447.

28. Ibid., 136.

29. Ibid., 127.

30. See http://www.comedy-zone.net/jokes/laugh/relation/relate17.htm.

31. Berle, *Milton Berle's Private Joke Files*, 324.

32. Rodney Dangerfield, *It's Not Easy Bein' Me* (New York: HarperEntertainment, 2004), 158.

33. See http://www.funny2.com.

34. Reproduced in Baird Jones, *Sexual Humor* (New York: Philosophical Library, 1987), 56.

35. Alan Dundes, *Cracking Jokes: Studies of Sick Humor Cycles and Stereotypes* (Berkeley, CA: Ten Speed Press, 1987).

36. Dundes, *Cracking Jokes*, 84.

37. Arnott and Haskins, *Man Walks into a Bar*, 287.

38. Berle, *Milton Berle's Private Joke Files*, 527.

39. Ibid., 325.

40. Holt, *Stop Me If You've Heard This Before*, 121ff.

41. Janie Chang, *When We Lived in Still Waters* (San Francisco, Blurb, 2009), 39–40.

42. Ogden Nash, "Everybody Loves a Bride, Even the Groom," in Nash, *The Private Dining Room* (Boston: Little, Brown, 1953), 13–14.

CHAPTER 18

Do Not Disturb

There comes a tumultuous supper, then dancing again, then the night cup. Even after midnight, scarce can the outworn bride and bridegroom seek their couch.

—Erasmus[1]

The typical bride in the United States today is 25 years old at the time of her first marriage (grooms' average age is 28), has cohabited with her partner, and is therefore not a virgin. Nevertheless, the typical bride does have a honeymoon, so there is still a wedding night.

Has the wedding night lost or kept its panache? A preliminary look at popular literature and Web sites finds a wide array of experience. While researching wedding nights past and cross-culturally, we asked many people who are or have wed for their private recollections. In this chapter, we scatter the gardenia petals and invite you to see what we were told. The result is a diverse collection of wedding-night experiences gathered from a population that continues to enrich itself by bringing wedding-night expectations from all over the world.

The men and women informally interviewed in 2010 bring to light something they previously had told their best friends or close relatives. Some were in the first year of marriage, and others shared what had been burnished by time. In either case, often when people recounted their experiences, it was as though Aladdin's lamp had been rubbed and had lit up a memory that had been sealed away for a year

In Chagall's painting, the young lady both dreams of her wedding night and awaits her groom in the nuptial bed. (Scala/Art Resource, New York.)

or 20 years but that, when revealed, felt as if it had happened just yesterday.

In the vignettes that follow, you'll see the foibles and gaffes, the romantically achieved and the thoroughly unplanned. You'll recognize the value of communication and of really liking the other person. As we lift the curtain on private experiences of the wedding night of contemporary couples, we'll see how people cast their minds back and recapture the joys that brought them to tears or the surprises that were too far-fetched to have been made up.

THE HARD PART WAS OVER

We arrived at the County Clerk's office with five minutes to spare before they locked the doors. Most of the guests were Catholic and, like me, unfamiliar with the rituals of our Russian Orthodox ceremony. It was a balmy 97 degrees in the church with no air conditioning, but we were married before friends and relatives who no doubt were ready to exit the sweltering heat and for the champagne and vodka. The reception was reasonably fun—lots of introductions as most people hadn't met Michael, polka, and banana cake. Tired, hungry (we hadn't eaten much), and dehydrated, we left the party at midnight and headed for our hotel, which was more suited for business than romance. And this is what I remember most: the welcoming smiles of the hotel staff and of guests in the lobby, who, because of my dress, knew we'd just been married. I remember this along with the incongruity of the hotel atmosphere with our occasion. It vaguely reminded me of me—a serious person who felt awkward and out of place around romance. But we did have a fabulous honeymoon suite. And I didn't have to worry about "trying" to be romantic or trying to make this night the most memorable of any night we'd ever had together. There was a level of comfort and acceptance of each other's ways. So, for us, the hard part (getting to the altar) was over. We ordered a large pizza with everything on it, including anchovies, which I discovered I don't like. We ate until we were full and made love partly out of desire and partly out of expectation. After completing the ritual—consummating a marriage in an already consummated relationship—we slept soundly. Six hours later, we were heading to the airport, certain we could handle our next big adventure.

—Cara, 40

TWO WEDDINGS BEFORE
THE HONEYMOON

The months of planning are concluded. The wedding has been joyous the entire day. As the couple moves to their quarters, they experience the after-effects of stress, lightheadedness, or letdown. She realizes she wore the wrong shoes, or he wonders if he toasted more than he ought to have. All the same, they probably have a rosy and gleeful sense of "We did it." Now they would just as soon drive away from the whole thing, run to the store in their wedding clothes for a pint of ice cream and two spoons, and then head off to the beach or a secluded spot—hold the flower petals and pedigree sheets. If they are young, one of them may be instinctively thinking, "Better to have fun before the kids come." If the couple has lived together or been a couple a considerable time, the wedding night has cachet, but not the ribbon-tied sort.

Sheila, a professional quilter, 68, says she is not very romantic, but her daughter and her son-in-law are, which explains why they wanted a big white wedding when they were already married (without telling). "Ari is English by nationality, and Hannah went to live with him in London. He wanted her very much to join him—they had met at work and had known each other only nine months. Over there, the only way for her to gain employment was for them to marry, so they did, but without telling anyone—the witnesses, two other couples (unmarried), were sworn to secrecy. Two years later, we had the big white wedding in our hometown. Hannah had thrown the bouquet and the car was waiting and then she said, 'Ari and I have something to tell you and Dad. This is not my first wedding, but it is our first honeymoon.'"

OLD HABITS, NEW HABITS

Dan, a librarian, recalled that, on their wedding night, his wife took a long shower. He grew tired of waiting for her and turned on the Rangers hockey game. She appeared in her negligee, but Dan had fallen asleep.

Even if our grandmothers had intercourse before the wedding, they probably had not spent an entire night in bed with a man. This gave many a bride cause to fret. What would he think when he saw her head full of rollers and bobby pins, tied up in a hairnet? Now he would see her bedtime beauty rituals. "I set my hair as usual," said Angela, who married in the 1960s. "As soon as he saw it he said, 'Would you please take those off?' To this day, 40 years later, I never put my hair in rollers again."

NERVES

Nerves can spoil the wedding night. A psychologist in suburban Washington, D.C. recalled:

> I'd played three hours of tennis the day before to de-stress and had lunged like all get-out in my serves. This seemed like a good idea: I was relaxed during the wedding and feeling good and full of desire. I remember how my wife put on a see-through nightie, and we began strenuous lovemaking. Then I don't remember much else but that my back went out. For days I was in serious discomfort; it made me grumpy and I knew it was my fault. I've heard other guys say they overdid from the same impulse right before the wedding and lived to regret it.

When Paul, a caterer, married Lauren, a graphics designer, they went to their room in the big Chicago hotel where the reception took place, and it was midnight. Paul immediately changed from dress shoes into sneakers; with an agitated look and a peck on Lauren's mouth, he disappeared down the hallway with an "I'll be a few minutes." Paul and Lauren had had a whirlwind courtship, and she began to wonder: had her family overwhelmed him; was he not ready? Suddenly, with their families gone, she felt lonely.

Paul hadn't gone out for ice because it was 45 minutes later when he reappeared—shirt tails falling out of his pants and panting. "Where did you go?" said Lauren, gripping his hand more tightly than usual. "Walking is good for stress," he said, "so I walked up and down the floor. Then I saw the exit, and went out, and ended up running up and down 31 flights of stairs. I feel great!"

Whereas Lauren could shift to being just the two of them instantly, Paul had to shake off his nerves. He understood what he needed, and she was learning.

HONEYMOON FIRST, WEDDING SECOND

Sandra, who runs an environmental engineering business with her husband, was leery of marriage.

So we went on the honeymoon first. It relaxed me and I was ready for the wedding, but we did it backwards—I think a couple should suit themselves. We spent the wedding night in a beautiful hotel, and then the ceremony followed the next day, and then we took everyone on a cruise around Manhattan, and that was the reception.

PARENTAL EXPECTATIONS

Nicole, a Chinese-Canadian who married a New Zealander, celebrated her wedding night on the eve of a big trip with her parents.

We flew to Vancouver for the wedding and stayed in my parents' house. Geoff and I had already been living together for some months, but my parents, in Chinese fashion, put us in separate bedrooms and sailed through the days prior to the wedding firmly maintaining the unspoken fiction that we had been celibate during courtship. All my life, neither of my parents ever mentioned sex. To this day I don't know the Chinese word for sex because my parents have never pronounced it in front of my brothers and me.

Our wedding night passed in champagne-enhanced bliss and cuddliness, just pleasant intoxicated feelings and the satisfaction that comes from having thrown a very good party. . . . The clap of thunder came after the honeymoon, when we returned to stay with my parents for a few days before our flight back to New Zealand. This time we were ushered into the guest room with the double bed. I lay in bed that night, and the thunderclap, when it came, said in horrified tones, "I'm in bed with a man and my parents want me to get pregnant!" Then I knew I was really and truly married.

OFF TO A POOR START

Gina had known her beau for five months. He was a new intern in the hospital where she worked. A defective condom—and she was pregnant with his child, and they both were ready to settle down:

I bought my wedding dress at Filene's Basement and shoes at T. J. Maxx. My mother, sisters and their spouses, and about five local friends came, as well as 50 or so of my husband's coworkers, not really "friends," but they filled the room. (Now my ex, he never actually had any friends, not then or now. Why didn't people warn me?) We married in my beautiful lakefront home, and the reception was at a club in the next town over. After the reception, which was a blur of smiling, and all-day morning sickness, we went home to my place, now *our* place. The plan was to quickly count the cash and deposit it along with any checks, so that a thief whose business was to know who was away on their honeymoon with the loot waiting at home for them would find nothing. Then my new husband and I were to drive to Bradley airport to stay in a hotel for about four hours, since the hotel stay entitled us to leave our car there for the trip, then fly out to St. Lucia for a honeymoon. That was the plan.

We got home and counted the money, and then the hubby went into the bathroom. He was in there for so long I actually began to worry that we might miss the plane the next day! I dared to question what the hell he was doing in there, on our wedding night for 30 or so minutes, when we were in a rush to go, and it angered him. The nerve of me to challenge him! And he never looked back. The ride to the airport was in angry silence. He pulled over suddenly and demanded that I drive. He didn't ask, he demanded. Not "I'm feeling really tired, honey, would you mind driving?" but "Drive." There was no consummating the marriage that night! The honeymoon was me feeling fat and him taking longer-than-normal runs, leaving me alone, incapable of running anymore since I was carrying his child. We spent much of the honeymoon in silence and sexual drought.

When we got back, I called my lawyer to see what, exactly, an annulment was, and could I get one?

Sad, isn't it?

Afterwards, I stayed with him until I was ready to get pregnant again. I needed to enjoy my daughter alone for at least a year. I used him for his sperm, and, once I had my second child, so that I would not have to rear my daughter as an only child with a single mother, I left.

The second wedding night? All seven in attendance, his three and my two, and all seven on the honeymoon. We did take the adjoining room for the wedding night. Then we put the kids in play-groups in the morning so that we could go back to bed. This marriage's sex life made up for the last, and this time I married for love and lovemaking!

Cynthia, a professional singer in musicals, recalled her long-ago wedding night, the start of a brief marriage not meant to be:

We left for the honeymoon three days late, that is, after the wedding. I had purchased a beautiful black lace satin nightgown, thinking it was the sexiest thing around. My new husband told me that he hated it and said he only liked white underwear. I didn't think that was a good omen for starting a marriage, and, unfortunately, I was right!

An established attorney in his fifties, Al recalled another ill-fated après-wedding:

A friend of mine had a big New York wedding and most of us stayed in the same big hotel. During the reception, the groom disappeared and the bride went looking for him. She found him having sex with one of the bridesmaids in a closet. She said, "I want an annulment in the morning."

LIFE INTERVENES

On his wedding night, Bob Kearns encountered an unexpected but not completely random life-altering event. A professor of engineering, he married a schoolteacher in Detroit in 1953. On their wedding night, his vision was impaired after a flying champagne cork hit him in the left eye. Nine years later, he was driving his Ford in the rain in Detroit, and the visibility was crummy, and Bob thought, "Why can't the windshield wipers work more like an eyelid?" With a love of gadgets, he conceived the idea of intermittent windshield wipers. His patent made him rich, and he became a hero who won a multimillion-dollar suit against Ford for stealing his invention.[2] His life story, beginning with the flying cork, was made into a movie called *Flash of Genius,* with Greg Kinnear in the role of Bob Kearns.

Gerald, an attorney about 50, had a midsummer wedding in Nantucket.

Family and friends congregated, the ceremony was in a little historic church, and my son (I'd been married before) was two years old and took part in it. A highlight was the rehearsal dinner, a lobster bake for 50, and it was a weekend of fun for everybody. But, at 2 A.M., we were awakened by a fight outside the window of the bungalow we had rented. The couple were slugging each other when I went out and got involved. The police came and put a stop to it, and I returned to my bride. One and a half years later, I had a call from the attorney of the abused woman, who turned out not to be a girlfriend but his wife. They were now divorcing, and he was running for a high political office. I gave a deposition. It was surreal. We were beginning our marriage, and they were ending theirs.

Renee grew up in a trailer in southwestern Florida. She was the youngest child of her father's second family, and her father was a fishing guide in the Everglades.

My wedding was six years ago. I was 35, and my dad was in his mid-eighties. I work for the EPA [Environmental Protection Agency] in Washington, where Hank and I had our wedding. We were buying a house, so we wanted to have a small wedding. But my parents insisted on a big one—elegant hotel, a top band, and so forth. No protests could dissuade them! I remember my parents and Hank and me waving goodbye from the balcony. As Hank and I started to withdraw to a hideaway suite, my mother leaned over and told me how much this had meant to her.

I knew something was wrong in her tone. She explained that my father was very sick. That night he went into the hospital. He had been diagnosed with inoperable pancreatic cancer.

LITTLE MISHAPS

Allen, a television writer, married Eliza, a graphics designer. After the reception, they went to the elevator to go to their car. Eliza, who is small, wore a dress that pouffed like a big silk artichoke. Allen had to squeeze her into the elevator, and the dress got stuck in the door after it closed. Their firstborn was a girl, but Allen jokes that if it had been a boy they would have named him Otis.

Either resistance is low before the wedding or the bride and groom don't pay attention to ordinary things, because numerous people spoke of accidents, sunburn and, yes, poison ivy.

Tricia's husband was clearing brush two days before the wedding. After the wedding, they went straight to the airport, bound for the Caribbean. That next morning, Rob started to break out with poison ivy between his fingers. Then there was a big storm, their flight was rerouted, and they ended up in an Atlanta hotel. Recalled Tricia,

> From the sweat dripping down as we sat hours in the runway in an overheated plane, my husband got poison ivy in the place which a man really needs on his honeymoon. Our 15-year marriage has been subject to Murphy's Law, and that first episode, where something disappointed and almost threw us, was saved by laughing about it, so it became just part of our story.

Poison ivy attacked Dana, a librarian, 36, who remembers well the circumstances.

> We were just out of college. We were hiking, and when I needed the facilities I went in the woods. All inside my upper legs was exactly where the poison ivy came out. Luckily, we went to the Bahamas a few days after the wedding, and the combination of the salt water and the sun dried it out.

It was rare that someone told a story he or she had told before, but when Paxton, a business college professor, 65, described his wedding night, it was clear he'd laughed at the memory many times before.

> I was a GI returning from Vietnam. We rented a car and drove to her parents' church from the airport. People tied cans to the car, and it had Just Married written on it. It was fun, once in a lifetime. We arrived at the Raleigh/Durham airport, parked the car, and raced into our hotel. We got a letter soon after. "Dear Mr. Miller, it appears during the time you had our car that you got married." They billed me for $37 to clean the car off.

Chris was marrying for the second time, Laurie the first. A few days before their wedding, in northern Virginia, the college student who had promised to take care of Chris's children canceled. Chris scrambled to find another sitter and, after the reception, dropped the twins at a neighbor's. Laurie remembered their relief as they headed south on I-95.

This was long before the Internet, and I had made phone reservations at a hotel near Richmond, just a short drive toward our honeymoon destination. We arrived late at night, and they had no record of our reservation. I am "Ms. Prepared" and had kept the reservation number. The hotel clerk acknowledged the hotel's error and gave us—yes, sometimes fantasies come true—the bridal suite. Chris carried me over the threshold into a suite of three rooms, much bigger than my apartment in southwest Washington, D.C. We made love and fell sound asleep. The magic was the next morning, the sunlight was pouring through the windows. We tried out the various couches and easy chairs, took a long shower in the spacious bathroom, and headed off for a week in historic Williamsburg.

THE SECOND TIME

Some of the people we interviewed would segue from "My first wedding night was like this" to "My second was like that." There seemed to be no correlation between wedding-night delights and the lasting marriage. Halstead, a stockbroker, compared the two.

For my second marriage in New York City, I was so tired by 1 A.M. that I fell asleep and didn't "consummate" the marriage until the morning. My first marriage had been more traditional, and I was younger. I had a two-year-long sexual history with my third wife, but the setting of that wedding night was magical—Newport, Rhode Island, in early June. After the wedding reception, a clambake on the water, a small launch to the mainland. We locked ourselves in the small bathroom of the boat and "did it." It was a real quickie, but it cemented our bond and enhanced the magic of the evening. When we got to our hotel, we undressed and fell asleep in each other's arms in a nonsexual way.

SWEET SEX

Joseph, 48, paid for the wedding ring in installments.

Every week in the months leading up to the wedding, I would walk to the jewelry store around the corner from where I worked and make a payment on the wedding ring. We were getting there, day by day, payment by payment. It was an estate piece, and Becky had picked it out after we picked the month of October for the wedding.

We chose to be married in an old hotel in downtown Philadelphia. The ceremony was in one of the smaller ballrooms down the hall from the lobby. The rabbi who presided was a professor at a local university who made a tidy living presiding over interfaith marriages.

In keeping with tradition, I did not see my bride in her wedding finery until she appeared on her father's arm. I was used to seeing her in fine clothes, but it was thrilling to see the white dress and the flowers in her slender hands.

After the ceremony, people moved to a larger ballroom downstairs that could accommodate dancing to a swing band and tables for dinner. Our song to dance together was As Time Goes By, which the older people recognized from Casablanca. We greeted every table, danced a little, and got picked up in chairs and carried around. We ate a bit of cake, the top layer of which was to be saved in the freezer for our first anniversary. After these rituals were completed, we exited upstairs.

Once we were alone in our suite, we looked around the room and peered out the windows. Neither of us had ever been in such a large room merely to sleep. There were champagne and chocolates and a pair of club chairs. We sat down and had a glass. After all of the people and noise, we just sat and talked quietly, happy to be with each other, happy to be going on a two-week honeymoon to Hawaii, paid for with many gifts of cash.

We had been living together for nearly a year and had already purchased a townhouse together. Our intimate life was settled—we made love three or four times a week. Nevertheless, we did make love on our wedding night. Our style of lovemaking was just that— lovemaking. We didn't pretend we were porn stars in the middle of a movie, playing a role within a role. Instead, we were two people in the middle of a bed, holding each other for dear life, greatly relieved to have found each other. Our lovemaking was part of our happiness together, and we were a refuge for each other. To be honest, though, our main objective was to sleep, with lovemaking as a prelude, since weddings can be exhausting.

Howard, an art dealer and collector, married Angi on the grounds of their new home in Bradenton, Florida. The ceremony was romantic, and, after the doves were set free and the rice was thrown, they took a limousine to their suite at the Ritz-Carlton in Sarasota.

I had arranged for rose petals to be scattered on our bed, a bottle of champagne on ice, and chocolate covered strawberries. Angi is a beautiful woman who rarely wears makeup, but I could not keep my eyes off her all day. She was so exquisite with her professionally done hair and tasteful makeup that I can still remember how she looked to this day. I insisted that she keep that look as we sipped our champagne, nibbled on our strawberries, and took lots of pictures with discreetly placed rose petals, and nothing else, covering Angi's body. It was a recipe for passion, role playing, and delicious lovemaking.

LET'S PARTY SOME MORE

Some recall being royalty for a day and night. Lena, a homemaker, 45, arrived at the Plaza Hotel, in New York City, with "Just Married" sprayed on back of the car.

When we checked in at the hotel, they knew we were newlyweds, and the woman at reception said, "You know this room has twin beds." No, I didn't. She checked and they didn't have a room with a double bed, so she gave us a deluxe suite the size of an apartment. I looked out the windows to Central Park and said to my husband, "I'd like our friends to see this. Let's have a party." So, even though the reception was over, we called a bunch of friends and had a second do. By the time we got to bed, it was one in the morning, and we found the bed was two beds pushed together. We turned out the lights, but we could not sleep side by side comfortably because of the gap. Then my husband got the idea of turning the mattresses crosswise.

GREEN WEDDING NIGHT

Before marrying, Ian had bicycled across America, taught water sports at a spa in Thailand, and learned Italian to go to medical school in Rome. Valerie had played the violin six hours a day at Juilliard since the age of 12. They were going to be a couple whose interests would separate them day in and day out most of their lives. Having met at a community garden, they decided to build an 8-by-24 foot greenhouse from a kit as a wedding present to the garden.

There were 2,000 pieces, counting the pegs. We spent the wedding night in the greenhouse. It had prop-open windows for air, and we had flowering shrubs that were not yet in the ground for privacy. We woke up to a policeman tapping on the greenhouse, but it was great.

VEGAS WEDDING NIGHT

Each wedding night is situated in an era. This one captures both the popular-music culture and the civil rights movement of the late 1960s.

Chelsea Brown was a budding young dancer and actress. She landed a job in Las Vegas as a backup dancer for Connie Stevens, who was starring at the Sands Hotel. Stevens had two backup dancers—Chelsea and Cheryl Weinberg. Chelsea was African American, and Cheryl was half-black and half-Jewish. Chelsea was marrying Gary Stromberg, a music publicist for rock stars—and a white man.

> Chelsea couldn't leave the show, so I flew to Vegas to marry her. It was an afternoon wedding, and Connie came with us as our witness. I went to the chapel and signed up. Chelsea wore a real wedding dress because it was a big occasion to her. Tipping her hat to tradition, Chelsea hid in a closet, ready to make a traditional entrance. Our turn came, and I was in front of a guy in a madras jacket who said, "Y'all getting married today?" A red flag went up—a guy from Dixie was going to marry us.
>
> The wedding chapel was tiny. The Dixie officiant put on a record of the wedding song and went to the podium. Suddenly Chelsea marched down the aisle. As the Dixie man looked up from the podium at Chelsea, I saw his jaw drop. Chelsea was beautiful in the dress and veil coming down the aisle, and here we were being married by someone I sensed was a bigot. But Chelsea didn't get it. I could see the tension in the man's face when he finished and said, "You can kiss the bride." I kissed Chelsea, and he winced.
>
> We walked out the door, and Connie threw rice at us. That night, Chelsea had to work, but Connie got us a suite at the Sands Hotel, and for the performance she got me a front row table. In the middle of the set, with Cheryl and Chelsea on stage, Connie said, "I'd like to introduce you to my backup dancers, Cheryl Weinberg and Chelsea Stromberg." It was the biggest laugh of the evening, and she did it on a nightly basis. The way she did it was so sweet. That was Chelsea's and my one-night honeymoon.

SUMMA NIGHT

According to Bonnie, a novelist, Peter is not a romantic kind of guy—except for one night. A Minnesota radio station had a yearly Valentine's Day promotion in which they invited people to submit letters stating why they should be selected to be married in a multiple matrimony ceremony at the Mall of America. The lure was a free ceremony and a chance to win a fantastic tropical honeymoon. Bonnie and her boyfriend and 91 other couples were chosen to be married on a frigid February morning in 1995.

We owned our own home, but the night before I stayed at my mother's house. Peter made our bedroom beautiful in my absence with everything clean, and on the bed were patterned blue sheets—it killed me a decade later to throw them out. He bought a beautiful cut-glass crystal vase in which he put a mix of roses from my garden and roses from a florist—all pink and white. My grandmother gave me a special wedding present of a crystal bowl that her bridesmaids gave to her 53 years before. She had asked me what I wanted for a wedding present, and I said, "Give me something special to you."

Peter knew I had an affinity for crystal. I'd go into a burning house for those two pieces. I kept the rose petals in the bowl for years. He has done nothing remotely as romantic since then. It was a one-shot deal, and I think at the time I understood that he was going outside his zone to show me his love.

This was not what I dreamed about as a young girl. Champagne and toasting the nuptials began about 10 A.M. After an impromptu wedding reception in Gatlins, a former nightclub in the Mall, we headed to Camp Snoopy, the indoor amusement park at the Mall for a roller-coaster ride in our wedding garb. After a morning and early afternoon filled with celebration, we headed to downtown Minneapolis to stay at the newly constructed Hilton Hotel. My brother-in-law was the hotel manager on duty that weekend, and he made sure everything was just right. We had course after course of delectable items, complete with glass after glass of red wine. I remember devouring some chocolate mousse. My next memory is being awoken with an undying thirst. And I mean a thirst that was never ending. As I surveyed the room searching for the ice bucket, I noted I was fully clothed lying on top of the comforter. My husband was snuggled under the comforter on the other side of the bed. As I ventured over to the ice bucket, my husband gave me a smile. We had endured our first evening together as husband and wife and would soon consummate our marriage to make it official. Looking back, something changed in our relationship that evening. Even though my husband used to say, "A marriage license is just a piece of paper," I knew by looking in his eyes that morning that it meant much more than that.

REAL AND IMAGINED

Many young women imagine their wedding night in advance of imagining their groom. Take, for example, the wedding-night plan the English actress Juliet Rylance had in girlhood: her wedding party would gather before dawn at the Globe Theater, which her stepfather, Mark Rylance, directs, and then go to a 12th-century church for the ceremony. "And then getting everybody in a boat, somehow, and sailing up to Oxford and staying in a barn, with lots of lights and candles, and everyone dancing. Camping out, fires. For a week."[3]

In her lovely dream scenario, she fantasized a protracted weeklong night of candlelit barn camp-out!

In actuality, Juliet married actor Christian Camargo on the closing night of *All My Sons*. His co-stars, Dianne Wiest and John Lithgow, serenaded the bride and groom, after which they took a cab to a rented apartment to get some much-needed sleep. "I realize the marriage is more important than the wedding," Juliet told a reporter for *The New Yorker* two years later, when she and her husband were starring together in a production of two Shakespeare comedies at the Brooklyn Academy of Music.

NOTES

1.   Quoted in Gordon Ratray Taylor, *Sex in History* (New York: Vanguard, 1970), 154.

2.   John Seabrook, *Flash of Genius and Other True Stories of Invention* (New York: St. Martin's Griffin, 2008), 7.

3.   Rebecca Mead, "All's Well," *The New Yorker*, August 26, 2010, http://www.newyorker.com/talk/2010/03/01/100301ta_talk_mead.

Appendix: Wedding Nights on the Silver Screen

This is an annotated list of films that feature a significant wedding night. Ordered by date, these films reflect a variety of first-night encounters, and are all available to rent or purchase.

THE WEDDING NIGHT (1935)

The Polish American tradition of breaking a plate with a coin takes place in this movie starring Gary Cooper as Tony Barrett, an urbane writer, and Anna Sten as Manya, a Polish American farm girl. Barrett has fled New York City for a cheaper life in rural Connecticut. There he meets his neighbors—Manya, her father, and the rest of the extended family. The film contrasts the urbanity of Tony with the unrefined earthiness of the Polish immigrants. In writing a novel based on the neighboring family, Tony falls in love with Manya, who is already promised to Fredrik, a fellow farmer, played by Ralph Bellamy. Manya turns her attentions to Tony and secretly visits him. When her father learns of this, he forces her to marry Fredrik, whom she does not love. The film features a Polish American wedding reception in which one of the men earns the first dance with the bride by breaking a plate she holds with a coin. As a way of flaunting his status as groom, Frederik taunts Tony into dancing with Manya, which he does but in a slow foxtrot rather than in the Polish style. Following old-country tradition, the married women escort Manya to the bedroom upstairs and prepare her for her first night as a married woman. Downstairs, the men drink and trade jokes about wedding-night pleasures. Frederik, thoroughly drunk, ascends to the bedroom and finds Manya unresponsive when he kisses her roughly. He accuses Manya of loving Barrett and storms out of the bedroom, vowing to kill the New York writer. Manya intervenes in the ensuing fight and dies in a fall down the stairs, leaving both men bereft.

LES DAMES DU BOIS DE BOULOGNE (1945)

Based on a story by Denis Diderot, an encyclopedist executed during the French Revolution, *Les Dames* features Helene, the jilted lover of Jean, who plots her revenge by arranging for Jean to meet and fall in love with Agnes, a cabaret dancer/prostitute whom Helene has rescued from her base profession on the condition that she live a reclusive life with her mother. Helene arranges for Jean to meet Agnes in the Bois de Boulogne, a woodland park in Paris. Trusting Helene's word that Agnes is of an "impeccable" background, Jean is smitten. But, because of her promise to Helene to live reclusively, Agnes resists Jean's attentions. The more she resists, the more Jean desires her. Helene is in the middle, manipulating both players in the romantic game of hide-and-seek. The climax of the movie comes when Agnes agrees to marry Jean but fails to disclose her past. After the wedding, Agnes is afraid to appear at the reception lest her old customers recognize her. At this point, Helene tells Jean that he has married a tramp. When Jean confronts Agnes in the bedroom, Agnes's shame causes her to faint. Jean is torn between his social status and his love for Agnes. At first he flees from the bedroom where Agnes lies on the nuptial bed, still dressed in her wedding gown and nearly unconscious. Later, he returns, and Agnes asks Jean for forgiveness and for time to show that she will be a loyal wife. Jean kneels by her side and declares his love for her, a love that puts the past aside. Agnes's faint smile shows him that she will live to fulfill her promise and his love.

Though melodramatic in style, this postwar film by Robert Bresson is shot in stunning black and white tableaus, whether in Helene's grand apartment or in the Bois de Boulogne, or in Agnes's modest apartment.

IT'S A WONDERFUL LIFE (1946)

In this much loved classic, George Bailey (Jimmy Stewart) and Mary Hatch (Donna Reed) marry after a rocky courtship. As they leave for the train station and their honeymoon, they see a commotion in front of the savings and loan formerly owned by George's late father and now run by George. George runs to the Savings and Loan and prevents a run on the S&L by explaining to worried depositors that the S&L lends out most of their savings so that other people can buy homes and that it can't be expected to cash out all the savings accounts at once. This mini-course in economics reassures most of the customers, and, to prove that the Savings and Loan is solvent, George cashes out a savings account, using the cash he had saved for the honeymoon. Having calmed the banking waters, he realizes that he has left Mary waiting to go on her honeymoon. He rushes to their new home, a dilapidated house that is leaking because it is raining. On the front door, he finds a sign that reads "Bridal Suite," and inside he finds a table set with candles and a bottle of champagne in an ice bucket. As the camera pans to the bedroom door, we see a carefully made bed with two pairs of slippers on the floor. It's clear that dessert will occur in the nuptial bed.

THE QUIET MAN (1952)

In this romantic John Ford film, Sean Thornton, played by John Wayne, returns to his native Ireland to reclaim a family farm. He meets Mary Kate Danaher, a fiery spinster, played by Maureen O'Hara. A tumultuous flirtation culminates in a long kiss in the rain. At the wedding reception, Mary Kate's brother, Red Danaher, refuses to hand over her full "portion." Mary Kate is enraged, but Sean, who had killed a man in the boxing ring in America, refuses to fight her brother even after Red levels him with a sucker punch. Back at their cottage, Sean's refusal to fight and his dismissal of the importance of Mary Kate's dowry—"It seems a lot of fuss over a little furniture and stuff"—leads to the couple's first wedded fight. Still in her wedding dress, Mary Kate tells Sean that, until he takes her brother to task, he will get "no bit of me" and then locks herself in the bedroom. Sean kicks down the door, throws back the counterpane, forcibly kisses his bride, throws her on the bed with such force that it breaks, and storms out of the room. So much for the wedding night. The rest of the movie tells of the stubborn couple's bumpy reconciliation as Sean finally confronts the brother, engages him in a couple of royal brawls, and gains Mary Kate's respect and love as a husband who protects what is rightfully hers.

YOURS, MINE, AND OURS (1968)

Helen North (Lucille Ball) and Frank Beardsley (Henry Fonda), navy widow and widower, meet, briefly court, and marry, blending together a family of 18 children. Their honeymoon is delayed when one of Helen's kids falls ill, so they spend their wedding night moving the large brood into their new home (an old house with a leaky roof). Helen and Frank valiantly orchestrate the logistics of the kids' first night living together in a new abode so that the newlyweds can spend their wedding night in private. To no avail. One of the bedrooms has a leak, and the small ones take refuge in the nuptial bed.

LOVERS AND OTHER STRANGERS (1970)

This film opens with a young couple, Susan, played by Bonnie Bedelia, and Mike, played by Michael Brandon, quarreling over their quickly approaching wedding. The two have cohabited on the sly, hiding that fact from their parents, for a year and a half. Mike is in a near panic at the prospect of marriage and summons personal and global reasons for sticking with cohabitation without the bonds of marriage: he doesn't think he can be faithful forever, Susan has fat arms, and the world has too many problems to afford permanent bonding. Just days before the wedding, at a barbecue at Susan's home, Mike puts his foot down—he wants out. Susan handles this gracefully, agreeing with Mike as long as he tells her father, played by Gig Young. In a wonderful scene, Susan's father listens to Mike as he confesses that he and Susan have been living together for over a year, that Susan is not a virgin, and that to have a wedding would be hypocritical. The father calmly explains to his future son-in-law that Susan has dreamed about her wedding since she was six and, as an eight-year old, dressed as a bride for a masquerade party. "Weigh your hurt against the hurt of everyone else" is the father's final counsel. Mike comes to his senses and agrees to the wedding. The night before the wedding, Mike and Susan are enjoying ice cream cones at a drive-in and ruing that they have to spend a night apart. Asserting her generation's new sexual freedom, Susan proposes, "Let's have our honeymoon now"—that they celebrate their wedding night *before* the wedding. The two check into the honeymoon suite at the very hotel where they will enjoy their wedding reception. Mike carries Susan over the threshold, and the two enjoy a final frolic of pursue-and-capture.

The other wedding-night joke involves Susan's sister, Wilma, and her husband, Johnny, who, though a physical fitness maven, has lost interest in sex with his wife. In bed, the muscular Johnny resists lusty Susan's attentions so that he can concentrate on the television, which is showing the movie *Spellbound*, a Hitchcock classic in which the psychiatrist, Ingrid Bergman, falls in love with the patient, Gregory Peck. The harder Wilma comes on, the more Johnny resists her caresses. As he turns out the light on his side of the bed, he tells Wilma that he "owes her one." Wilma reminds him that he already owes her from the week before and receives the final brush-off—"I'm not in the mood right now." This reversal of traditional bedtime roles is only one of the film's scenes that looks at marital love and how families handle it. *Lovers and Other Strangers* takes up other family and romantic relations—the father is having an affair with his wife's sister, Mike's brother and his wife are separated and about to file for divorce, a bridesmaid and an usher fall in love—as it moves through the wedding and wedding reception and, at last, Susan and Mike's "official" wedding night. This time in bed, the groom is so engrossed in *Spellbound* that he resists Susan's sexual attentions. Mirroring Wilma and Johnny, they quarrel, with Susan declaring that she "wants out." But the two easily reconcile and slip into a nuptial embrace.

THE RULING CLASS (1972)

Jack, the 14th Earl of Gurney, played by Peter O'Toole, takes over the family estate when his father accidentally hangs himself while reenacting famous moments in British military history. However, Jack abhors his name and prefers to go by J.C. or the Lord. He is grandly delusional and has spent most of his life in an insane asylum run by a slightly Germanic psychiatrist who likes to experiment with his paranoid rats and patients. In this wacky sendup of the British aristocracy, Jack's uncle arranges for his nephew to meet and fall in love with the uncle's mistress, an erstwhile stripper named Grace Shelly, played by Carolyn Seymour, who takes on the persona of the Lady of the Camellias, Jack's fantasy lover. Although she does not speak French, Grace plays the part well enough that Jack falls in love with her as a flesh-and-blood woman and agrees to marry her. The uncle's plan is that J.C. and Grace will produce a male heir, and then the uncle will have Jack recommitted to the asylum, the uncle taking control of the estate. After a quickie wedding presided over by an inept bishop, played by Alastair Sim, Grace retires to the bedroom, which is dominated by a four-poster the size of a small ship. Confessing "I always get first-night nerves, any performer does," Grace performs a striptease for the camera, including some early pole dancing with a monstrously large bedpost. As she lies in bed in her negligee, J.C. arrives, riding a three-wheel hobby horse. But, unlike Catherine the Great's Peter (chapter 4), J.C. ascends to the amorous bed and declares, "God loves you, God wants you, God needs you." In a tender yet comic moment scored by Tchaikovsky's *Pathetique*, the newlyweds consummate with a kiss.

The next morning, Grace is wolfing down a large bowl of corn flakes. Jack's uncle—now her "former" lover—wonders aloud how the nuptial night went. The new bride, while asking for more cereal—"Keep pouring, I'm starving, it was a damn long night"—tells him that J.C. was up all night riding a "three-wheel bicycle." "Well, first his bike, then me. His mind may be wonky, but there's certainly nothing wrong with the rest of his anatomy." The wedding night does produce an heir, and the rest of the movie sails along toward J. C.'s rehabilitation as just "Jack" and his relapse into another delusional persona, Jack the Ripper.

PRIVATE BENJAMIN (1980)

This film opens with the second wedding of Judy Benjamin, played by Goldie Hawn. (The first, to an adventurer who was after her father's money, lasted six weeks.) The second wedding scene establishes Judy as an "American Jewish princess," overly concerned with the fabric and fluting of an ottoman for her soon-to-be husband's study. The groom, Yale, is hyperactive, exiting the reception to telephone a real estate client, and hypersexually needy, begging Judy to relieve his headache, not the kind treated by Tylenol, by giving him oral sex in the limo parked outside the reception. The wedding night finds them in their apartment undressing for bed, Yale at first on the phone with another client and then embracing Judy from the rear as she washes her face at the sink. Judy suggests that they move their lovemaking to the bed—"It's not real romantic making love in a sink"—but Yale takes her to the floor, where they consummate the marriage, if not the relationship. Yale is spent—after all, it's his second ejaculation in a few hours—and lies heavily on his new bride. This intercourse quickie leaves no time for Judy to enjoy a petite mort, but Yale's postcoital slumber is the big death—he's dead à la Valley of the Dolls.[1]

After Yale's funeral, Judy retires to the family bedroom to grieve and to ponder her future. In a send up of the royal parade (where notables used to pay call on a regal nuptial bed), a series of family women enter the bedroom to console Judy. As she lies on the bed in her mourning dress, she receives such wisdom as "que sera sera" and "when you fall off the horse, you have to get right back on." Yale's mother arrives to tearfully ask, "What were Yale's last words?," to which Judy responds, "I'm coming."

Judy slips out of the house and checks into a motel, where she seeks consolation and advice by calling a nighttime radio talk show. She confesses that she has been dependent on men since she was two, and her eight days in the motel mark the first time she has been on her own. The call-in leads to an interview with an army recruiter who promises Judy a private room, a posting to Europe, and a paid 30-day vacation. Judy signs up and, as Private Benjamin, earns her independence in an army that has left Vietnam behind and enjoys peacetime antics. In a lovely scene during a mock battle, the women recruits sit around a campfire and share marijuana and stories of their first orgasmic sex. Judy tells her troopmates that she was married twice, the first ending after six weeks and the second after only six hours while having sexual intercourse. One of the women wonders what one would do after that, to which Judy replies, "Join the army."

The movie winds down with Judy falling in love with Henri, a wealthy but inappropriate French fiancé—he abuses his dog, sleeps with the maid, obsesses over an old lover, requires Judy to sign a prenuptial contract leaving him all his property in the event of a divorce—but this time, at the altar, Judy realizes her impending mistake, breaks off the wedding by flooring Henri with a sucker punch, and, dressed in a white gown, walks away from family and wedding guests into an unknown future on her own terms.

MARY SHELLEY'S FRANKENSTEIN (1994)

The movie has a different feel and mobility from the book. Rather than rely on the Prometheus plot of Victor's downfall from the godlike height of creation, the movie emphasizes the coming of age of Victor Frankenstein, played by Kenneth Branagh, and his adopted sister, Elizabeth, played by Helena Bonham Carter. When they reach maturity, Victor proposes to Elizabeth. But they are too much brother and sister, and Elizabeth demurs, pushing him to study science in Ingolstadt while she takes on the role of substitute for Victor's mother, who has died giving birth to a baby boy. Mary Shelley's point is that they need to mature as adults before they can share a bed. In Ingolstadt, Victor becomes obsessed with using electricity to create life—"No one need ever die"—and stops sending letters back home. Alarmed, Elizabeth travels to Ingolstadt to persuade Victor to leave the cholera-stricken city and marry her back in Geneva, but Victor, fully the mad scientist, chooses his work in the lab over his love. So, the wedding night is delayed a second time. Elizabeth returns home and drapes her wedding dress in black.

Victor succeeds in creating a new being by combining parts of various cadavers and applying voltage, and of course his monster escapes the lab and roams the countryside as an unwanted creature. After observing a peasant family, the monster comes to the realization that he needs a mate, a bride. Victor returns to Geneva to wed Elizabeth, and there the monster confronts him and orders him to create a companion female monster. But the process is too much for Victor, who finally refuses the request. The monster, without prospect of a bride, vows revenge on Victor's loved ones. Victor marries Elizabeth and walks into an action-packed wedding night. In the midst of passionate embraces on the nuptial bed, Victor is called to defend the estate against the marauding monster. He leaves Elizabeth alone, and the monster attempts to rape her. Victor intervenes, and, in a rage, the monster tears out Elizabeth's heart and flees. At this point, the movie departs from the book. In the movie, during the wedding night, Victor returns to his lab and restores life to his bride by attaching her head to a cadaver that has a heart. The result is a monstrous Elizabeth, grossly stitched together and deformed. In a bizarre scene, Victor tries to restore her affection for him by dancing with her. Again, the monster enters the wedding night and invites Elizabeth to join him as his mate. Elizabeth is torn between the two men, between herself as human and as monster. She resolves the test of male wills by immolating herself. Thus ends Victor's wedding night, several times postponed and never consummated.

BRAVEHEART (1995)

Both the Best Director and the Best Picture Oscars for 1995 went to Mel Gibson and his epic adventure *Braveheart*, in which Gibson also starred as the 13th-century Scottish hero Sir William Wallace, who led Scotland's rebellion against English rule. In 2009, the film was second on a list of "the most historically inaccurate movies" that appeared in the English newspaper *The Times*, but the writer of the screenplay, Randall Wallace, a descendant of the real Braveheart, defended his work by claiming that he got the spirit of the times right.

A romance precedes the battles and sets the plot in motion.

In an early scene, King Edward I of England, known as Edward Long-shanks because he is tall and skinny, supervises the wedding of his son to Isabelle, the daughter of the rival king of France. It is rumored that, for the princess to conceive, Longshanks has to do the honors himself. We presume that Longshanks has the disgusting idea of bedding his son's bride in that the role of French princess is played by the lovely Sophie Marceau. A connection is then made with a political strategy Edward devises to quash the Scottish rebellion—that the king will grant *primae noctis*; that is, an English landowner will have the right to have sex on the first night with any common girl who marries. The king's pithy line in the script is "If we can't get them out, we'll breed them out!"

Cut to a village wedding where the English lord demands *primae noctis*. He makes a speech to explain to moviegoers what's at stake—"As lord I'll bless the marriage by taking the bride into my bed the first night." One of the soldiers holds a knife blade to the throat of the bridegroom until the bride, wearing her crown of orange blossoms, gives her new husband a long kiss and, to save their lives, goes off on the saddle with the overlord in obedience to the law.

Braveheart is portrayed as a young man who has traveled, who woos his love in poetic French, and who wants to farm and raise a family, not fight. He and his beloved are married secretly by a priest—even with the girl's father's consent, they would otherwise have to cope with the royal decree of *primae noctis*. But soon the couple is indiscreet, the English discover their "lawlessness," and theirs becomes the match that strikes the light of the rebellion.

MARIE ANTOINETTE (2006)

The latest of several movie versions of the life of the famous queen, this one includes the formal bedding of the princess, played by Kirsten Dunst, and the dauphin, played by Jason Schwartzman. Several dozen courtiers surround the nuptial bed as the royals seat themselves on the spacious bed. The priest gives the Church's blessings, and the king stands at the foot of the bed and pronounces, "Good luck and good work." The next morning, the king's mistress tells him that nothing occurred. In the bedroom, Marie Antoinette awakes to find the room filled with her ladies-in-waiting. In a funny scene, the dauphine is undressed and stands naked before the French ladies as the lady in charge of protocol, played by Judy Davis, decides which lady-in-waiting has sufficient rank to hand the Austrian princess her undergarments. Covered at last, Marie Antoinette observes of the proceedings, "This is ridiculous." To which the mistress of protocol responds, "This is Versailles."

THE HEARTBREAK KID (2007)

In this remake of the 1972 hit, Eddie, played by Ben Stiller, is facing a life of lonely bachelorhood when he fails to prevent a mugger from stealing a passerby's purse. The owner of the purse, Leila, played by Malin Akerman, shows up at Eddie's sporting goods store, and romance ensues. Urged by his father and his best friend to marry the beautiful woman, Eddie quickly proposes, and they head to the altar. On the honeymoon, Eddie discovers that he and Leila are not a good match. Driving to their honeymoon destination, Leila obsessively sings along to the radio, whereas Eddie would like to drive in silence. They disagree on how to spend their time at the resort. To relieve the growing tension, Leila proposes that they stop at a motel for a sexual romp. In the first night (afternoon, really), Leila is sexually dominant, asking Eddie to engage in such acrobatics as the jackhammer, Swedish helicopter, and inverted corkscrew, all the while instructing him, "Tell me how you like it." When Eddie inquires whether they could just do it in the missionary position, Leila asks, "What's that?" She agrees, as long as Eddie can power-drive her. The next morning at breakfast, Leila is ravenous and chatty, whereas Eddie is quiet and pensive. Their hasty marriage is headed for quarrels and misunderstandings, complicated by Eddie's falling in love with another woman at the honeymoon resort.

NOTE

1.   Jacqueline Susann's *Valley of the Dolls* made famous the dangers of male sexual overexertion during sex.

Index

About the Authors

JANE MERRILL lives on the St. George Peninsula in Maine. She is the author, with David Knox, of *When I Fall in Love Again* (Praeger). She has written or collaborated on books on history, beauty, sexual technique, child rearing, bilingualism, jewelry, Chinese recreation and arts, and recovery from addiction. In addition, Jane has published articles on popular culture, art, style, and relationships in dozens of national magazines, including *Cosmopolitan, New York, The New Republic, Town and Country, Redbook, Connoisseur, Modern Bride,* and *Vogue.* Educated at Wellesley, Harvard, and Columbia, she has three master's degrees in literature and librarianship.

CHRIS FILSTRUP is a research librarian at Stony Brook University on Long Island. He earned his bachelor's degree at Haverford College and has two master's degrees: one from Harvard, in Middle East studies, and one from Columbia, in library science. His library career includes administrative positions at the New York Public Library and the Library of Congress. He is the author of *Beadazzled: The Story of Beads* and *China: From Emperors to Communes.*